"The authors skilfully guide readers through the key concepts and applications of attachment theory. It is an invaluable primer for students, professionals, researchers and interested readers in a wide range of areas including psychology, child development, mental health and applied social sciences."

–**Dr Angus MacBeth**, *CPsychol, AFBPsS; Senior Lecturer in Clinical Psychology; Director of Research, School of Health in Social Science, University of Edinburgh; 2022 UNICEF Innocenti Senior Research Fellow*

"The accessible writing style and embedding of early theory and research within the biographical histories of the key figures involved in the development of this fascinating theory, makes for compelling reading."

–**Professor Jane Barlow**, *Professor of Evidence Based Intervention and Policy Evaluation, University of Oxford*

"This is a much-needed, contemporary guide to attachment theory across the lifespan, which beautifully summarises a complex and messy topic as clearly as I have ever read it. Whether you are a Professor of Attachment or a student starting out on your psychology journey – there are nuggets of knowledge for everyone."

–**Dr Camilla Rosan**, *Consultant Clinical & Research Psychologist, Anna Freud Centre*

ATTACHMENT THEORY

THE BASICS

This book provides a comprehensive and accessible introduction to key concepts of attachment theory, from the work of its founder John Bowlby to the most recent research within the field.

The first part of the book gives readers a clear understanding of attachment theory during infancy, childhood, adolescence, adulthood and in bereavement. The second part of the book illustrates how attachment theory can be used to inform clinical interventions with children in different contexts, adults, and within wider health, social and educational systems. Using case examples throughout, the authors provide the reader with a practical understanding of the clinical applications of attachment theory across the lifespan and in varying health, social care and educational systems.

Attachment theory is one of the most important lifespan development theories and is relevant to students and practitioners from a wide range of disciplines, including medicine, nursing, psychology, child development, mental health and applied social sciences.

Dr Ruth O'Shaughnessy is a consultant clinical psychologist and clinical lead for the award-winning Cheshire and Merseyside Specialist Perinatal Service and for the North West Coast Perinatal Clinical Network.

Professor Katherine Berry is Professor of Clinical Psychology at the University of Manchester and a practicing clinical psychologist. She has published over 100 papers on attachment theory in adulthood and has edited two previous books on attachment theory in adult mental health.

Professor Rudi Dallos is Emeritus Professor of Clinical Psychology at the University of Plymouth and works as a family therapist in his own private practice.

Dr Karen Bateson is an independent clinical psychologist with a 30-year career which has included working clinically in the NHS, developing interventions for the NSPCC, and as Head of Clinical Strategy and Development for the Parent-Infant Foundation.

The Basics

The Basics is a highly successful series of accessible guidebooks which provide an overview of the fundamental principles of a subject area in a jargon-free and undaunting format.

Intended for students approaching a subject for the first time, the books both introduce the essentials of a subject and provide an ideal springboard for further study. With over 50 titles spanning subjects from artificial intelligence (AI) to women's studies, *The Basics* are an ideal starting point for students seeking to understand a subject area.

Each text comes with recommendations for further study and gradually introduces the complexities and nuances within a subject.

PHILOSOPHY OF RELIGION
SAMUEL LEBENS

SEX THERAPY
CATE CAMPBELL

PLAY DIRECTING
DAMON KIELY

CLASSICAL MYTHOLOGY
RICHARD MARTIN

SOCIAL WORK
MARK DOEL

EDUCATIONAL NEUROSCIENCE
CATHY ROGERS, MICHAEL S. C. THOMAS

SEXOLOGY
SILVA NEVES

ARCHAEOLOGICAL THEORY
ROBERT CHAPMAN

SPECIAL EDUCATIONAL NEEDS AND DISABILITY
JANICE WEARMOUTH

ENGLISH VOCABULARY
MICHAEL MCCARTHY

INFORMATION SCIENCE
JUDITH PINTAR, DAVID HOPPING

DRAMATURGY
ANNE M. HAMILTON, WALTER BYONG-SOK CHON

DIGITAL RELIGION
HEIDI A. CAMPBELL, WENDI BELLAR

DEATH AND RELIGION
CANDI CANN

HINDUISM
NEELIMA SHUKLA-BHATT

ISLAMIC PSYCHOLOGY
G. HUSSEIN RASSOOL

RELIGION IN AMERICA
MICHAEL PASQUIER

FINANCE
ERIK BANKS

BEHAVIORAL ECONOMICS
PHILIP CORR, ANKE PLAGNOL

ATTACHMENT THEORY
RUTH O'SHAUGHNESSY, KATHERINE BERRY, RUDI DALLOS, KAREN BATESON

For a full list of titles in this series, please visit www.routledge.com/The-Basics/book-series/B

ATTACHMENT THEORY

THE BASICS

Ruth O'Shaughnessy, Katherine Berry, Rudi Dallos and Karen Bateson

Routledge
Taylor & Francis Group
LONDON AND NEW YORK

Designed cover image: Getty Images

First published 2023
by Routledge
4 Park Square, Milton Park, Abingdon, Oxon OX14 4RN

and by Routledge
605 Third Avenue, New York, NY 10158

Routledge is an imprint of the Taylor & Francis Group, an informa business

British Library Cataloguing-in-Publication Data
A catalogue record for this book is available from the British Library

ISBN: 978-1-13856-999-7 (hbk)
ISBN: 978-1-13857-001-6 (pbk)
ISBN: 978-0-20370-387-8 (ebk)

DOI: 10.4324/9780203703878

Typeset in Bembo
by Taylor & Francis Books

CONTENTS

ILLUSTRATIONS

FIGURES

TABLES

CONTRIBUTORS

Dr Karen Bateson is an independent psychologist with more than 25 years' experience of clinical work, development and leadership of child and family services, teaching, research and writing. Karen had a twenty-year NHS career as a clinical psychologist specialising in work with children under five, a researcher and workforce trainer. Then at NSPCC, Karen led the national roll out of an antenatal programme for families facing adversity and developed a place-based systems-change programme to prevent child maltreatment. Most recently, Karen was Head of Clinical Strategy and Development at the Parent-Infant Foundation, supporting infant mental health services across the UK. Karen has published articles on parenting groups, engaging fathers, infant mental health, and Adverse Childhood Experiences (ACEs) and has contributed to multiple podcast and media publications.

Professor Katherine Berry is a professor and clinical psychologist who is based at the University of Manchester. After completing her clinical psychology training in 2003, she went on the study for a PhD on attachment theory in psychosis. She has published over 100 papers on attachment theory in adulthood and has edited two previous books on attachment theory in adult mental health and attachment theory and psychosis. She currently works as a professor on the University of Manchester clinical psychology training programme, is involved in the running of a number of trials of psychological therapies for people experiencing psychosis within the NHS and practices as a clinical psychologist in adult mental health services.

Professor Rudi Dallos is Emeritus Professor of Clinical Psychology at the University of Plymouth and works as a family therapist in his own private practice. He has engaged in research into aspects of attachment theory, including eating disorders, autism and self-harm and has developed Attachment Narrative Therapy (ANT) as an approach for working clinically with young people and their families. He has published a range of papers and books, including; *Attachment Narrative Therapy, An Introduction to Family Therapy, Formulation in Psychology and Psychotherapy, Working Systemically with Attachment Narratives* and *Don't Blame the Parents: Positive Intentions, Scripts and Change in Family Therapy.*

Dr Ruth O'Shaughnessy is a consultant clinical psychologist and clinical lead for the award-winning Cheshire and Merseyside Specialist Perinatal Service. She is clinical lead for the North West Coast Perinatal Clinical Network, NHS England. Her interests include the clinical applications of attachment theory, family mental health and relationships in the perinatal period, and community psychology. She has a particular interest in relational leadership and developing responsive services using asset-based approaches. Ruth is author of several papers and book chapters in the field of parental mental health, infant mental health and attachment.

ACKNOWLEDGEMENTS

General acknowledgements
To Hilary Kennedy for reviewing and commenting on the VIG material in Chapter 11.

Special thanks to Dr Ruth Butterworth for being our biggest cheerleader and for her contributions to the book concept, structure and content during the first phase of the book.

In addition, to all the people and families we have worked with over the years.

Ruth's acknowledgements
With thanks to my mum and dad, who fostered both my drive to learn and tenacity to finish what I start. And my brothers and sister – David, John, Daniel and Rebecca – for their no-nonsense advice and good humour. To my children – Felix, Martha and Malachy – without whom this book would have been completed two years ago. Most of all thanks to my husband Jamie for his support and encouragement, especially during moments of self-doubt.

Karen's acknowledgements
With thanks to my husband and children, who have taught me many important things and have been such a source of joy, learning and healing. I dedicate my contribution to this book to my parents and grandparents.

Katherine's acknowledgements
For my family and especially my boys, Jacob, Ethan and Benjamin, who have brought attachment theory to life for me and taught me more than any text book could.

1

ATTACHMENT AND CAREGIVING

Dr Ruth O'Shaughnessy

INTRODUCTION

Attachment theory is one of the most productive and influential theories of human development and describes a field of scientific research within the social sciences. Attachment theory was first proposed by John Bowlby in the late 1960s. The first empirical evidence was provided by Mary Ainsworth, a colleague of Bowlby's, in the 1970s. This chapter summarises John Bowlby's seminal trilogy and life's work *Attachment* (1969), *Separation* (1973) and *Loss* (1980a) and outlines key theoretical ideas. Starting with an overview of Bowlby's life and key influences, it describes key concepts including attachment figures, attachment behaviours, attachment and affectional bonds and internal working models in an accessible and coherent way. The overall aim of this chapter is to tell the story of the first phase of attachment theory development in a way that is accurate, understandable and relatable.

THE ORIGINS OF ATTACHMENT THEORY – A POTTED HISTORY OF JOHN BOWLBY'S LIFE AND WORK

John Mostyn Bowlby was born in London in 1907 to wealthy, well-connected parents Sir Anthony Bowlby (the King's surgeon) and May Mostyn. John was the fourth of six children and, as was typical for many affluent parents of that generation, the care of their children was delegated to a nanny. He was profoundly affected by the departure of 'Nanny Minnie' – his primary

DOI: 10.4324/9780203703878-1

caregiver from birth until the age of four – describing this later as the tragic loss of his mother (Van Dijken, 1998).

John and his siblings were talented and had a wide range of interests. A love of nature and knowledge of the natural world were passed down through generations and instilled in the Bowlby children from an early age. John remained a passionate naturalist throughout his life and his propensity for curiosity and observation provides an insight into the mind behind the theory.

The First World War broke out in 1914, and seven-year-old John was sent to boarding school, an experience which he later described as "barbaric" (Holmes, 1993, p. 17). In 1925 John went to study medicine at Trinity College, Cambridge where he won several awards and graduated with a first-class degree. Reluctant to follow in his father's footsteps, he made the unconventional decision to accept a job in a school for maladjusted children where he was first alerted to the possible connection between early separation and the onset of psychological difficulties in children. This is historically important because his development of this idea marks a departure from the prevailing psychoanalytic view of the time that distress is primarily an intrapsychic (internal) phenomenon unconnected to negative life experience.

After completing medical studies in 1933, John embarked on training in adult psychiatry and psychoanalysis and was later appointed to the London Child Guidance clinic at the Tavistock – an early child and family mental health service. Child guidance clinics sought to promote children's mental wellbeing through prevention and work with parents. Here, John became interested in the idea of transgenerational transmission of mental distress in which unresolved problems from the parent's past contribute to the development of their child's difficulties. He wanted to show that negative events in childhood can have negative consequences in later life. From this point, John increasingly stressed the role of the environment, arguing that factors such as separation from the mother, maternal mental illness and family breakdown are causative (Bowlby, 1944).

World War II broke out in 1940, and John joined a group of army psychiatrists to support the war effort. In 1944 he joined the newly established War Office's Research and Training Unit where he started a famous collaboration with James Robertson to study the effects of separation on young children. At the time, children would typically be left in hospital alone without their parents. In 1952 Robertson recorded the now infamous film *A Two-year-old Goes to Hospital* (clips can be found on YouTube) which starkly portrays the extraordinary distress young children experience when separated from their parents (Bowlby, Robertson & Rosenbluth, 1952). These videos are as shocking to watch now as when they were first shown to audiences in the 1950s. Renowned contemporary psychotherapist Graham Music describes how the children "started off relatively composed, expecting to have their attachment needs met, but soon protested, crying and screaming and later slowly but painfully sunk into a despairing state, and eventually into a cut-off one" (Music, 2011, p. 60). Thankfully, John Bowlby and Robert Robertson's work liberalised hospital practices and mothers were thereafter able to stay overnight with their hospitalised children.

Mary Ainsworth had arrived at John's research unit in 1950 and she was involved in the analysis of Robertson's video tapes. She was impressed by John's approach to naturalistic observation and decided to focus her research career on the empirical validation (where evidence is provided through a series of experiments) of his "ethological notions" (Ainsworth, 1989, personal communication to John).

A keen naturalist, John saw there were clear links between his clinical practice, his emerging theory about attachment and separation and new findings from ethology (the study of animal behaviour). He was particularly interested in the imprinting phenomenon described by Konrad Lorenz in 1952 whereby new-born goslings follow their mother and show symptoms of anxiety (cheeping, searching) when separated, even though she does not directly provide food.

A second major influence on John's ideas was the work of Harry Harlow and his famous "wire mother" monkeys (Harlow, 1958). Through a series of laboratory-based experiments, Harlow separated infant monkeys from their mothers at birth and reared them with the help of "surrogate wire mothers". In one famous experiment, the baby monkeys were given a choice of (1) a wire-only mother with a feeding bottle; or (2) a cuddly mother (soft cloth attached) with no feeding bottle. The prevailing view at the time, that of Behaviourism, would predict the baby monkey's preference for the wire-only mother, owing to the reinforcement of food.

Harlow showed that the baby monkeys overwhelmingly chose the cuddle mother, clinging to her for around 18 hours per day. Taken together, Lorenz and Harlow's work demonstrated an attachment and bonding system independent to feeding and the vital importance of proximity, comfort and closeness during infancy and the early years.

John's established reputation as an expert in child mental health led to an invitation from the World Health Organisation to provide international guidance on the mental health of post-war homeless children. John and his expert reference group published *Maternal Care and Mental Health* (Bowlby, 1951) which was published again in a popular edition as *Child Care and the Growth of Love* (Bowlby, 1953b) and became an international bestseller. What marks out this publication in the history of social reform is its emphasis on psychological and relational factors as opposed to economic, nutritional, medical or housing difficulties as a root cause of distress (Holmes, 1993). Contemporary thinking in mental health stresses the importance of understanding a person's unique history and combination of multiple, inter-related factors (biology, parenting, family, social circumstances etc) in making sense of distress (e.g., Black & Hoeft, 2015).

From 1964 to 1979, John dedicated time to writing his epic trilogy *Attachment and Loss* (Bowlby, 1969; 1973; 1980a) in which he outlines the basic tenets of the theory. He went on to hold numerous positions and received many honours and awards throughout his career. He retired from the NHS in 1972 but continued to supervise, lecture and write until his death in 1990. John Bowlby was a pioneer, an original thinker and a fierce advocate for children. He disliked the way in which children were denied love and affection in the name of 'not spoiling' them and insisted on the everlasting nature of dependency as an essential part of human relationships and not as something to 'grow out of' (Holmes,1993).

KEY CONCEPTS IN ATTACHMENT THEORY

A key feature of attachment theory is its theoretical diversity which integrates findings from ethology (study of animal behaviour), evolutionary biology (study of evolution), psychoanalysis (theories and therapies that focus on the unconscious mind), cognitive neuroscience (study of brain processes, cognition, memory and mind) and systems theory (study of systems and groups and how they interrelate). Bowlby knitted together an extraordinary range of ideas which, taken together with findings from his clinical practice, provide the foundation for key tenets of attachment theory. Bowlby's life work was vast and included the *Attachment and Loss* trilogy (Bowlby, 1969; 1973; 1980a), *The Making and Breaking of Affectional Bonds* (Bowlby, 1979) and *A Secure Base* (Bowlby, 1988a). What follows is an outline of the key ideas and core concepts in attachment theory.

WHAT IS "ATTACHMENT"? WHAT IS "CAREGIVING"?

"Attachment" has both a lay and a technical meaning. Oxford Languages define the lay meaning of attachment as *"affection, fondness, or sympathy for someone or something"*. However, Bowlby's use of the word was in fact not synonymous with love, affection, relationship or bond. In attachment theory, "attachment" has a specific meaning: a bond or tie between a child and an "attachment figure" based on the need for safety, protection and comfort (Prior & Glaser, 2006). Its meaning was further developed by Bowlby and Ainsworth to emphasise attachment as a protection from threat, enhancing survival and ultimately genetic replication. This is critical during infancy and early childhood when a human baby is completely dependent on their caregivers for survival. It is important to note that because of the precise meaning of attachment, it is not recommended for practitioners to use the word attachment in their practice unless they have specific additional training and expertise.

An "attachment figure" is the person who cares for the baby such that the baby's chances of survival are increased. Typically, this is a parent, and the attachment is strengthened when care is safe, sensitive and comforting. However, a baby cannot survive without an attachment to someone who will keep them alive, even if their attachment figure provides suboptimal care. So, babies will attach to attachment figures who are unpredictable, neglectful, hostile or even dangerous, if necessary.

The reciprocal tie, from carer to baby, is known as the "caregiving bond", and this ideally involves a commitment to be responsive and protective to a child's distress.

ATTACHMENT AND EVOLUTIONARY SCIENCE

Attachment theory is an evolutionary theory in that Bowlby argued that humans come into the world biologically pre-programmed to form attachments with others to survive. A key insight from evolutionary theories is the recognition that any behaviour that increases the chances of survival is passed onto the next generation. Bowlby termed the environment in which a person adapts "the environment of evolutionary adaptedness". Early hunter-gatherer humans found some safety living in small groups at a time when big cats, bears and wolves presented the biggest threat. Mary Main later summarised "in contrast to those mammals for whom a special place (burrow or den) provides the infant's haven of safety, then, for the primate infant the attachment figure is the single location that must be sought under stress" (Main, Hesse & Kaplan, 2005).

ATTACHMENT BEHAVIOUR AND THE ATTACHMENT BEHAVIOURAL SYSTEM

"Attachment behaviour" is any behaviour by the baby that induces proximity-seeking to the attachment figure when feeling distressed, threatened, frightened or unsafe. These types of physical or emotional threats activate attachment behaviours whose *set goal* is to achieve closeness or proximity to their caregivers because that increases safety and therefore survival. Attachment behaviours in infants include crying, reaching, clinging - any behaviour that attracts attention from caregivers and brings them closer. Collectively, these behaviours act as a motivational system to achieve or maintain proximity to the attachment figure. This is known as the "attachment behavioural system" (Bowlby, 1969).

According to Bowlby, the conditions that activate threat in infants fall into three groups:

1 External dangers (the presence of a stranger, a loud noise, shouting and arguing, rapid approaches from people or animals, unfamiliar places, etc.).
2 Internal dangers (feeling unwell or ill, high temperature, too hungry, too cold, too hot, physically uncomfortable, overtired, pain, etc.).

3 Behaviour, responsiveness and whereabouts of the attachment figure (attachment figure leaving or absent, discouraging or punishing proximity / attempts to be close, physical and/or psychological absence).

Though Bowlby originally described the attachment behavioural system as a 'start-stop' system (1969, p. 258), it is now generally agreed that it is continually active, where activation can range from low to intense depending on the nature and severity of threat. To 'turn-off' the attachment system would render the infant at too much risk. Attachment behaviour varies according to the intensity of the threat (and the extent to which the attachment behavioural system is activated):

- Example of low activation: A parent who becomes distracted during a play interaction and turns attention to another activity, the baby may grumble (low activation) in an attempt to reconnect with their carer and continue the game (set goal).
- Example of high activation: A parent who abruptly leaves during a play interaction leaving the baby with an unfamiliar neighbour while visiting their home, the baby may quickly resort to crying and flailing (attachment behaviour) in an attempt to bring their parent back into the room and pick them up (set goal).

In either case the set goal is proximity – closeness to the attachment figure brings relief, regulation, and comfort (down-regulation of attachment behavioural system). George and Solomon (1996) coined the term *"caregiving system"*, referring to the reciprocal response of a parent to their baby's attachment behaviour. Common behaviours found in the caregiving system include reaching, picking-up, stroking, rocking, smiling, eye-contact, following, using a soothing voice or singing.

PROTEST, DESPAIR AND DETACHMENT

Another Bowlby collaborator, Robert Hinde (ethologist, zoologist and psychologist), showed that baby monkeys removed from their mothers first protested then fell into despair and eventually became cut-off and subdued (Hinde, 1970). The children in Robertson's videos showed remarkably similar patterns of behaviour and emotions. Robertson and Bowlby identified three phases of a separation response: protest, despair and denial or detachment. When attachment behaviours fail to achieve sufficient proximity, the attachment system becomes overwhelmed: children can become physically and emotionally dysregulated using whatever resources available to recover their caregiver. This might involve anger, tantrums and crying. A behavioural interpretation might describe this as "attention-seeking" but to attachment theorists this is better described as "attachment-seeking".

If loss or separation is prolonged (remember the children in Robertson's videos) children enter a despairing and hopeless state, with evidence of increased apathy and withdrawal from social contact. There may also be accompanying difficulties with sleeping and eating. However, if the loss continues or becomes permanent (for example death of a parent), this can lead to detachment. In older children or adults, this may present as depression.

THE DEVELOPMENTAL SEQUENCE OF ATTACHMENT

Together, Bowlby and Ainsworth outlined four phases in the development of an attachment relationship (Table 1.1) though the boundaries between these are imprecise and influenced by family context and culture.

Children form attachments with more than one caregiver. The notion of multiple caregivers makes evolutionary sense in the context of our hunter-gatherer ancestors who lived in small groups. Adults (and even older siblings) who are regularly involved in looking after a child such as grandparents, an auntie or uncle, or childminder are likely to earn status as an attachment figure. However, there tends to be an overall *hierarchy* where children can use their attachment figures quite flexibly, with a primary attachment figure achieving most prominence in the hierarchy. The primary attachment figure is the main carer, usually the mother or father. Bowlby makes this case quite powerfully when he describes

Table 1.1 The development of attachment

Developmental stage	*Phase*	*Key features*
0–8 weeks	Pre-attachment	Attachment behaviour is indiscriminate. Baby's signals are directed towards anyone.
8 weeks – 6 months	Attachment-in-the-making	Baby can discriminate between adults and shows a preference for familiar attachment figure(s). Baby actively listens and looks out for familiar attachment figure(s).
Starts in second half of first year and lasts until approximately age 2 or 3	Clear-cut attachment	Baby's behaviour is focussed on proximity towards their attachment figure especially during stress or threat. Patterns of parent-infant relationships become established.
Starts age 2 or 3	Goal-corrected partnership	Child comes to understand that parents are separate and have their own motives and needs. Relationship becomes more complex and reciprocal – a partnership.

his work with Wendy, a four-year-old girl who has lost her mother:

> "About four weeks after her mother had died, Wendy complained that no one loved her. In an attempt to reassure her, father names a long list of people who did (naming those who cared for her). On hearing this Wendy commented aptly, "But when my mommy wasn't dead I didn't need so many people – I needed only one."
>
> (Bowlby, 1988b, p. 280)

ATTACHMENT AND AFFECTIONAL BONDS

As children grow, attachment underpins "affectional bonds" with key adults. This might include childminders, teachers, or family relatives from whom the child has experienced care and safety.

Mary Ainsworth later identified five criteria for affectional bonds between individuals:

1 An affectional bond is lasting, not transient
2 An affectional bond is directed towards a particular person
3 An affectional bond has a significant emotional component
4 The individual wants to maintain proximity or contact with the person
5 The individual feels a degree of sadness at involuntary separation from the person

(Ainsworth, 1989)

As described earlier, an attachment bond is characterised by a bond or tie between a child and an attachment figure specifically based on the need for safety, protection and comfort.

SECURE BASE, SAFE HAVEN AND EXPLORATORY BEHAVIOURAL SYSTEM

In its early development, attachment theory was essentially a spatial theory: the closer the parent was, the happier and more relaxed the child. Bowlby and Ainsworth saw the attachment figure as both "a safe haven" (Ainsworth, 1978) and a "secure base" (Bowlby, 1980a). Safe haven refers to the physical distance required to make the child feel safe. For newborn babies, this might require skin-to-skin contact, while for older toddlers that might simply require visual contact. It is a sign of healthy development that mobile children test the limits of their safe haven, venturing further away but constantly checking back. The attachment figure provides a safe haven to which the child can return when feeling uneasy, stressed, overwhelmed, or unsafe. The presence of responsive, available parental care enables the child to ask for help and to learn that he or she will be comforted, protected and regulated. These interactional patterns enable the child to build confidence because they know that within their safe haven they will find their attachment figure as a *secure base*. Knowing that they can return to a safe haven promotes exploration. Without the confidence of a safe haven, children's exploration may be reduced. Children who lack the experience of a safe haven and secure base (Figure 1.1) can grow up to feel much more anxious about engaging in relationships and the world on their own, including childcare and school.

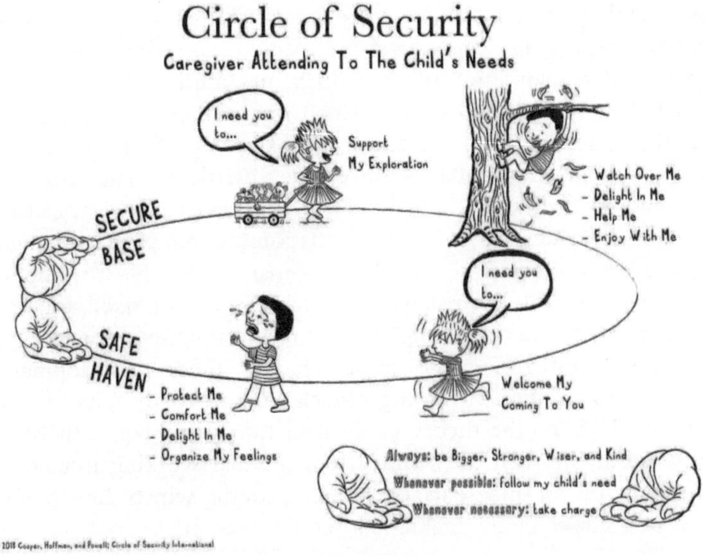

Figure 1.1 Circle of Security, an evidence-based intervention for families, illustrates the dynamic nature of attachment relationships and the child returning to their safe haven and exploring from their safe base. Reproduced with permission from Circle of Security International.

INTERNAL WORKING MODELS

Attachment theory initially concentrated on observable behaviours. However, it became clear that children process their attachment experiences cognitively, leading to the formation of internal predictions about how relationships work. Bowlby described these expectations or blueprints as an "internal working model", a mental map the child develops about themselves, others and relationships. Children develop this map based on how the world has worked in the past (attachment history) and is therefore likely to work in the future. These mental representations or maps tend to include predictions about:

1 Self
2 Other people
3 The relationship between the self and another person

As a child's brain develops, it seeks to make sense of patterns in relationships, cause and effect in relationships, the 'why's and 'how's of relationships: When I do x, my mother does y/When my father does x, then I do y/When my mother does x, I feel y. As the child grows up and starts to make sense of the world at a more cognitive and reflective level, they use their mental maps to understand the world, to anticipate, to manage and negotiate. Internal working models act as relationship templates to guide future relationships with friends, partner(s) and family. It is important to note that internal working models are not fixed and can change over time depending on new relationship experiences.

During this first phase of attachment theory development, Bowlby used internal working models to describe the inner world of the child. As the theory evolved in his partnership with Mary Ainsworth, he used the construct of internal working models to account for the different attachment patterns which Ainsworth's research subsequently established (see Chapter 2).

SUMMARY

This chapter describes the origins of attachment theory, key influences and events and core tenets of the theory as they evolved from the work of John Bowlby and key collaborators. Bowlby's research was primarily observational and used small samples, which by present-day standards would not be deemed sufficient or scientifically rigorous (e.g., no control groups). However, Bowlby's extraordinary capacity for naturalistic observation and meticulous note-keeping provides data that enabled adults to see the world through a child's eyes in a powerful, irreplaceable way. In the next chapter, we turn our focus to the second phase of attachment theory Mary Ainsworth's Strange Situation Procedure and the empirical evidence for attachment theory.

RECOMMENDED READING

Holmes, J. (2014). John Bowlby and attachment theory. Routledge.
Prior, V. and Glaser, D. (2006). Understanding attachment & attachment disorders: Theory, evidence, and practice. Jessica Kingsley Publishers.

REFERENCES

Ainsworth, M. S. (1989). Attachments beyond infancy, *American Psychologist*, 44: 709–716.

Black, J. M. & Hoeft, F. (2015). Utilizing biopsychosocial and strengths-based approaches within the field of child health: what we know and where we can grow. *New Directions for Child and Adolescent Development* (147): 13–20.

Bowlby, J. (1944). Forty-four juvenile thieves: Their characters and home life. *International Journal of Psychoanalysis*, 25, 107–127.

Bowlby, J. (1951). *Maternal care and mental health.* World Health Organization Monograph.

Bowlby, J. (1952). Maternal care and mental health, *Journal of Consulting Psychology, 16(3)*: 232.

Bowlby, J. (1953). *Childcare and the growth of love.* Penguin Books.

Bowlby, J. (1969). *Attachment and loss, Vol. 1: Attachment.* Basic Books.

Bowlby, J. (1973). *Attachment and loss, Vol. 2: Separation.* Basic Books.

Bowlby, J. (1980a). *Attachment and loss, Vol. 3: Loss, Sadness and Depression.* Basic Books.

Bowlby, J. (1988a). *A secure base: Parent-child attachment and healthy human development.* Basic Books.

Bowlby, J. (1988b). Changing theories of childhood since Freud. In E. Timms and N. Segal (eds), *Freud in exile* (p. 280). Yale University Press.

Bowlby, J., Robertson, J. & Rosenbluth, D. (1952). A Two-Year-Old Goes to Hospital. *The Psychoanalytic Study of the Child*, 7(1): 82–94.

George, C. & Solomon, J. (1996). Representational models of relationships: links between caregiving and attachment, *Infant Mental Health Journal*, 17: 18–36.

Harlow, H. (1958). The nature of love, *American Psychologist*, 13: 673–685.

Hinde, R. (1970). *Animal behaviour: A synthesis of ecology and comparative psychology.* McGraw Hill.

Holmes, J. (1993). *John Bowlby and attachment theory.* Routledge.

Howe, D (2011). *Attachment across the lifecourse: a brief introduction.* Palgrave Macmillan.

Lorenz, K. (1952). *King Solomon's ring.* Methuen.

Main, M., Kaplan, N. & Cassidy, J. (1985). Security in infancy, childhood, and adulthood: a move to the level of representation. *Monographs of the Society for Research in Child Development*, 50(1–2): 66–104.

Main, M., Hesse, E. & Kaplan, N. (2005). Predictability of attachment behaviour and representational processes at age 1, 6 and 18 years of age: the Berkeley Longitudinal Study. In K. E. Grossman, K. Grossman & E. Waters (eds), *Attachment from infancy to adulthood* (p. 204–245). Guilford Press.

Music, G. (2010). *Nurturing natures: Attachment and children's emotional, socio-cultural and brain development* (1st ed.). Psychology Press.

Prior, V. & Glaser, D. (2006). *Understanding attachment & attachment disorders: Theory, evidence, and practice.* Jessica Kingsley Publishers.

Van Dijken, S. (1998). *John Bowlby: His early life: a biographical journey into the roots of attachment theory.* Free Association Books.

2

INDIVIDUAL AND CULTURAL DIFFERENCES IN ATTACHMENT

Dr Ruth O'Shaughnessy

INTRODUCTION

Without Mary Ainsworth, her perceptive observations of children and parents, and development of the Strange Situation Procedure (SSP) it is unlikely that attachment theory would occupy the central position in developmental psychology that it does today. This chapter outlines the seminal work of Mary Ainsworth on assessing individual differences in attachment using the SSP. It introduces the reader to attachment styles (including Mary Main's later work on disorganised attachment) and their relationship to the construct of maternal sensitivity. There is an overview of how recent research has developed our understanding of the antecedents of attachment security including "mentalization" and "mind-mindedness". This chapter's emphasis is that all attachment patterns are functional and develop to support the infant getting his or her needs for protection met. We conclude with a brief appraisal of attachment theory and its application in different cultural contexts.

THE EMPIRICAL EVIDENCE FOR ATTACHMENT THEORY – AN OVERVIEW OF MARY AINSWORTH AND THE STRANGE SITUATION

Born in Ohio in 1913, Mary was the eldest of three girls born to Mary (a nurse) and Charles (a successful businessman) Salter. The family re-located to Toronto, Canada, when Mary was five years

DOI: 10.4324/9780203703878-2

old. Both parents placed a high value on education and expected their children to exceed academically. Mary was a precocious child, able to read from age three, she excelled in school and secured a place at the University of Toronto at age sixteen to study psychology. Mary completed her masters and doctoral degrees in the 1930s. Her PhD was entitled "An Evaluation of Adjustment Based on the Concept of Security" in which she concludes that "*where family security is lacking, the individual is handicapped by the lack of secure base from which to work*" (Salter, 1940, p. 45) – evidence of early theorising on the role of parent-child relationships and child outcomes.

Like John Bowlby, Mary joined the war effort in 1942 and served in the Canadian Women's Army Corps, reaching the rank of major in 1945. After the war she secured a teaching position at the University of Toronto and subsequently married Leonard Ainsworth (PhD graduate) in 1950 (they divorced ten years later). The couple soon re-located to London, a transition that enabled Mary to apply for a post at the Tavistock Clinic with John Bowlby. It was Mary's experience at Bowlby's research unit (1950–53) and particularly the remarkable observational skills of James Robertson (see Chapter 1) that re-set the direction of her professional career to focus on a series of experiments which would provide the evidence to validate attachment theory. It was also the beginning of a lifelong friendship and one of the most prolific partnerships in the history of social sciences. Or as Mary put it, "What can I say?....we liked each other!" (Ainsworth & Marvin, 1995, p. 4).

In 1954 the Ainsworths moved to Uganda so that Leonard could take up employment with the East African Institute of Social Research. With support from the same institution, Mary managed to secure enough funds to support herself and an interpreter to lead a small research project focussed on infant-mother behaviour in Ugandan families. Mary learned enough Lugunda (one of the major languages spoken in Uganda) to be able to describe her research to local tribal leaders and families and successfully recruited twenty-eight pairs of mothers and babies (age one to two years old). For several months, Mary went from village to village observing mothers and infants, taking continuous notes on every interaction (separations, reunions, exploration, sleeping, feeding, toileting, etc.) in context (the wider family, village and customs). It was through these intimate observations of the daily 'back-and-forth' between mothers and babies that Mary started to see Bowlby's theory of attachment come to life (Ainsworth, 1967).

The Ainsworths left Uganda in 1955, re-locating to Baltimore, USA, where Mary took a teaching position at John Hopkins University. Here she started to sort through hundreds of hours of observation of Ugandan families, where infant behaviour organised itself into three categories: sixteen pairs (57%) she labelled "secure" (infants that cried infrequently and enjoyed playing and exploring with their mother's near-by); seven pairs (25%) were labelled "insecure" (infants that cried a lot and were not easily soothed by their mothers and did not explore much); and five pairs (18%) were labelled as "not yet attached" (infants that didn't seem to have a 'special' relationship with their mother). Critically, while Mary found that all mothers had demonstrated warmth towards their babies, those infants categorised as secure had mothers' who were sensitive and responsive to their cues and had the most insight into their children. These mothers readily answered questions about their babies and provided spontaneous detail and enthusiastically offered descriptions to highlight examples of their babies' behaviour. This incredibly important research pointed towards caregiver sensitivity as worthy of future investigation (Ainsworth, 1967).

During this time, Mary also started a second observational study with a group of twenty-six middle-class mothers and their babies from Baltimore (Ainsworth, 1977). Recruited during pregnancy, the families participated in eighteen home visits (four hours per visit) between the baby's first month and approximately nine months old, producing around seventy-two hours of data collection per family. Mary's naturalistic observational approach emphasised identification of meaningful interactional patterns in context, rather than frequency counts or checklists of specific behaviours (e.g., quantitative data).

The Baltimore study yielded two ground-breaking innovations which retain a central role in attachment theory: the Strange Situation Procedure and the first explicit conceptualisation of "maternal sensitivity" (these are described in the next section).

Although the assessment methods were slightly less sophisticated in the Uganda project, the infants in both samples showed the same types of attachment styles in roughly the same proportions. Taken together, the Uganda and Baltimore observations provided the first data suggesting that babies can develop individual differences in attachment pattern based on parenting practices.

In 1975, Mary began teaching at the University of Virginia where she stayed for the remainder of her impressive career. For decades, John Bowlby and Mary Ainsworth frequently exchanged letters and manuscripts and continued their collaboration until John's death in 1990. Mary received several honours for her contribution to developmental psychology. She died aged eighty-five from a stroke.

THE STRANGE SITUATION PROCEDURE (SSP) AND THE CATEGORICAL MODEL OF ATTACHMENT ("ABCD")

One of Ainsworth's major innovations was the development of a laboratory procedure to measure and classify the child's attachment to his or her caregiver (usually the mother), known as the Strange Situation Procedure (SSP). This signals the second phase of attachment theory. Until this point, little was known about how individual children differed in their developing attachment. Building on Bowlby's ideas of proximity and survival, Ainsworth hypothesised that parenting styles influence children's attachment patterns and how they learn to be in relationships. In other words, Ainsworth's work suggested it is the quality of the parent-child interaction more than the quantity that determines attachment patterns (Holmes, 2014). Ainsworth's Strange Situation Procedure was essential in providing the empirical evidence for Bowlby's theory and continues to be used widely in global infant attachment research.

The early origins of the Strange Situation Procedure (SSP) emerged in Uganda. As reimbursement for their time, Mary offered to drive the mothers and babies to the local health clinic for their routine appointments. Here she was able to sit with babies in a strange, new setting to observe how they managed this slightly scary situation with new people (strangers) and to watch how their mothers responded to them. Similar 'strange situations' include a child's first day at school or nursery or visiting a friend's house without a parent. These clinic observations helped Ainsworth think about how "security" in a relationship is related to both "sensitivity" of care received and emotional self-management under stress. She used these ideas to devise a way to assess security in the attachment relationship.

Earlier researchers had used separation and stress as a method to investigate children's fear and had started to notice links to the security of the mother-child relationship. For example, a researcher called Jean Arsenian used various procedures of mother-infant separation to observe child behaviour in the 1940s, reflecting the post-war social changes of increased female employment and out-of-home childcare. But it was Ainsworth who first connected these ideas to the categorisation of attachment. In 1963 Ainsworth formally designed the SSP for use with the Baltimore mothers and babies. It consists of a twenty-minute session, which meant that lengthy naturalistic observations could be replaced by a much shorter, standardised procedure to categorise patterns of attachments. It is divided into eight episodes lasting for three minutes each:

1 Infant and caregiver enter the laboratory setting (a comfortable room with a couple of chairs and a selection of toys).
2 Caregiver encourages infant to explore but does not participate.
3 After one minute, a stranger enters the room and chats to the mother then tries to interact with the infant.
4 First separation experience: The caregiver conspicuously leaves the room, leaving the infant with the stranger for three minutes.
5 First reunion experience: The caregiver returns and tries to comfort the infant.
6 Second separation experience: The caregiver leaves for a second time, this time the stranger also leaves, and the infant is left alone.
7 The stranger re-enters the room and offers comfort to the infant.
8 Second reunion experience: Finally, the caregiver returns and tries to comfort the infant.

These episodes incrementally increase stress to the infant thereby activating the attachment behavioural system. The procedure is videotaped and rated, focusing particularly on the infant's response to separation (stress) and reunion (comfort). What is intriguing is the individual differences that babies have in coping with stress and the corresponding caregiving patterns demonstrated by their mothers. Ainsworth categorised these distinct reactions into three main groups: securely attached (group B) and two types of insecure attachments known as avoidant (group A) and ambivalent (group C). A fourth group (group D) was added later through the work of Mary Main (Main & Solomon, 1990). Each group had remarkable consistency with parental patterns, specifically a mother's responsiveness to infant's distress and exploratory behaviour (see Table 2.1). This was an important finding; that a young child's attachment pattern can be reliably predicted from how effectively the parent provides sensitivity and security. Ainsworth was the first to suggest that the babies of sensitive mothers would become securely attached, and the babies of insensitive mothers would become insecurely attached.

Research has confirmed an association between parental sensitivity and attachment category (Juffer, Bakermans-Kranenburg and IJzendoorn, 2008). Generally, more sensitive parents do tend to have more securely attached children, but the relationship is perhaps less strong that Ainsworth hypothesised (De Wolff & van IJzendoorn, 1997). Other suggestions include that the infant's temperament may moderate attachment patterns (e.g., Kagan, 1984) and Patricia Crittenden, a later student of Ainsworth's, suggested that attachment categories are more adaptable than first thought (e.g., Crittenden, Landini & Spieker, 2021). Lamb (1977) pointed out that the Strange Situation Procedure only assesses a young child's attachment to their mother, but children might have different attachment patterns with different carers (dad, grandparent, aunt, childminder, etc.). However, Ainsworth's development of attachment theory was ground-breaking because she used detailed observation of mother-infant interactions to develop insights into the individual differences in attachment patterns, identified common categories of attachment security and devised a brief, standardised tool to measure them.

Table 2.1 Caregiving patterns and corresponding attachment styles

Parental or caregiving pattern/Sensitive responsiveness	*Attachment classification and origin*	*Behavioural description*
Key features: Consistently available Sensitive to infant's distress Offers comfort Not overwhelmed by infant's distress Child learns: My parent is reliable and trustworthy, my feelings are important, I matter	B – Secure attachment 65% of Ainsworth's sample, Ainsworth et al. (1978)	These babies cried (attachment behaviour activated) when their mother left the room and were relieved or quickly soothed when she returned and offered comfort. Babies returned to play and exploration once regulated (calm, attachment behaviour deactivated).
Key features: Consistently rejecting to infant's distress (e.g. minimising, 'pull your socks up' Fewer interactions with infant Child learns: There's no point in crying because no one notices or cares, it's better to figure things out myself, rely on myself. Feelings don't matter.	A – Insecure-Avoidant attachment 21% of Ainsworth's sample, Ainsworth et al. (1978)	These babies didn't seem to notice when their mother left the room and didn't show overt signs of distress. Tended to ignore their mother when reunited, especially during the second episode (stranger) where the stress is greater. These babies tended to be inhibited in their play. Can be described as 'hypo-activating' or 'shutting down' their distress (attachment behaviour).
Key features: Inconsistent – sometimes available, sometimes not Intrusive interactions, generally unpredictable Child learns: I don't know what to expect so it's better keep 'my heart on my sleeve' - this gives me the best chance at getting some connection and comfort.	C – Insecure-Ambivalent attachment 14% of Ainsworth's sample, Ainsworth et al. (1978)	These babies tended to be clingy to their mothers even before she left the room, became very distressed by separation and not easily comforted when reunited. Babies often wanted contact, but then resisted by kicking, turning away or refusing toys. These babies found it hard to return to play. Can be described as 'hyper-activating' their distress (attachment behaviour).

Parental or caregiving pattern/Sensitive responsiveness	*Attachment classification and origin*	*Behavioural description*
Key features: Frightening to or frightened by their infants Associated with trauma and abuse Child learns: The person who is supposed to look after me is scary / hurts me and should not be trusted. I don't know how to get my needs met Over time I'll learn to control other or look after others so that the world feels a bit more predictable	D – Disorganised attachment Main and Solomon (1990)	These babies did not fit easily into the above categories and showed a range of unusual behaviours including freezing in presence of mother, approaching then moving aside, disorientation, stereotyped movements such as rocking or curling up into a ball during reunification.

A NOTE ON DISORGANISATION

Mary Main, who was a student of Mary Ainsworth, and colleagues transformed the field of attachment in two ways: first, they extended the study of infant attachment to adults by devising the Adult Attachment Interview (George, Kaplan & Main, 1985) (see Chapter 6), and second, Main and Solomon identified a fourth category of attachment – disorganised attachment – expanding the theory into contemporary clinical theory and practice. Main's theory of disorganised attachment is summarised in a classic paper (Main & Solomon, 1990) hypothesising that the parents of infants classified as disorganised are frightening to or frightened of their infants – and that this is because of *their own* unresolved loss or trauma (see Chapter 8). A series of meta-analyses (Cyr, Euser, Bakermans-Kranenburg & van IJzendoorn, 2010) shows the destructive impact of child maltreatment for attachment security as well as disorganisation, but also that the accumulation of socioeconomic risks appears to have a similar impact on attachment disorganisation.

This highlights that socioeconomic adversities can contribute to disorganisation and that parental behaviour is not the only causal factor.

According to Mary Main, disorganised infants lack a coherent strategy for getting their needs met – there is nowhere safe for them to turn, and they are left with an irresolvable paradox in which the caregiver is both the *"source and the solution to its alarm"* (Main & Solomon, 1990, pp 163). Main and Hesse (1990) called this "*fright without solution*". However, they argued that over time children do in fact develop strategies to manage either by aggressively controlling or by providing care (e.g., controlling via "role-reversal") to their parent. For these children the world does not generally feel safe unless they are in charge. Hence, the word disorganised may be a misnomer; while one "organised" strategy may not be possible in the face of unpredictable, hostile or dangerous carers, the child is still organising their behaviour, albeit seemingly chaotic or aggressive behaviour, to give themselves the best chance of security and survival.

It is important to remember that attachment patterns are functional – children have learned to adapt to their environment and work out the best way to keep their caregivers close by and get their needs met. We now understand that children are resourceful and adaptable in such a way that their attachment style reflects their best attempt to elicit safe and responsive care from their caregiver.

Main's work led to new research into the study of child maltreatment and early life relationships. In middle-class community samples, around 14% of children might be classified as disorganised (van IJzendoorn, Schuengel & Bakermans-Kranenburg, 1999). But this figure rises dramatically as children find themselves in more stressful situations such as experiencing poverty, parental mental illness, or environmental stress. Rates of disorganised attachment have been found between 22% (Vasileva & Petermann, 2018) and 90% (Cicchetti, Rogosch & Toth, 2006) in children known to have been abused or neglected. Links between frightening caregiver behaviour and disorganised attachment are well established, accounting for 13% of the variance in disorganisation (Madigan et al., 2006). Infants classified as disorganised have a significantly elevated risk of negative developmental and mental health outcomes (see Chapter 4), the most well-evidenced finding is an association with externalising problems such as aggression (Fearon, Bakermans-Kranenburg, van IJzendoorn, Lapsley & Roisman, 2010; Sroufe, Egeland, Carlson & Collins, 2009).

Patricia Crittenden was a student of Mary Ainsworth's around ten years later than Mary Main and was interested in the links between attachment category and danger in the caregiving environment. Crittenden (1995) rejected the construct of "disorganisation" and suggested that children showed highly organised combinations of avoidant and resistant attachment strategies, leading to the development of the Dynamic Maturational Model of attachment, a somewhat different classification of attachment organisation, retaining the A, B and C categories, but substituting A/C for D.

MATERNAL SENSITIVITY AND ATTACHMENT SECURITY

Ainsworth had hypothesised that a child's attachment style is dependent on the behaviour the mother shows towards them (Ainsworth, Blehar, Waters & Wall, 1978). She was interested in four aspects of early care: sensitivity to infant signals, cooperation vs. interference with ongoing behaviour, psychological and physical availability, and acceptance vs. rejection of infant's needs. Specifically, she proposed that the most important aspect of maternal behaviour is sensitive responsiveness to infant cues and communications.

Mary Ainsworth developed the Maternal Sensitivity Scale to use as a measure in her Baltimore longitudinal study. Her method uses a nine-point scale (nine being very high and one being very low) in several important maternal traits and behaviours organised into four scales (see Table 2.2). For this measurement to be accurate, it is essential that the researcher has developed good observations and insight into the behaviour of the caregiver (Benson & Haith, 2009). The Maternal Sensitivity Scales provide a global measure of parental sensitivity and tap into "the extent to which a particular mother is able to gear her interaction with a particular baby in accordance with the behavioural signals he gives of his states, needs, and eventually, of his wishes and plans" (Ainsworth et al., 1978, p. 152).

Table 2.2 Maternal Sensitivity Scales

Scale	*Description*
Scale 1 Sensitivity V Insensitivity to the baby's signals	Awareness of baby's signals (engagement signals like eye-contact, smiling / disengagement signals like looking away, losing interest in an activity or getting tired), accurate interpretation of the signal, and a prompt and appropriate response e.g. noticing that baby looks down and rubs his eyes, mother might say "oh maybe you're getting tired, is it time for a nap?" and then picks up the baby to offer comfort.
Scale 2 Cooperation V Interference with baby's ongoing behaviour	The extent to which a mother's behaviour functions to support baby's play (tuned in and led by baby) or cuts-across/intrudes (overhandling, poking, intruding, restraining). Cooperative behaviour might be a mother who facilitates play without interfering, or who gradually slows down the pace of play before bedtime, bringing the baby into a relaxed state in anticipation of bedtime. Interfering behaviour might be picking up a baby who is content playing on the floor.
Scale 3 Physical and Psychological Availability V Ignoring and Neglecting	The central issue here is the mother's accessibility to the infant – being aware of the baby even when busy with other tasks, ability to readily switch attention, ability to regulate own feelings and respond to baby, always alert to what baby's needs. Inaccessible mothers can be unaware of baby's signals (e.g., do not perceive them in the first place) or are aware but do not respond to them (ignore).
Scale 4 Acceptance V Rejection of Baby's Needs	This scale deals with the balance between a mother's positive and negative feelings towards her baby – and the extent to which she can integrate or manage these normal feelings. It is assumed that there are positive and negative aspects in all mother-baby relationships – ambivalence is normal. The issue is the way in which a mother acknowledges and balances these out (e.g., what is lost and gained from becoming a parent).

TRANSMISSION OF ATTACHMENT

Once Ainsworth, Main and others had established the idea of attachment categories and the role of maternal sensitivity, researchers began to ask whether the same patterns could be passed from one generation to the next. Over the past thirty years, the dominant school of thought has evolved to focus on the construct of "reflective functioning" (Fonagy, Steele, Moran, Steele & Higgitt, 1991) also known as "mentalization" (Fonagy, Gergely, Jurist & Target, 2002) as the primary mechanism of the transmission of attachment. Peter Fonagy and Mary Target first coined the term "mentalization" to describe a person's "ability to make sense of one's own and other's mental states, and to reflect on these, and to realise that behaviour is driven by psychological and emotional factors" (Music, 2010, p. 66). Mentalizing is about having insight into one's feelings and the reasons for them, especially difficult emotions such as anger or sadness. Mentalization has also been described as trying to "understand misunderstandings". It involves looking beyond behaviour and considering what the *reason* for the behaviour is (Slade, 2006). Everyone mentalizes to a degree, but some more than others, and we are rarely aware of it.

Major developments in attachment research over the past thirty years have introduced parental mentalization as a predictor of infant-parent attachment security. Research in infant attachment has found a significant association between maternal reflective functioning and infant attachment security assessed using the SSP (Slade, Grienenberger, Bernbach, Levy & Locker, 2005; Camoirano, 2017). A meta-analysis by Zeegers, Colonnesi, Stams & Meins (2017) examined the relationship between parental mentalization, parental sensitivity and attachment security. The results showed a positive relationship between parental mentalization and infant attachment security, and between parental mentalization and sensitivity. This means that parents who are better at mentalizing and responding sensitively to their baby are more likely to find their infant has a secure attachment.

Closely related to reflective functioning / mentalization is the construct of "mind-mindedness" (Meins, Fernyhough, Fradley & Tuckey, 2001) which is defined as the parent's ability to read their child's mental states and verbalise this during interactions (e.g., make 'mind-related' comments). Examples of mind-related comments might include a parent wondering out loud what might be wrong if their baby suddenly starts to cry "oh dear, that must have startled you" or "oh dear, you thought I had disappeared but I'm right here". Meins coded the spontaneous language that mother's use to describe their children's experience, reflecting their ability to recognise that their child has their own mind. She found that mothers of avoidant children (group A) made few mind-related comments whereas mothers of ambivalent children (group C) made mind-related comments that were often inaccurate. Secure children (group B) had mothers who made accurate mind-related comments, hypothesising that the experience of having your own mental states reflected in an attuned and coherent way helps the child to build awareness of their own and other's mental states (Music, 2010). By contrast, having your mental states go unattended or inaccurately misinterpreted negatively influences one's sense that the world is responsive and trustworthy.

During the first phase of attachment theory, John Bowlby had drawn attention to the idea that every child needs proximity to a safe caregiver as the basis for emotional security. The second phase of attachment, spearheaded by Mary Ainsworth and followed by a rich tradition of attachment research, demonstrated that individual children develop a particular pattern of attachment in response to the quality of care they have received but which might be modified by factors such as infant temperament, the amount of stress in their environment or how well their carers can mentalize or 'mind-read'. This focus on psychological wellbeing being related to actual experiences of care challenged the psychoanalytical view from the early 1900s that *internal, psychic* experiences lay at the heart of psychological distress or disturbance. We conclude the chapter by now examining the role cultural differences can make in the development of attachment.

BRIEF APPRAISAL OF ATTACHMENT THEORY AND APPLICATION ACROSS CULTURES

All theories evolve during a particular time in history and within a specific cultural context, so it is crucial to critically appraise attachment theory's applicability today and in different contexts and cultures. There have been several helpful reviews (Prior & Glaser, 2006; van IJzendoorn & Sagi-Schwartz, 2008; van IJzendoorn & Bakermans-Kranenburg, 2010) which point towards the conclusion that attachment is a universal phenomenon therefore applicable across cultures. This makes good sense; Bowlby started from the evolutionary perspective that every baby is innately driven to attach to a carer who can maximise their chance of survival. Indeed, attachment behaviour is similarly seen in other species (Mesman, 2016). However, international studies show that what may differ are the nuances of attachment relationships. In other words, while there is a large degree of *universality* in attachment, there are also some *contextual* elements related to culture. How do attachment security and insecurity differ across cultures and in what ways are those differences related to culture-specific parenting practices?

We do not yet have a well-developed body of research which looks at cultural differences within communities, villages or even countries ("intra-cultural"). There are more studies comparing differences between countries ("cross-cultural"). One study which looked at both types of cultural differences is Van IJzendoorn and Kroonenberg (1988) who conducted a meta-analysis (an analysis of multiple other studies) of nearly two thousand Strange Situation classifications from eight countries. Table 2.3 shows a summary of their data on attachment classifications in different countries.

Table 2.3 Cross-cultural patterns of attachment (IJzendoorn and Kroonenberg, 1988)

	Attachment classification, %		
Country (no of studies)	*Secure*	*Avoidant*	*Ambivalent*
USA (18)	65	21	14
UK (1)	75	22	3
Holland (4)	67	26	7
Germany (3)	57	35	8
Japan (2)	68	5	27
China (1)	50	25	25
Israel (2)	64	7	29
Sweden (1)	74	22	4

Results indicate that the average findings were broadly consistent with Ainsworth's original research in as much as secure patterns predominate, typically occurring at rates of 50–75%. This shows that in all countries studied, secure attachments tend to be the norm suggesting that broadly speaking, reliably sensitive parenting predominates. This also supports Bowlby's idea that attachment is a universal phenomenon.

The proportion and distribution of the two insecure patterns varies between cultures with variation linked to differences in child-rearing practices and parenting goals for that particular culture. For example, Western cultures tend to show higher percentages of avoidant classifications, which might be generally associated with unresponsive parenting and more aligned to a drive for early independence and individualism.

Van IJzendoorn and Kroonenberg's findings are in line with other cross-cultural research which shows that "the different types of attachment appear to be present in various Western and non-Western cultures. Avoidant, secure and resistant attachments have been observed in African, East Asian and Latin American studies" (Mesman, van IJzendoorn & Sagi-Schwartz, 2016). However, Van IJzendoorn and Kroonenberg also found that "intra-cultural" differences were about 1.5 times greater than "cross-cultural" differences. In other words, subgroups of families looked a lot more similar to subgroups in other countries than they did to some of the families in their own country.

Children are cared for in a way that is culturally defined, and this care is the basis for the attachment relationship (Morelli et al., 2017). It is therefore critical for the attachment relationship to be understood in context and for practitioners to appreciate the extraordinary richness of cultural diversity and avoid the trap of assuming that one way of parenting is better than another. Beliefs about the 'best' way to bring up a baby differ across cultures and shapes many aspects of how we take care of babies, feed them, keep them safe and communicate with them. Parenting does not occur in a vacuum and the extent to which a culture values independence or inter-dependence profoundly shapes caregiving and parenting practices (see Table 2.4).

The distinction between collectivist and individualistic cultures is a helpful one, even if the distinction describes a spectrum rather than any absolute differentiation (Geertz, 2017; Music, 2010). Heidi Keller and colleagues (2007) found that German babies spent

Table 2.4 Overview of collectivist and individualistic societies, values and practices

Society	*Sociocentric or collectivist cultures*	*Egocentric or individualistic culture*
Community	Non-western communities	Western communities
Values	Relationships Inter-dependence Social and community goals Needs of group above self	Autonomy Independence Self-control Individual goals Achievement
Caregiving behaviours or practices	Co-sleeping, breast-feeding for longer and on-demand, carrying baby and anticipating needs, little or no separation, teaching child to have sense of duty and attentiveness to feelings and needs of others	Independent sleeping / sleep 'training', shorter breastfeeding relationship / bottle feeding, use of buggies, teaching child to 'self-soothe' and to be independent and self-reliant

forty percent of their time out of reach of their mothers, whereas babies in rural, Cameroonian communities were never alone – in fact separation was unimaginable (Keller, Abels, Borke, Lamm, Su, Wang & Lo, 2007). Cameroonian mothers kept their infants close-by, anticipated their needs and immediately offered comfort via breastfeeding. When shown videos of German mothers trying to comfort their children without breastfeeding, they were shocked and even wondered if they were their real mothers! The finding that Germans have higher rates of avoidant attachment makes sense – children are parented in a way that shapes self-reliance, compliance and independence – broadly reflective of Western culture and values.

SUMMARY

Starting with changes in hospital visiting procedures across Europe, Bowlby's and Ainsworth's pioneering work has continued to influence large-scale public health and policy change in the UK and globally (e.g., Early Head Start in the US, Sure Starts in the UK and more recently The Best Start for Life initiative). The availability of the Strange Situation Procedure has led to a formidable explosion of clinical research and the subsequent development of effective therapeutic interventions designed to enhance caregiver sensitivity and prevent attachment disorganisation (see Chapters 10–12 about applications). Mentalization, reflective functioning and mind-mindedness all refer to the ability of parents to be responsive to their children – crucial to the development of secure attachments and happy children. These more recent developments have continued to support Bowlby's original assertion that attaching is a universal phenomenon and Ainsworth's demonstration that despite culture-specific parenting practices, secure attachment predominates.

RECOMMENDED READING

Howe, D. (2005). Child abuse and neglect: Attachment, development and intervention. Palgrave Macmillan.

Howe, D. (2011). Attachment across the life course: A brief introduction. Palgrave Macmillan.

Keller, H. (2022). The myth of attachment theory: A critical understanding for multicultural societies. Routledge.

Saltman, B. (2020). Strange Situation: A mother's journey into the science of attachment. Random House.

REFERENCES

Ainsworth, M. D. S. (1967). *Infancy in Uganda: infant care and the growth of love.* Johns Hopkins Press.

Ainsworth, M. D. S. (1977). Infant development and mother-infant interaction among Ganda and American families. *Culture and infancy* (pp. 119–149).

Ainsworth, M. D. S., Blehar, M. C., Waters, E. & Wall, S. (1978). *Patterns of attachment: A psychological study of the strange situation.* Lawrence Erlbaum.

Ainsworth, M. D. S. & Marvin, R. S. (1995). On the shaping of attachment theory and research: An interview with Mary D. S. Ainsworth (Fall, 1994). *Monographs of the Society for Research in Child Development*, 60(2/3): 3–21.

Benson, J. & Haith, M. (2009). *Social and emotional development in infancy and early childhood* (1st ed.). Academic.

Camoirano, A. (2017). Mentalizing makes parenting work: A review about parental reflective functioning and clinical interventions to improve it. *Frontiers in Psychology*, 8(14): 1–12.

Cicchetti, D., Rogosch, F. & Toth, S. (2006). Fostering secure attachment in infants in maltreating families through preventive interventions. *Development and Psychopathology*, 18(3): 623–649.

Crittenden, P.M. (1995). Attachment and psychopathology. In S. Goldberg, R. Muir & J. Kerr (Eds), *John Bowlby's attachment theory: Historical, clinical, and social significance* (pp. 367–406). Analytic Press.

Crittenden, P. M., Landini, A. & Spieker, S. J. (2021). Staying alive: A 21st century agenda for mental health, child protection and forensic services. *Human Systems*, 1(1): 29–51.

Cyr, C., Euser, E. M., Bakermans-Kranenburg, M. J. & Van IJzendoorn, M. H. (2010). Attachment security and disorganization in maltreating and high-risk families: A series of meta-analyses. *Development and Psychopathology*, 22(1): 87–108.

De Wolff, M. S. & IJzendoorn, M. H. (1997). Sensitivity and attachment: A meta-analysis on parental antecedents of infant attachment. *Child development*, 68(4): 571–591.

Fearon, R. P., Bakermans-Kranenburg, M. J., Van IJzendoorn, M. H., Lapsley, A. M. & Roisman, G. I. (2010). The significance of insecure attachment and disorganization in the development of children's externalizing behavior: a meta-analytic study. *Child Development*, 81(2): 435–456.

Fonagy, P., Steele, M., Moran, G., Steele, H. & Higgitt, A. (1991). The capacity for understanding mental states: The reflective self in parent and child and its significance for security of attachment. *Infant Mental Health Journal*, 13: 200–216.

Fonagy, P., Gergely, G., Jurist, E. L. & Target, M. (2002). *Affect Regulation, Mentalization, and the Development of the Self* (1st ed.). Routledge.

Geertz, C. (2017). *The interpretation of cultures* (3rd ed.). Basic Books.

George, C., Kaplan, N. & Main, M. (1985). *Adult Attachment Interview*. Unpublished manuscript. Berkeley, CA: University of California.

Holmes, J. (2014). *John Bowlby and Attachment Theory* (2nd ed.). Routledge.

Juffer, F., Bakermans-Kranenburg, M. & IJzendoorn, M. (Eds). (2008). *Promoting positive parenting: an attachment-based intervention*. Psychology Press.

Kagan, J., Reznick, J. S., Clarke, C., Snidman, N. & Garcia-Coll, C. (1984). Behavioral inhibition to the unfamiliar. *Child development* (pp. 2212–2225).

Keller, H., Abels, M., Borke, J., Lamm, B., Su, Y., Wang, Y. & Lo, W. (2007). Socialization environments of Chinese and Euro-American middle-class babies: Parenting behaviors, verbal discourses and ethnotheories. *International Journal of Behavioral Development*, 31(3): 210–217.

Lamb, M. E. (1977). The development of mother-infant and father-infant attachments in the second year of life. *Developmental Psychology*, 13: 637–648.

Madigan, S., Bakermans-Kranenburg, M. J., Van IJzendoorn, M. H., Moran, G., Pederson, D. R. & Benoit, D. (2006). Unresolved states of mind, anomalous parental behavior, and disorganized attachment: A review and meta-analysis of a transmission gap. *Attachment & human development*, 8(2): 89–111.

Main, M. & Solomon, J. (1990). Procedures for identifying infants as disorganized/disoriented during the Ainsworth Strange Situation. In M. T. Greenberg, D. Cicchetti & E. M. Cummings (Eds), *Attachment in the preschool years: Theory, research, and intervention* (pp. 121–160). The University of Chicago Press.

Main, M. & Hesse, E. (1990). Parents' unresolved traumatic experiences are related to infant disorganized attachment status: Is frightened and/or frightening parental behavior the linking mechanism? In M. T. Greenberg, D. Cicchetti & E. M. Cummings (Eds), *Attachment in the preschool years: Theory, research, and intervention* (pp. 161–182). The University of Chicago Press.

Meins, E. & Fernyhough, C. (1999). Linguistic acquisitional style and mentalising development: The role of maternal mind-mindedness. *Cognitive Development*, 14(3): 363–380.

Meins, E., Fernyhough, C, Fradley, E. & Tuckey, M. (2001). Rethinking maternal sensitivity: mother's comments on infants' mental processes predict security of attachment at 12 months. *Journal of Child Psychology and Psychiatry and Allied Disciplines, 42(5)*: 637–648.

Mesman, J, van IJzendoorn, M. H. and Sagi-Schwartz, A. (2016). Cross-cultural patterns of attachment. Universal and contextual dimensions. In J. Cassidy and P. Shaver (Eds), *Handbook of attachment: Theory, research and clinical applications* (3rd ed.). Guilford Press.

Morelli, G. A., Chaudhary, N., Gottlieb, A., Keller, H., Murray, M., Quinn, N., Rosabal-Coto, M., Scheidecker, G., Takada, A. & Vicedo, M. (2017). Taking culture seriously: A pluralistic approach to attachment. In H. Keller & K. A. Bard (Eds), *The cultural nature of attachment: Contextualizing relationships and development* (pp. 139–169). MIT Press.

Music, G. (2010). *Nurturing natures: Attachment and children's emotional, social and brain development.* Taylor & Francis.

Prior, V. & Glaser, D. (2006). *Understanding attachment and attachment disorders: Theory, evidence and practice.* Jessica Kingsley Publishers.

Salter, M. (1940). *An evaluation of adjustment based upon the concept of security.* University of Toronto Press.

Slade, A.Grienenberger, J., Bernbach, E., Levy. D. & Locker, A. (2005). Maternal reflective functioning, attachment, and the transmission gap: a preliminary study. *Attachment and Human Development*, 7(3): 283–298.

Slade, A. (2006). Parental Reflective Functioning. *Psychoanalytic Inquiry*, 26: 640–657.

Sroufe, L. A., Egeland, B., Carlson, E. A. & Collins, W. A. (2009). *The development of the person: The Minnesota study of risk and adaptation from birth to adulthood*. Guilford Press.

Steele, H., Steele, M. & Fonagy, P. (1996). Associations among attachment classifications of mothers, fathers, and their infants. *Child Development*, 67(2): 541–555.

Van IJzendoorn, M. H. & Kroonenberg, P. M. (1988). Cross-cultural patterns of attachment: A meta-analysis of the Strange Situation. *Child Development*, 59(1): 147–156.

Van IJzendoorn M.H., Schuengel, C. & Bakermans-Kranenburg, M.J. (1999) Disorganized attachment in early childhood: meta-analysis of precursors, concomitants, and sequelae. *Developmental Psychopathology*, 11(2): 225–249.

Van IJzendoorn, M. H. & Bakermans-Kranenburg, M. J. (2010). Invariance of adult attachment across gender, age, culture, and socioeconomic status? *Journal of Social and Personal Relationships, 27(2)*: 200–208.

Van IJzendoorn, M. H. & Sagi-Schwartz, A. (2008). Cross-cultural patterns of attachment: Universal and contextual dimensions. In J. Cassidy & P. R. Shaver (Eds), *Handbook of attachment: Theory, research, and clinical applications* (pp. 880–905). The Guilford Press.

Van IJzendoorn, M. H. & Kroonenberg, P. M. (1988). Cross-Cultural Patterns of Attachment: A Meta-Analysis of the Strange Situation. *Child Development*, 59(1): 147–156.

Vasileva, M. & Petermann, F. (2018). Attachment, development, and mental health in abused and neglected preschool children in foster care: A meta-analysis. *Trauma, Violence, & Abuse*, 19(4): 443–458.

Zeegers, M. A. J., Colonnesi, C., Stams, G.-J. J. M. & Meins, E. (2017). Mind matters: A meta-analysis on parental mentalization and sensitivity as predictors of infant–parent attachment. *Psychological Bulletin*, 143(12): 1245–1272.

3

THE NEUROBIOLOGY OF ATTACHMENT

Dr Ruth O'Shaughnessy

INTRODUCTION

In the past thirty years, burgeoning research has provided insight into brain areas involved in processing and managing emotions, and crucially how the human brain develops in response to our first relationship experiences. Scientific advances, particularly Positron Emission Tomography and functional Magnetic Resonance Imaging brain scans, suggest that the way parents interact with their child can have long-term effects on multiple aspects of their health and development. In short, research suggests that the attachment relationship is a major organiser of brain development (Schore, 2001), and that sensitive, responsive parenting can shape brain systems optimally, enabling children to better enjoy and achieve in life.

This chapter will provide a basic overview of brain structure and function, and an introduction to the more relevant and accessible findings from research in the field of attachment and neurobiology.

THE STRUCTURE AND EVOLUTION OF THE HUMAN BRAIN

Our nervous system is made up of our brain, our spinal cord and all our nerves. The basic building blocks of our nervous system are nerve cells called neurons. There are about one hundred billion neurons in a newborn baby's brain which means that neurons must be made at a rate of a quarter of a million cells per second throughout pregnancy (Ackerman, 1992).

DOI: 10.4324/9780203703878-3

Neurons have long, thin cell bodies that carry electrical and chemical messages around the brain and to and from the nerves, and this is how our body communicates both internally and with the outside world. The nervous system takes in information through our senses, processes the information and triggers reactions, such as making your muscles move or causing you to feel pain. For example, if you touch a hot plate, you reflexively pull back your hand and your nerves simultaneously send pain signals to your brain (Yam et al., 2018). Similarly, when a baby senses danger in his or her environment, distress signals are sent to their brain simultaneously activating the attachment behavioural system (see HPA axis theory below).

The human brain is infinitely complex so unless you are a neuroscientist it is helpful to adopt a simpler model to describe it. MacLean (1990) suggests we think of the brain as having three main parts; the basal ganglia (which he called the reptilian brain), the midbrain (which he called the mammalian brain and is sometimes referred to as the limbic system) and the cortex. MacLean calls this the triune brain theory and suggests that these three distinct 'brains' emerged during different phases of our evolution as the reptilian brain, the paleo-mammalian brain and the neocortex. They now co-exist in the skull of modern humans, developing largely separately during pregnancy.

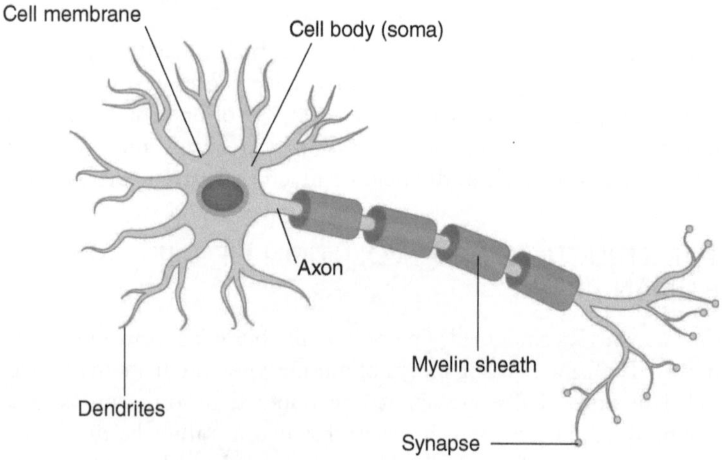

Figure 3.1 A neuron

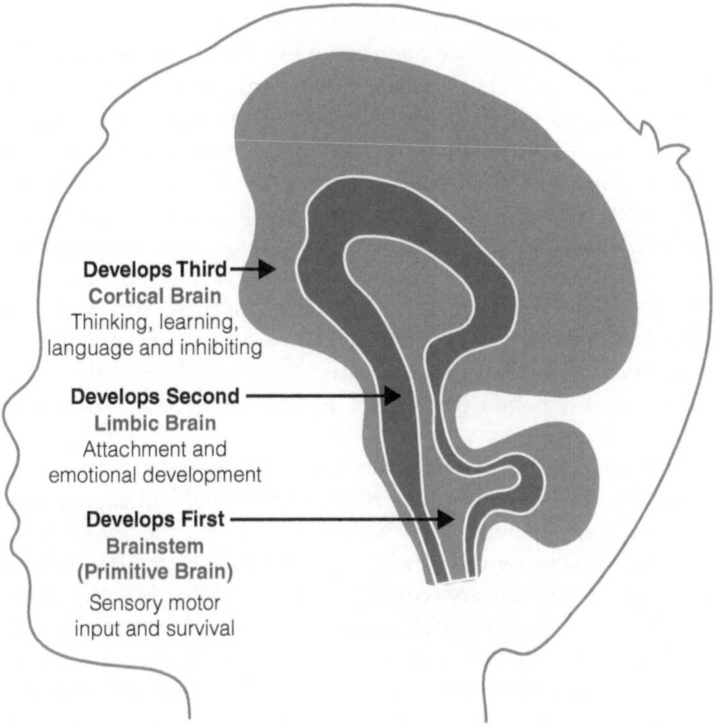

Figure 3.2 The triune brain

MacLean proposed that each of these brain systems have distinct functions but are also connected to each other by multiple networks of neurons. The reptilian brain is the oldest of the three and evolved around three hundred million years ago. It controls vital internal functions such as heart rate, breathing, digestion, temperature, and balance – all the functions which keep us alive without us having to think consciously about them. Our reptilian brain includes the main structures found in a reptile's brain: the brainstem and the cerebellum. The reptilian brain is predominantly concerned with managing our internal biology to ensure our survival, and so the functions of this area take priority over our higher brain areas. For example, when we are in danger, the reptilian brain quickly signals our body to prepare to 'fight, flight or freeze' while our conscious brain is still thinking about what's happening. The brain stem is reliable and learns fast but tends to be somewhat rigid and compulsive (Naumann, et al., 2015). The reptilian brain is the deepest and oldest structure within the human brain and is largely unchanged by evolution (Naumann et al., 2015).

The paleomammalian or limbic brain emerged in the first mammals, around one hundred and fifty million years ago. It is a collection of brain areas concerned with emotions, memory, feeding, reproduction and caring for young (Queensland Brain Institute, 2019). These include the hippocampus, which is strongly connected to memory, and the amygdala, which plays a central role in emotional responses and how we remember emotional experiences. The amygdala is particularly sensitive to the facial expression of emotion (Benuzzi et al., 2007) especially fearful faces (Thomas et al., 2001).

Between its various components, the limbic system can record memories of interactions that produced good and bad experiences, so it is broadly responsible for forming emotional memories. Fearful memories can be laid down very quickly and strongly, and this makes good evolutionary sense; if we once encountered something which threatens our survival, we need to remember it very clearly so that we can be on high alert next time. Hence, the limbic system is responsible for comparing our immediate experience with memories of past threats, and will activate the "fight, flight or freeze" response when required. The limbic components are also responsible for the value judgments that we make, often unconsciously, that exert such a strong influence on our behaviour.

Lastly, the neocortex, commonly known as the cortex, emerged only around two or three million years ago in primates and culminated in the human brain around two hundred thousand years ago. It is the pinkish-grey crinkly area that you would recognise as the human brain. The cortex is the thinking brain or "smart brain" (Sunderland, 2006) responsible for the development of human language, abstract thought, imagination, self-awareness, planning, organisation, and reflection. The cortex tends to be flexible and has almost infinite capacity for learning. Together, the cortex, and the limbic structures make up the right and left cerebral hemispheres of the brain. The two hemispheres are connected by a bundle of nerves called the corpus callosum, which facilitates efficient communication between the two sides of the brain.

Table 3.1 Summary of major brain areas and their components and functions

Name of brain area	*Key Components*	*Functions*
Reptilian brain	Cerebellum Brainstem	Preparing for fight, flight or freeze Hunger, thirst Digestion Breathing Circulation Temperature Balance, movement Territorial instincts Assessing threats
Paleomammalian brain or Limbic brain	Hippocampus Amygdala Hypothalamus and thalamus Pituitary Gland	Surveilling threats Joy, pleasure Exploration, playfulness Fear Rage Distress (separation distress) Social bonding
Cortex or neocortex	Grey matter White matter Corpus callosum	Thought Reflection, reasoning Language Imagination, creativity Self-awareness Problem-solving Kindness, empathy Planning and organisation

The triune theory of the brain has been criticised for over-simplifying how very complex our brains are (e.g., Deacon, 1990), but it has also been welcomed as a useful metaphor for how the various parts of our brain compete and communicate. For example, in the triune theory, the feelings connected to our memories of love and care, those connected to our primitive survival, would typically override later rational thought. This might explain the enduring strengths of our early attachment experiences. Coan (2008) points out that so many different brain structures are involved in human emotional and social behaviours, that "it is possible to think of the entire human brain as an attachment structure" (p. 244).

THE 'BABY BRAIN'

All babies are born 'early'. Because of the size of the birth canal and the heavy metabolic burden a baby places on his or her mother in-utero, a baby's head can only grow to a certain size before birth. This means that babies are born with underdeveloped brains that are hungry for stimulation and which are ready to be profoundly shaped by their interactions with the world (Music, 2010).

For a baby, their parent *is* their world – their brain and mind are influenced by both negative and positive parent–child interactions. It is no surprise then that the first three months of life have been referred to as the "fourth trimester" (Karp, 2002), which speaks accurately to the vulnerability and malleability of the new-born human.

Babies are born with pretty much all the neurons they will ever have, estimated at 200 billion and nearly twice the number of the adult brain (Sunderland, 2006). In the first three years of life the human brain grows faster than any other part of the body (Huttenlocher, 2002). At birth, a baby's brain is about one-third the size of the adult brain, and within three months it more than doubles its volume (Nowakowski, 2006). Though the infant brain has an overabundance of neurons, there are relatively few connections between them. At birth, each neuron has about two thousand five hundred connections (called synapses) but this will increase rapidly to around fifteen thousand per neuron by the age of around three years (Gopnik, Meltzoff & Kuhl, 1999).

Everything a baby experiences, including the attachment relationship, forges neural connections. In a stroke of evolutionary genius, the infant brain will adapt – for better or for worse – to the local environment. When things go well, the triune systems work together harmoniously, enabling us to flourish and function optimally in different circumstances. However, when things go wrong, one brain system can hijack the others, impacting our ability to cope and be resilient in the face of perceived challenge.

Crucially, parenting and the quality of attachment relationships make up a major aspect of a new baby's environment. They exert a major influence on how a child's brain systems adapt and learn to interact together, with opportunity in early childhood to lay down robust foundations for lifelong health and wellbeing. Hence, attachment plays a significant role in the brain development of the baby.

KEY PRINCIPLES OF THE GROWTH OF THE DEVELOPING BRAIN

Here, we will simplify three key principles of brain development drawing on the work of Bruce Perry (1998) and Allan Schore (2001), world leaders in the field of neurobiology and attachment.

PRINCIPLE 1: THE BRAIN DEVELOPS IN A SEQUENCE

The brain develops over time from the bottom-up (Perry, 1998) thus the first areas to develop are the brain stem and cerebellum which are 'on-line' from before birth. These regions are responsible for processing sensory information and influencing internal processes to keep the baby alive, physically and psychologically safe from harm. Hence at birth, sensory experiences are of paramount importance for the baby's comfort and sense of safety. The limbic system develops next with the cortex last to mature although capable of adapting throughout life, a process known as neural plasticity.

From a parenting point of view, this sequence is important to understand because during infancy and toddlerhood, the lower brain is 'in charge' and the cortex is not yet developed sufficiently to take charge and regulate arousal. What this means in practice is that a distressed or upset baby is *dependent* on their caregiver for physical and emotional comfort, and to bring their body and brain systems back into balance.

PRINCIPLE 2: BRAIN DEVELOPMENT HAS SENSITIVE PERIODS

The development of brain functions can have "sensitive" periods, sometimes called windows of opportunity, during which the baby needs rich, specific experience to make the necessary connections and pathways and achieve a developmental goal (National Scientific Council on the Developing Child, 2007).

The exact timing and duration of sensitive periods differ by function. For example, the sensitive period for being able to pick out the sounds of our native language closes at only six months of age while the window for learning new vocabulary never closes (Shriver, 2001). Animal research has provided clear evidence of the critical role of early life attachment in programming cognitive and emotional health. For example, Harry Harlow and his colleagues (see Chapter 1) were working with rhesus monkeys and assessing the effects of being reared without a mother but providing basic food, water and warmth (Harlow & Harlow, 1965). This work clearly highlighted the importance of the infant's social interactions with the mother during a sensitive period in development since, without the caregiver, infants showed emotional and cognitive difficulties that were reminiscent of human children reared in inadequate orphanages without an attachment figure (Teicher et al., 2016).

Importantly, while the brain retains the ability to adapt and modify its neural circuits throughout life, it becomes far harder to alter neural circuits after the sensitive period has ended (National Scientific Council on the Developing Child, 2007). Applied to attachment, this suggests that what we learn about attachment relationships before the age of two will persist through life, but that later learning is also possible. One of the hopeful findings from neuroscience is that the brain remains plastic throughout life (Doidge, 2008) and that to some degree new learning and the associated brain changes are possible throughout the life course.

PRINCIPLE 3: BRAIN DEVELOPMENT IS EXPERIENCE-DEPENDENT

Though the brain is not a muscle, it can be helpful to think of brain functions as exactly that – a muscle that either gets stronger and grows or weakens and withers according to how much it is used. As discussed, the infant brain has an abundance of neurons, but these are relatively unconnected through neural circuits. How these connections are made largely depends on the environment, which for a baby is largely directed by the caregiving environment. Put simply, the way a parent listens, talks, and comforts are vital in shaping brain pathways.

The overproduction of neurons facilitates a wide range of potential responses from the baby but is followed by a pruning back and elimination of unused pathways. This allows the most strongly reinforced or most frequently used pathways to be strengthened, through a process called myelination. Underused neural pathways become downgraded, allowing raw materials to be recycled and the brain to operate with improved efficiency.

Neural pathways that are repeatedly used are strengthened, becoming part of the brain's architecture (National Scientific Council on the Developing Child, 2007). For example, if most times a baby is upset, they are comforted by his or her parent, pathways are formed and strengthened between the emotional centre in the lower parts of the brain and the cortex (thinking, rational). Through repeated interactions such as this, neural networks create a stronger pathway between the emotions and the memory that one can anticipate a caring, helpful response. This helps the baby learn that care is on the way and that difficult emotions can be managed. This co-regulation, being shown how to soothe oneself by a caring other, lays down the foundations of future self-regulation and of being able to use this blueprint to soothe oneself. Similarly, if a baby is not regularly comforted, he or she might experience prolonged distress, thereby establishing an oversensitive stress response pathway in the brain. It is worth noting that the amygdala, the relevant areas of the cortex and the connections between the two are not mature enough to facilitate self-soothing until around seven to nine months (Hershkowitz, 2000). No matter how sensitive and responsive a parent might be, most babies are incapable of anything more than rudimentary self-soothing until that age.

ATTACHMENT, PARENTING AND THE BRAIN

The essential task of the first year of life is to form an attachment relationship (Bowlby, 1953) so that the chances of survival are maximised. Infants deploy a range of attachment behaviours to promote their chances of attachment; being cute, clinging, engaging in social interaction and crying to signal distress. Infants cannot regulate their own distress and are completely dependent on their attachment figures to help them manage their arousal and return to baseline. A distressed infant's attachment behaviour has a goal of re-connecting with their parent and achieve relief, comfort and regulation. The ways in which parents regulate their infant's physical and physiological arousal, respond to their joy or distress, have profound and long-lasting implications for all aspects of children's development – neurological, cognitive, physical and psychological (Sunderland, 2016). Children who are helped to regulate their arousal in the context of consistent and emotionally responsive parenting, gradually learn to regulate themselves, and eventually learn to think about feelings (Fonagy, Gergely, Jurist & Target, 2002). Hence, this process of "co-regulation" (Feldman, 2003) strengthens attachment relationships. Caregiver co-regulation allows parents to facilitate children's emotional regulation by providing them with external support. These experiences serve as scaffolds for children to develop their own ability to deal with emotional distress in later life.

In this next section, we will focus on the neurobiology of stress and comfort, and the power of the parent–child connection in shaping children's development.

THE NEUROBIOLOGY OF INFANT STRESS

Difficulties in regulating stress and arousal in very early life are a risk factor for the development of mental health and relational difficulties in later life (e.g., Keenan, 2000). There is now compelling evidence that one potential pathway to early dysregulation is the programming of the hypothalamic-pituitary-adrenal (HPA) axis during the last trimester of pregnancy (Glover, O'Connor & O'Donnell, 2010) through to the end of the second year of life (Maniam, Antoniadis & Morris, 2014).

Allan Schore has coined the term "relational stress" (Schore, 2001) and subsequently distinguished between "big T trauma" and "little t trauma". Big T traumas are catastrophic, life-threatening, and intensely distressing events that are typically associated with the word 'trauma' – an accident, violence, abuse, neglect or witnessing the trauma of others. Little t trauma refers to relatively smaller, more interpersonal, distressing events or interactions that are usually not life-threatening. Shore describes how little t trauma may not be so obvious to the observer, but that it too negatively impacts infant brain development, the effects of which need to be better understood. In early childhood, little t trauma essentially refers to when the primary caregiver is chronically "mis-attuned" in his or her responses to the infant. This might be in the form of an intrusive interaction style (e.g., fussing, correcting, interrupting baby's play) or in the form of "benign neglect" where the parent is not emotionally responsive to the baby's cues and communication. The latter can be subtle and harder to identify, with babies often developing a withdrawn position in the attachment relationship – an infant state often misinterpreted as 'an easy baby'. This is why it is crucial for clinicians and front-line practitioners to build expertise in the assessment of early relationships.

Now let's look in more detail to what happens inside an infant's body and brain when they are exposed to too much stress or mis-attunements in the attachment relationship. In the early years, young children need to learn to tolerate both positive feelings – like intense joy or excitement – and negative feelings – like stress and boredom. Research has shown that even in the best functioning mother-infant pairs, they were in an attuned state just thirty per cent of the time (Tronick, 2007). When things go well, parents and babies match each other's rhythms, make eye contact, and share moments of joy. Attuned caregivers also know when to take a break or step back from an interaction and allow space for the infant to look away for a moment of respite. However, perfect parental attunement is not possible, and in daily interactions there is a constant cycle of rupture (mis-attunement) and repair (attunement). Even in securely attached relationships, babies spend a lot of time learning to tolerate mis-attunement. We can recall from Chapter 2, in Ainsworth's Strange Situation Procedure, that separations and reunions play an important role in building attachments. In the Strange Situation, the separation and reunion are *physical*. Mis-attunements in the interaction between parent and infant can be thought of as *emotional* separations and reunions. When the parent and infant fall out of attunement, in other words when the parent is not responding accurately to the baby's cues and communications, the baby is temporarily emotionally separated and therefore stress will start to build. How the dyad reconnects, sometimes called the *repair* of mis-attunement, is key. If the adult can notice the rupture in mis-attunement, and get the interaction back in tune, the baby's stress comes down and he has learnt that temporary emotional separation can be managed.

These inevitable relational mismatches are valuable stress-tolerance practice opportunities for the young child. Infants use manageable stress experiences to grow, develop, and build resilience to later life stressors. However, when these mis-attunements are chronic, the stress becomes developmentally dangerous leading to hypersensitivity of brain regions and hormonal pathways such as the HPA axis.

INFANT STRESS AND THE HPA AXIS

The HPA axis is a complex neuro-hormonal system that manages our reactions to stressful situations. As distress levels build up in a crying baby, a hormonal chain reaction is activated, involving the adrenals, the pituitary gland, and the hypothalamus.

The **hypothalamus** is a small part of the brain that does a very big job, responsible for body temperature, energy levels, and sleep cycles. It is located in the limbic system and its function is to send messages from the brain to the pituitary, the adrenals and other organs. It is usually considered the starting point of the HPA axis.

The **pituitary gland** is about the size of a pea and is physically connected to the hypothalamus and situated at the base of the brain. The pituitary gland has overall control of the body's hormone production.

The **two adrenal glands** are located each above our kidneys. The adrenals also produce hormones, critically stress hormones including cortisol. The hormones produced by the adrenals control chemical reactions throughout our bodies, including some involved in the 'fight, flight, freeze' response.

Activation of the HPA axis starts when an infant's experiences stress. Stress for an infant can have obvious sources (e.g., loud noise, shouting) but can also be difficult to pin-point (e.g., interactive mismatches, boredom, neglect).

Stress activates the hypothalamus to produce a hormone (corticotrophin-releasing hormone) which in turn sends a message to the pituitary gland. This stimulates the pituitary to release adrenocorticotropin, which then prompts the adrenals to make cortisol (Coan, 2008). Among other things, cortisol raises sugar in the baby's bloodstream and prepares his or her body for the 'fight, flight, freeze' response that they are anticipating. This is thought to

Table 3.2 Infant stressors

Environmental	*Physical state of infant*	*Relational states*
Loud noises	Hungry, thirsty	**"Little t"**
Too bright or over-stimulating	Too cold/too hot	Separation from parent
Shouting e.g., Domestic violence	Tired	Mis-attunement, mismatches
Not safely held	Wet/dirty nappy	Boredom
	Feeling ill, temperature	Over- or under-stimulation
		High parental stress
		"Big T"
		Major separation or loss of parent
		Chronic mis-attunement & absence of interactive repair
		Chronic boredom, neglect
		Chronic over stimulation
		Parental mental illness
		Child abuse

be at least one of the mechanisms through which significant stress during infancy raises the risk of adolescent obesity and insulin resistance (Kaufman et al., 2007).

The baby's adrenals also release adrenaline, which raises heart rate and increases blood pressure. A crying baby has a highly activated HPA axis that will keep producing cortisol which can only be 'switched off' by comfort, holding and soothing. Brain scans show that chronic stress in infancy can cause the HPA axis to become permanently wired for stress and cause cell death in brain structures such as the hippocampus (a brain region central to memory) (Bremner, 2002).

THE NEUROBIOLOGY OF COMFORT AND THE ATTACHMENT RELATIONSHIP

Infants and young children cannot control physical and emotional arousal states so they are dependent on their parent to do this for

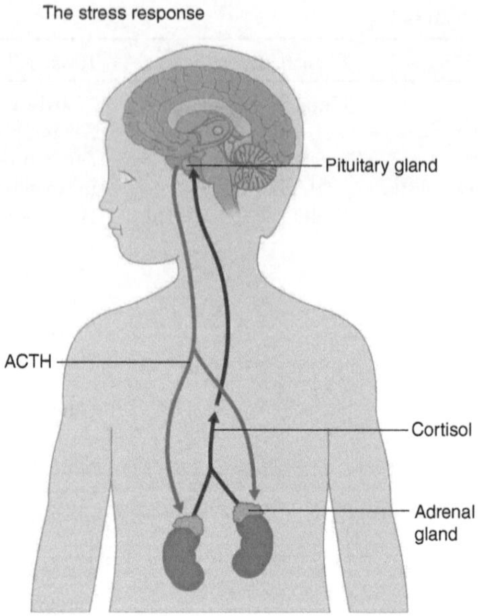

Figure 3.3 HPA axis

them. In effect, a parent functions as an "external frontal lobe" (e.g., Green, 2005) until the young child's cortex is mature enough to manage. Research has shown that babies who receive regular touch have stronger neuronal connections and greater overall well-being (Maitre et al., 2017). In one study with premature babies, the more babies experienced pleasant, nurturing touch (such as breastfeeding or skin contact) the greater the brain response to touch as measured by electrodes (Maitre et al., 2017). Conversely, unpleasant touch, such as skin punctures and tube insertions, were associated with reduced brain activity. In another study, a study of ninety-two seven- to nine-year-olds, who had previously been studied in pre-school, showed that those who had received more nurture and comfort by their mothers had a ten per cent bigger hippocampus than those who were not as well nurtured (Luby et al., 2012). This was the first research of its kind to show the link between early nurturing and changes in the hippocampus, which is a key brain structure important to learning, memory and stress response.

A recent human study supports previous animal studies which show that comforting babies can positively affect babies at a molecular level (Moore, 2017). Parents of ninety-four babies were asked to keep diaries of their touching and cuddling habits from five weeks after birth, as well as logging the behaviour of the infants – sleeping, crying, and so on. Nearly five years later, DNA swabs were taken of the children and differences between "high-contact" children and "low-contact" children were found at five specific DNA sites, two of which were within genes: one related to the immune system, and one to the metabolic system. These results show that greater human contact postnatally can have positive biological effects on the baby, including for the immune and metabolic systems.

What happens in a baby's body and brain when they experience loving comfort? In early life, it is the parent's responsibility to bring their baby back 'into balance' and regulate infant arousal. Comforting a distressed infant activates his or her vagus nerve. The vagus nerve is in the brain stem and is the longest cranial nerve in the human body. It runs alongside the spinal cord, sending out fibres from the brainstem to the major organs. As a parent comforts their baby, the vagus nerve is activated and starts to restore order in baby's brain and body – rebalancing major systems impacted by stress including heart rate, breathing, digestion, and immune system functioning. Research has shown that good vagal tone is linked with a range of psychological, cognitive and physical benefits including emotional balance, clear thinking, better attention, better immune system function, and better digestive system function (Porges, Doussard-Roosevelt & Maiti, 1994; Graziano & Derefinko, 2013). So powerful are these findings that psychotherapist Margot Sunderland described how "one of the greatest gifts you can give your child is good vagal tone" (Sunderland, 2006, p. 45).

The vagus nerve effectively tells a baby's body to relax by releasing hormones such as acetylcholine, vasopressin, and the popularised "feel good" hormone oxytocin. Oxytocin in particular promotes warm and affiliative feelings, with research showing that levels increase when we are with someone we love (Parmar and Malik, 2017). Specifically, infant research has shown that parents can stimulate oxytocin through touch and massage, movement and rocking, cuddling, breastfeeding, and keeping baby warm (Sharma,

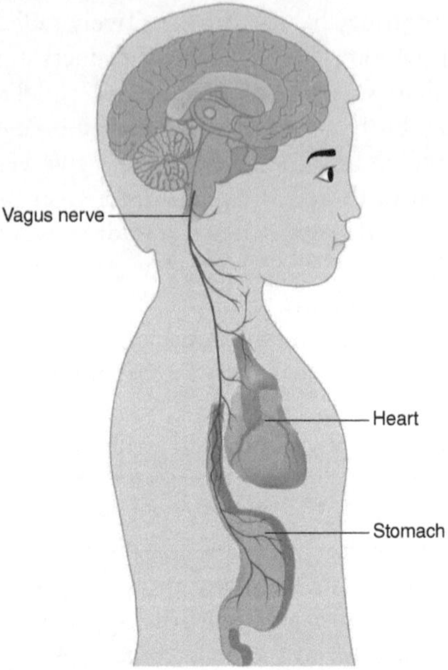

Figure 3.4 Vagus nerve

Gonda, Dome & Tarazi, 2020). Interestingly adult research has found that people with higher oxytocin levels were more trusting, generous and contented (Baumgartner, Heinrichs, Vonlanthen, Fischbacher & Fehr, 2008) leading to trials of oxytocin treatment for a range of problems. However, human biology is rarely that straight forward; oxytocin has also been shown to be increased in women in distressing adult romantic relationships. This led Shelley Taylor to suggest the 'Tend and Befriend' hypothesis; that during stress, oxytocin signals women to tend (to their young) and befriend someone (Taylor, 2011).

SUMMARY

With advances of neuroscience, we now have vital information about how the human brain develops, in particular that the baby brain is "unfinished" and open to being moulded by both positive and negative interactions. Attachment is a biological evolutionary system contributing to infant survival. In children, a secure attachment is vital to healthy brain and stress response system development. With emotionally responsive and attuned parenting, hormones are released in the baby's body, more receptors for these 'good' hormones are established, and a template for future emotional experiences is set up which have life-long benefits.

RECOMMENDED READING

Gerhardt, S. (2004). Why love matters: how affection shapes a baby's brain. Routledge.

Music, G. (2010). Nurturing natures: Attachment and children's emotional, sociocultural and brain development. Psychology Press.

Sunderland, M. (2016). The science of parenting: How today's brain research can help you raise happy, emotionally balanced children (2nd Ed.). Dorling Kindersley.

REFERENCES

Ackerman, S. (1992). *Discovering the brain*. National Academies Press.

Baumgartner, T., Heinrichs, M., Vonlanthen, A., Fischbacher, U. & Fehr, E. (2008). Oxytocin shapes the neural circuitry of trust and trust adaptation in humans. *Neuron*, 58: 639–650.

Benuzzi, F., Pugnaghi, M., Meletti, S., Lui, F., Serafini, M., Baraldi, P. & Nichelli, P. (2007). Processing the socially relevant parts of faces. *Brain Research Bulletin*, 74(5): 344–356.

Bowlby, J. (1953). *Childcare and the growth of love*. Penguin Books.

Bremner, J. D. (2002). Neuroimaging of childhood trauma. *Seminars in Clinical Neuropsychiatry*, 7(2):104–112.

Coan, J. A. (2008). Toward a neuroscience of attachment. In J. Cassidy & P. R. Shaver (Eds), *Handbook of attachment: Theory, research, and clinical applications* (pp. 241–265). The Guilford Press.

Deacon, T. W. (1990). Rethinking mammalian brain evolution. *American Zoologist*, 30(3): 629–705.

Doidge, N. (2008). *The brain that changes itself: stories of personal triumph from the frontiers of brain science*. Penguin.

Feldman. R. (2003). Infant-mother and infant-father synchrony: The coregulation of positive arousal. *Infant Mental Health Journal*, 24(1): 1–23.

Fonagy, P., Gergely, G., Jurist, E. L. & Target, M. (2002). *Affect regulation, mentalization, and the development of the self* (1st Ed.). Routledge.

Glover, V., O'Connor, T. G. & O'Donnell, K. (2010). Prenatal stress and the programming of the HPA axis. *Neuroscience and Biobehavioral Review*, 35(1): 7–22.

Gopnik, A., Meltzoff, A. & Kuhl, P. (1999). *The scientist in the crib: what early learning tells us about the mind*. Harper Collins Publishers.

Graziano, P. & Derefinko, K. (2013). Cardiac vagal control and children's adaptive functioning: A meta-analysis. *Biological Psychology*, 94(1): 22–37.

Green, B. (2005). Cited in C.Y. Johnson, Parents get look at teens' brains. *Boston Globe*, 10 November.

Harlow, H. & Harlow M. (1965). The affectional systems. In A. Schrier, H. Harlow & F. Stollnitz (Eds). *Behavior of nonhuman primates* (Vol. 2, pp. 287–334). Academic Press.

Herschkowitz, N. (2000). Neurological bases of behavioral development in infancy. *Brain & Development*, 22(7): 411–416.

Huttenlocher, P. (2002). *Neural plasticity: The effects of the environment on the development of the cerebral cortex*. Harvard University Press.

Institute of Health. (2018). What are the parts of the nervous system? Eunice Kennedy Shriver National Institute of Child Health and Human Development (linkingin.co), accessed 20 June 2022.

Karp, H. (2002). *The happiest baby on the block*. Bantam Dell.

Kaufman, D., Banerji, M. A., Shorman, I., Smith, E. L., Coplan, J. D., Rosenblum, L. A. & Kral, J. G. (2007). Early-life stress and the development of obesity and insulin resistance in juvenile bonnet macaques. *Diabetes*, 56(5): 1382–1386.

Keenan, K. (2000). Emotion dysregulation as a risk factor for child psychopathology. *Clinical Psychology: Science and Practice*, 7(4): 418–434.

Luby, J. L., Barch, D. M., Belden, A., Gaffrey, M. S., Tillman, R., Babb, C., Nishino, T., Suzuki, H. & Botteron, K. N. (2012). Maternal support in early childhood predicts larger hippocampal volumes at school age. *Proceedings of the National Academy of Sciences of the United States of America*, 109(8): 2854–2859.

MacLean, P. D.(1990). *The Triune Brain in Evolution*. Plenum Press.

Maniam, J. M., Antoniadis, C. & Morris, M. (2014). Early-life stress, HPA axis adaptation, and mechanism contributing to later health outcomes. *Frontiers in Endocrinology*, 5(73): 1–17.

Maitre, N., Key, A., Chorna, O., Slaughter, J., Matusz, P., Wallace, M. & Murray, M. (2017). The dual nature of early-life experience on somatosensory processing in the human infant brain. *Current Biology, 27 (7)*, 1048–1054.

Moore, S. R., McEwen, L. M., Quirt, J., Morin, A., Mah, S. M., Barr, R. G. & Kobor, M. S. (2017). Epigenetic correlates of neonatal contact in humans. *Development and Psychopathology*, 29(5): 1517–1538.

Music, G. (2010). *Nurturing natures: attachment and children's emotional, social and brain development.* Taylor & Francis.

National Scientific Council on the Developing Child. (2007). The timing and quality of early experiences combine to shape brain architecture: Working Paper No. 5. Retrieved from www.developingchild.harvard.edu on 30 June 2022.

Naumann, R. K., Ondracek, J. M., Reiter, S., Shein-Idelson, M., Tosches, M. A., Yamawaki, T. M. & Laurent, G. (2015). The reptilian brain. *Current Biology*, 25(8): 317–321.

Nowakowski, R. S. (2006). Stable neuron numbers from cradle to grave. *Proceedings of the National Academy of Sciences of the United States of America*, 103(33): 12219–12220.

Parmar, P. & Malik, S. (2017) Oxytocin: The hormone of love. *Journal of Pharmacy and Biological Sciences, 12(6)*: 1–9.

Perry, B. (1998). Homeostasis, stress, trauma and adaptation: a neurodevelopmental view of childhood trauma. *Child and Adolescent Psychiatric Clinics*, 7(1): 33–51.

Porges, S. W., Doussard-Roosevelt, J. A. & Maiti, A. K. (1994). Vagal tone and the physiological regulation of emotion. *Monographs of the society for research in child development*: 167–186.

Queensland Brain Institute. (2019). The limbic system. Retrieved from https://qbi.uq.edu.au/brain/brain-anatomy/limbic-system on 30 June 2022.

Sharma, S., Gonda, X., Dome, P. & Tarazi, F. (2020). What's love got to do with it: Role of oxytocin in trauma, attachment and resilience. *Pharmacology & Therapeutics*, 214(7): 107602.

Schore, A. N. (2001). Effects of a secure attachment relationship on right brain development, affect regulation and infant mental health. *Infant Mental Health Journal*, 22(1–2): 7–66.

Shriver, E. (2001). Brain development and mastery of language in early childhood years. Intercultural development research association. www.idra.org/resource-center/brain-development-and-mastery-of-language-in-the-early-childhood-years. Accessed 9 May 2022.

Sunderland, M. (2006). *The science of parenting: How today's brain research can help you raise happy, emotionally balanced children* (2nd Ed.). Dorling Kindersley.

Taylor, S. E. (2011). Tend and befriend theory. In A. M. van Lange, A. W. Kruglanski & E. T. Higgins (Eds). *Handbook of Theories of Social Psychology* (pp. 32–49). Sage Publications.

Teicher, M. H., Samson, J. A., Anderson, C. M. & Ohashi, K. (2016). The effects of childhood maltreatment on brain structure, function and connectivity. *Nature Reviews Neuroscience*, 17(10): 652–666.

Thomas, K. M., Drevets, W. C., Whalen, P. J., Eccard, C. H., Dahl, R. E., Ryan, N. D. & Casey, B. J. (2001). Amygdala response to facial expressions in children and adults. *Biological psychiatry*, 49(4): 309–316.

Tronick, E. (2007). *The neurobehavioral and social emotional development of infants and children*. Norton.

Yam, M. F., Loh, Y. C., Tan, C. S., Khadijah, A. S., Manan, N. & Basir, R. (2018). General Pathways of Pain Sensation and the Major Neuro-transmitters Involved in Pain Regulation. *International Journal of Molecular Science*, 19(8): 2164.

4

MIDDLE CHILDHOOD AND CHILD OUTCOMES IN ATTACHMENT

Dr Karen Bateson

INTRODUCTION

Chapters 1 and 2 describe how babies are born with instinctive motivation to organise their behaviour to maximise attachment security with their caregiver, which in turn increases the chances of survival to child-rearing age. This evolutionary strategy draws upon multiple neurobiological systems including those related to feeding, social interaction, exploration, movement, fear and memory. Babies and toddlers instinctively use attachment behaviours such as clinging, wariness and returning to the "safe haven" of their carer during stress, because these protect them from a wide range of dangers. Very young children are also cute and sociable in ways which strengthen and expand the network of attachment figures who will provide them with protection (Marvin, Britner & Russell, 2016).

In this chapter, we describe how attachment develops from toddlerhood to adolescence and summarise some of the longer-term outcomes of attachment status where it was measured before the age of three. We will show how attachment patterns relate to important developmental milestones such as starting school, making new friends and becoming more independent. One of the biggest debates in the attachment field is whether a person can change attachment categories in response to new life experiences. Can you be securely attached as a baby and then become insecure as an older child, or vice versa? In this chapter we will review research about the stability and potential for change in attachment styles during middle

DOI: 10.4324/9780203703878-4

childhood. This is a theme which will be picked up in the later chapters on attachment in adolescence and adulthood.

ATTACHMENT DURING PRE-SCHOOL YEARS (2–5 YEARS)

Infancy is a time of developmental sensitivity for attachment when much of the baby's behaviour is oriented towards attaching. By around the age of twelve months old, babies' attachment patterns are stable enough to be measured through observing certain interactions, such as separation and reunion. As described in Chapter 2, where the baby's care-seeking behaviour has received a predominantly predictable and positive response, the baby is likely to have formed a secure attachment pattern. If, however, care-seeking has been followed by neglect, hostility or confusing responses from the caregiver, the attachment pattern formed is more likely insecure or disorganised. After twelve months of age, the baby is still able to form new attachments and (re)organise existing ones. However, infants placed in foster care after twelve months of age show more rejection behaviours towards their new carers than younger babies (Dozier & Rutter, 2016), suggesting that past experiences of care are already capable of directing present and future relationship behaviour.

For early experiences of care to become organised into behavioural attachment patterns, babies must have a way to remember and make sense of relationships. Bowlby theorised that babies must develop a cognitive representation or model which eventually takes over from instinct to shape and direct care-seeking behaviour in the context of that unique parent-infant relationship. In other words, babies quickly learn, remember and adjust to key aspects of their carer's behaviour using cognitive representations. Bowlby described this cognitive mechanism as the "internal working model" (Chapter 1), an unconscious model in our minds of what we have learnt to expect in care-seeking (and later caregiving) situations.

Bowlby (1969) believed that while the intensity and frequency of attachment behaviour remained fairly constant during the child's second and third years of life, their exact expression changes in line with other aspects of development. For example, toddlers are more mobile than babies and can now walk and run further from their carers. Attachment behaviours such as retreat to a carer and clinging are still frequent and necessary, but new behavioural strategies develop, such as shouting or delaying, to maintain parental attention and engagement. This was often previously described as "attention-seeking" behaviour in toddlers but is more accurately described as "attachment-seeking" behaviour (Chapter 1). Bowlby (1969) described this early pre-schooler behaviour as goal-directed (directed towards changing the caregivers' behaviour directly). As the child's language develops, so does their ability to understand and tolerate the needs and goals of others and understand that good relationships are based on both parties considering each other's needs.

Ainsworth and others (Ainsworth, 1967; Ainsworth, 1990; Marvin, 1997) suggested that as children grow, they juggle a complex dynamic balance between four behavioural systems: attachment, fear/wariness, exploration and sociability. When wariness is activated, as it is when the child is frightened or stressed, the fear system typically shuts down exploration and sociability and activates attachment behaviours so that the child increases proximity to the carer. This is easily observed in a toddler who clutches onto a parent in a new environment.

Toddlers want to be more autonomous and independent but still need close care and protection so their exploration system continues to be tempered by their wariness and attachment systems. You can see this when a toddler insists on being allowed to feed themself (exploration) but then they protest if the caregiver moves away from the table to be with another child (attachment). Being a toddler is all about managing this balance of dependence and independence against a backdrop of rapid physical and cognitive development.

There seems to be a developmental turning point around the age of three, when children start to decide much more for themselves how close or far from their attachment figure they can manage (Marvin, Britner & Russell, 2016). They also become better at tolerating brief separations especially if they are with a friendly adult and are more likely to cautiously engage with unknown adults rather than ignore them (Greenberg & Marvin, 1982). Typically, a three- or four-year-old can manage being left in (good-quality) childcare more easily than a two-year-old, although that is not to say they do not find it anxiety-provoking still.

A secure attachment in infancy seems to help the pre-school child dampen the reactivity between wariness and attachment and increase the relationship between wariness and sociability, thereby facilitating exploration. An example is when a securely attached child can calm down quickly after the initial wrench of nursery drop-off, whereas an insecurely attached child might need more help and take longer to regulate their anxiety before they can go and play. Having learnt during infancy that primary caregivers could be trusted, their internal working model of relationships acts as a blueprint for new relationships with adults. Hence, the secure pre-schooler is more able to build trust with other adults and move on to the important business of world exploration.

By the age of four, children typically understand that their attachment figure has their own internal thoughts, feelings and goals and that these can differ from their own (Marvin, 1977). They are beginning to be able to inhibit their attachment behaviour a little to join in with their carer's needs and goals. Four-year-olds typically understand that their relationship with their attachment figure endures even during separations, but they still cherish close proximity during everyday interactions, retreating to the comfort of the attachment figure during times of tiredness, pain and other moments of low ebb. Established patterns of attachment continue to be observable during separations and reunions.

An example of attachment in action might be the first day of school, when four- and five-year old children cling to their parents, unsure of what separation into school means for them. This is clearly the wariness system activating the attachment system and is a healthy and typical response. As children spend the next few days and weeks in the routine of school, getting to know which adults can be relied on for care, comfort and protection, their anxiety is successfully co-regulated, and they can begin to interact with the other children and explore the classroom. In this scenario, securely attached children may resist the initial separation, but their internal working model of relationships with caregivers helps them to form relationships with the teacher, deactivate wariness and fear, and to activate sociability and exploration. In children with an avoidant attachment pattern, wariness conversely tends to dampen down the attachment system in favour of the exploration system. This might be seen in the child who gregariously explores the classroom environment without reference to or apparent need for an attachment figure, and persistently runs away to play during later reunion with a carer. A child with an ambivalent attachment pattern might be very distressed at separation, increasing their attachment behaviours such as staying very close to the teacher for a long time. Their exploration system is dampened, but they might then seem angry, hostile or inconsolable when parent(s) return for pick-up. In children with a disorganised attachment pattern, all four systems might be activated in different and unpredictable ways, leading to confusing and contradictory behaviours during stress, separation and reunion.

Sometimes, in situations of wariness and fear activation, a "transitional object" (Winnicott, 1953) can help some children regulate themselves. This is an inanimate object which has already acquired some attachment meaning and helps the child activate the soothing feelings of attachment even in the absence of their attachment figures. A transitional object might be their cherished teddy from home or a security blanket. For slightly older children, temporary transitional objects might act as a talisman to elicit feelings of closeness and support when needed. For example, a small keyring or discrete token from their parent might help an older child returning to school following an extended absence, to help them manage the transition.

The quality of a child's attachment to their primary carer is also associated with school readiness across a range of academic skills including literacy, reading comprehension and maths skills, as well as socioemotional skills such as emotional and behavioural self-control, problem solving and social skills (see Williford, Carter & Pianta, 2016, for a review). This is probably related to several different factors; a securely attached child's enhanced experience of parent-infant interaction, having a secure base from which to safely explore, and benefitting from the early establishment of attachment security which then promotes early exploration and sociability.

These types of emotional, social and behavioural differences between securely and insecurely attached children tend to widen over primary school, especially where insecure children face additional challenges such as poverty (Williford et al., 2016). A secure attachment pattern also promotes better quality child-teacher attachment which contributes to academic success (Williford et al., 2016).

Bowlby (1969) suggested that attachment was fully organised by around school entry age. However, this is not the end of the attachment story. We will see in the following section that later researchers believe attachment continues to be malleable across the course of one's life.

ATTACHMENT DEVELOPMENT DURING MIDDLE CHILDHOOD (6–12 YEARS)

Middle childhood is a distinct but often overlooked phase of attachment development, typically being neither mainly family-centric like early childhood and nor mainly peer-centric like adolescence. In middle childhood, the world rapidly expands to include multiple short and long-term relationships with new adults and children, longer separations from attachment figures, the prospect of sleepovers away from home (where friend's parents may not be established as formal attachment figures) and, towards the end of middle childhood, the development of puberty. Parenting transitions from constant close supervision to supporting increased independence. By the time middle childhood ends, the child is typically more self-reliant, more peer-focussed and spending decreasing amounts of time with their early attachment figures.

THE FOUR KEY FEATURES OF ATTACHMENT DURING MIDDLE CHILDHOOD

Kerns and Brumariu (2016) note that there are four key features of attachment development during middle childhood. Firstly, the child's focus changes from proximity to an attachment figure to availability of an attachment figure. The child no longer needs to be able to see their carer, but they do need to know a carer is available when required. A securely attached child is now able to manage longer separations and the feelings activated. The need for an adult to be present to help regulate feelings of fear and wariness is being gradually replaced with the capacity for self-regulation.

Secondly, children still see their parents as their primary attachment figures even though multiple new relationships are forming with peers and other adults. Thirdly, the child is more intentionally collaborative with their attachment figure, using their carer to help solve problems, not just looking for the problem to be solved by the adult. Finally, attachment is still serving the dual function of a secure base from which one can go out and explore, and a safe haven to return to in times of distress. This typically changes to predominantly the latter during adolescence. Parents that can support secure attachment are more likely to be successfully balancing the tension between ongoing care for their child and encouraging them to explore, try new things and take measured risks (Kerns et al., 2015).

ATTACHMENT STABILITY DURING MIDDLE CHILDHOOD

Bowlby, Ainsworth and multiple other researchers have provided convincing evidence that attachment patterns are well organised by the time a child enters school. However, that is not the same as saying that they are "fixed", never to be changed again. It makes good evolutionary sense for attachment to continue to be changeable during childhood (Belsky, 1997). Evolution requires individual adaptation to the environment to maximise the chances of at least some genes passing to the next generation. If a child develops a particular attachment pattern in early life but then finds that pattern is poorly adapted to their environment outside the family, they are vulnerable to not forming relationships and so less likely to have children of their own and pass on their genes to the next generation. Therefore, we might expect middle childhood to be a time when children are trying to work out how to adjust their attachment behaviour to the environment outside of their family. Attachment patterns which were fully adaptive to the family context may be significantly mismatched to the school environment.

Secondly, if attachment patterns develop in response to caregiver behaviours, then all children in one family are likely to develop the same attachment pattern (we will see in later chapters that this is not necessarily the case). Without some capacity for change and adaptation, all children from the same family would face the same risk of not passing on genes if they are equally poorly suited to finding a mate. Therefore, evolutionary theory predicts that some change in attachment patterns beyond early childhood is possible, and that different children raised by the same parents should be able to develop attachment patterns different from one another.

We might, therefore, reasonably expect to see siblings diverge from the same attachment pattern during middle childhood.

There is evidence to demonstrate that change in attachment patterns is possible, albeit often slowly (see also Chapter 6). Attachment stability over time is greater over the age of six than under the age of six, suggesting that up until school age, attachment is still forming and changing (Pinquart, Fuessner & Ahnert, 2013). After six, further adaptation is still possible, but the likelihood and rate of any changes slows. Pinquart et al.'s (2013) large meta-analysis found that securely attached children are the least likely to change attachment category. This is also found to be the case for adults (see Chapter 6). However, while attachment stability tends to be high over a period of up to five years, it is far less stable over fifteen years or longer. This suggests that while one's attachment pattern during infancy forms a blueprint for relationships, it can change, albeit slowly, over the life course dependent on a range of factors.

Groh et al. (2014) report a large study on attachment stability which finds that attachment disorganisation also shows some stability between infancy and late adolescence but happily not particularly strongly. In other words, some of the toddlers found to have a 'disorganised' attachment have improved by the time they reach their late teens. As you will read in Chapter 6, research suggests that where attachment patterns change, the mechanism of that change is most likely that additional internal working models have developed alongside the original one and have come to predominate.

Drawing these findings together, it seems that while individual circumstances and attachment patterns can change, and sometimes quite considerably, that tends not to happen for most children. This is probably because for most children their caregiving environment is broadly constant. However, the evidence described above that individual attachment patterns can change is important good news as this gives cause for optimism for those children with insecure or disorganised attachments.

DISTRIBUTION OF ATTACHMENT PATTERNS DURING MIDDLE CHILDHOOD

Research about attachment in middle childhood tends to use the four categories from Ainsworth, Main and Solomon which are secure, avoidant, ambivalent and disorganised. In one example, Boldt, Kochanska, Grekin and Brock (2016) followed one hundred and two two-parent, intact, American families for ten years. Multiple measures of parent-child interaction, parental responsive care, child behaviour, child receptiveness to parental values and attachment were taken at ten key points between age seven months and ten years (Boldt et al., 2016). The Iowa Attachment Behavioural Coding (IABC) was used at age ten years to assign children to secure, avoidant, ambivalent and disorganised attachment patterns. The IABC is an observational coding system developed out of the Minnesota Longitudinal Study (Sroufe et al., 2005), in which an eighty-minute interaction between the child and parent was recorded and then coded according to twelve attachment-related behavioural codes. The findings broadly supported the same distribution of attachment patterns at age ten that have been largely demonstrated by studies of one-year olds, suggesting moderate constancy during middle childhood. This supports the Pinquart et al. (2013) meta-analysis and is an important finding; it suggests that during middle childhood, aspects of attachment become a "feature of the individual" rather than a "feature of a specific relationship". As Thompson (2016) notes, attachment theory suggests that security begins as a feature of a relationship (external) and slowly becomes a feature of one's personality (internal).

Boldt et al. (2016) also found that children tend to be more avoidant with fathers and more ambivalent or disorganised with mothers, possibly reflecting higher emotional expression in mother-child relationships. These findings support the theory that we develop multiple different internal working models of relationships during childhood. As expected, a history of parental responsive care had significant influence over whether attachment patterns were broadly more secure or insecure. Those children with the greatest cumulative attachment insecurity throughout their early and middle childhoods were more likely to have behaviour problems and tended to be less receptive to parental values.

Put together, these studies give us some insight into how early insecure or disorganised attachment can become a cumulative difficulty throughout middle childhood. If the caregiving environment remains about the same, then the child's attachment patterns will do too and will become internalised as part of the older child's personality, leading to a range of difficulties in adolescence and adulthood. However, if the childhood caregiving environment changes, attachment change remains possible.

In this chapter so far, we have seen that middle childhood is a time of expansion in attachment relationships and new modalities of expressing attachment behaviour. We now turn to the developmental consequences of attachment patterns through middle childhood and beyond.

CHILD OUTCOMES IN ATTACHMENT

When we compare groups of babies with different attachment patterns, how might we expect their development over their future years to be similar or different? Thompson (2016) notes that research from the 1970s and 1980s into the long-term developmental outcomes of attachment broadly supported Bowlby's prediction that attachment affects later relationship behaviour with peers and partners, personality development, behavioural problems and mental health. However, Bowlby also notes that it is a child's cumulative experience of care over their childhood that is the best predictor of later development. In other words, the best outcomes are seen when parental sensitivity and support persist throughout childhood.

There is now copious research to demonstrate that significant stress during early life, such as that associated with insecure or disorganised attachment, can wreak a heavy toll on later physical and mental health (e.g., Center on the Developing Child at Harvard, 2016) and that a secure attachment supports better outcomes. This link between attachment and later outcomes occurs through at least four routes; neurobiological foundations, protection from stress, support to explore and enhancement of social support.

As described in Chapter 3, secure attachment supports the biological and neurological development of the child in multiple ways. One way is through building the brain architecture of good emotional co-regulation (the process of helping the child learn how to notice, acknowledge, label, understand and ultimately manage strong feelings). A parent who can provide repetitively sensitive and nurturing responses to the child's distress helps brain pathways form which underpin good emotional regulation and reduced stress reactivity. The brain is optimally receptive to learning about emotional regulation during infancy (Gee, 2020) so an ongoing secure attachment characterised by helpful and healthy management of feelings lays the foundation for good emotional regulation in adulthood.

Another way attachment influences later outcomes is by protecting the infant from toxic stress (levels of stress which are overwhelming to the nervous system). Parents who provide a safe haven and protection in the face of physical and emotional threats reduce exposure to unmanageable levels of stress. Toxic stress during early life begins a snowball effect of altered neurobiology and relationship behaviours (e.g., McCrory, De Brito & Viding, 2011).

A third route is by providing sensitive encouragement to engage with the world and its developmental opportunities. A child who is securely attached feels safe to venture into the world, ready to learn and engage, secure in the knowledge that parents are there if needed. An insecurely or disorganised attached child still needs to use some attention and cognitive resource to establish a more secure and organised attachment strategy; she does not have access to robust emotional co-regulation to help down-regulate wariness and attachment, and activate exploration and sociability. In a study of two hundred and fifty-five children between fifteen months and two years of age, Bernier, Beauchamp and Cimon-Pasquet (2020) found a direct link between secure attachment and improved school readiness.

Finally, parents who provide good early experiences of relationships, help a child to build better relationships and maintain improved social support throughout life. One example is that better attachment security is a good predictor of higher marital satisfaction (Diamond, Brimhall & Elliot, 2018). Children who benefit from good early attachment relationships are therefore more likely to have the cumulative benefit of their parents' ongoing social support and of making and maintaining other attachment relationships.

INFANT ATTACHMENT AND LATER RELATIONSHIP OUTCOMES

Securely attached young children are more likely to go on to have more harmonious and collaborative relationships with their parents, better social competence with peers, reduced peer conflict, less loneliness and to be better at creating and eliciting the support of social networks (Thompson, 2016).

INFANT ATTACHMENT AND PHYSICAL HEALTH

Given the essential role of attachment in helping regulate the stress of young children, it is not surprising that non-securely attached children experience later problems with the physical impact of stress. Puig et al. (2013) followed 163 people who were assessed at ages twelve and eighteen months old using the Ainsworth Strange Situation Procedure and then at age thirty-two years using a questionnaire about physical illnesses. This study did not use the disorganised category, dividing all children into secure, anxious resistant, or anxious avoidant. They found that children who had been insecurely attached were at least four times more likely to report inflammation-based illness (e.g., cardiovascular disease, asthma) and increased non-specific symptoms of illness at age thirty-two. In a related study, Farrell et al. (2017) found that stress during early childhood and/or adolescence predicts adult health outcomes at age thirty-two and that parenting interventions which promote maternal sensitivity may avoid some of those risks. These findings are consistent with neuroscientific studies which show that early childhood and adolescence are times of maximal brain sensitivity to our internal and external environments (e.g., Sawyer et al., 2012; Gold, 2017) such that a failure in emotional co-regulation during these times can undermine lifelong ability to cope with and respond to stress.

INFANT ATTACHMENT AND PERSONALITY

Attachment begins as a feature of an external relationship but over time becomes internalised as a feature of personality (e.g., Thompson, 2016), hence attachment is found to be one of several factors in adolescent personality development. The Minnesota Study of Risk and Adaptation from Birth to Adulthood (Sroufe, Egeland, Carlson & Collins, 2005) was a valuable study because it started studying people three months before they were born and followed them up until they were age thirty-four. Participants were assessed at various ages, in a variety of different ways, thus providing a prospective longitudinal multi-measures study of change from infancy to adulthood. Attachment at twelve to eighteen months of age was found to be related to self-esteem, emotional health, resilience and social competence during adolescence.

Carlson, Egeland & Sroufe (2009) found that in a sample of families living in poverty, disorganised attachment during early childhood was one of a number of predictive factors for the diagnosis of Borderline Personality Disorder (BPD) at the age of twenty-eight. BPD is described as a severe mental disorder characterised by persistent and pervasive emotional dysregulation, difficulties with one's identity and disturbances in social functioning such that relationship are frequently difficult and/or stressful (Bohus et al., 2021). More recently, BPD has been referred to as Emotionally Unstable Personality Disorder instead (EUPD). BPD/ EUPD is often associated with having experienced childhood abuse and there is significant debate ongoing about whether or not it is in fact a complex presentation of post-traumatic stress disorder. Interestingly, Carlson et al. (2009) found the other predictive factors for BPD were childhood maltreatment during infancy, maternal hostility during preschool years and general life stress up to the age of forty-two months.

INFANT ATTACHMENT AND ADULT MENTAL HEALTH OUTCOMES

The types of interaction between parents and babies which form a secure attachment also lay down the foundations of mental health, through both neurobiological mechanisms (as above) and through cognitive representations. This is addressed in detail in Chapter 6. What children learn very early on about themselves, others and relationships, establishes beliefs and expectations which then influence how a person experiences and predicts the world. For example, a child securely attached during early life is more likely to have learnt that attachment figures can be relied upon during times of stress and to have our best interests at heart. An insecurely attached child may grow up believing that the intentions of attachment figures and their support during times of stress are not to be relied upon. Hence, later in life, a securely attached person diagnosed with a life-threatening illness is more likely to seek support from loved ones, trusting that it will be provided with best intentions.

An insecurely attached person may worry much more about asking for support, may be less certain of receiving it and may worry that their loved ones will not be reliable.

In their comprehensive review of attachment and adult mental health, Stovall-McClough and Dozier (2016) conclude that adult psychiatric disorders "are nearly always" associated with non-secure attachment patterns (which they describe as "attachment states of mind"). They find support for Bowlby's (1973) "branching railway lines" ideas, that is that we encounter decisive junctures throughout life, at which our lives can take a more positive or more negative turn. Attachment can start us off on a better or worse track but also then influences which direction we choose to throughout our various life stages. A child who had a difficult start but whose environment changes for the better during childhood will have better outcomes than a child maintained in a poor caregiving environment.

This idea has been extended by Professors McCrory and Viding to describe the theory of latent vulnerability (McCrory & Viding, 2015), which suggests that our early life experiences influence us in ways which change how we then interact with the world. Early adversity, such as an insecure or disorganised attachment, changes a child's biology and behaviour in deleterious ways which makes that child less likely to accurately appraise threat, less likely to develop and maintain a strong social network, and more likely to recall their negative memories. These changes then alter how a child approaches and engages with the world, in ways which might be more or less adaptive to the environment. This suggests that mental health outcomes of early adversity emerge over time as a result of complex iterations between how the environment cares for the child and how the child then adapts at each of Bowlby's "branching lines".

THE GENETICS OF ATTACHMENT OUTCOMES

It is right to consider whether later outcomes might not be directly caused by infant attachment security but simply correlated with it, in the same way that shoe size does not cause height, but these two things are correlated with each other. Rather than secure attachment leading to better development, perhaps certain genes promote both attachment security and better outcomes?

Despite broad international consistency in the distribution of attachment categories, there is no strong evidence that genes play a significant role in determining attachment category. The various published studies of Glenn Roisman and his multiple collaborators (e.g., Roisman et al., 2013; Roisman & Fraley, 2008; Fearon & Roisman, 2017) concludes that at present, attachment is unusual among aspects of development in being shaped largely by environment with very little evidence of genetic influence. This finding holds steady throughout repeated high quality twin studies on the matter (see Fearon & Roisman, 2017 for a review).

While genes may not determine attachment category, there is some evidence that some children are more genetically susceptible to sub-optimal care than their peers. This is known as the differential susceptibility hypothesis (Belsky, 1997, 2005; Bakermans-Kranenburg & van IJzendoorn 2007), based on the idea that there is an interaction between genes and caregiving environment. Children with "susceptibility" genes are both more vulnerable to a poor caregiving environment and more likely to flourish in a positive caregiving environment, when compared to children without susceptibility genes. Those without susceptibility genes tend to be less susceptible to either kind of environment and tend to fare well-enough in later life irrespective of the kind of caregiving they received early on. Another way of saying this is that those children who carry "susceptibility" genes will be more badly affected by poor caregiving but will also benefit far more from help and support (Bakermans-Kranenberg & van IJzendoorn, 2016). This opens an interesting avenue for future research to explore whether the same children who are more susceptible to poor parental care might also be more vulnerable to other environmental adversity. Equally, whether some children might benefit from attachment interventions differently depending on their genetic make-up.

SUMMARY

In infancy, attachment patterns are directly and predictably related to the quality of caregiving from primary caregivers. This provides an organising principle which is taken into middle childhood, where it influences how the child approaches and engages with the world. Children who have learnt to trust attachment figures and to venture away from their secure base knowing that they have a safe haven to return to in the face of life's ups and downs, are more likely to be ready to learn, form healthy new attachments and cope with separation and stress. Those children who continue to experience caregiving which is unpredictable, unreliable and/or hostile demonstrate poorer outcomes during middle childhood and beyond.

If the environment continues to provide the same kind of care, the child's attachment pattern is likely to stay broadly the same. Over the relatively short span of time from early childhood to adolescence, big changes in attachment pattern are usually related to big changes in the caregiving environment. Where life is cumulatively good or bad, so will be the attachment. Bowlby (1973) referred to this as the "branching railway lines" metaphor. In other words, certain developmental pathways become more or less likely with cumulative experience. Attachment sets the direction, but life provides junctions at which thing can get considerably worse or considerably better.

As adolescence approaches, features of the external attachment relationship from early childhood start to become internalised as part of the child's cognitive and behavioural presentation. In this way attachment plays a role in personality development.

While an early secure attachment initiates a virtuous cycle of healthy relationships, healthy biology and healthy outcomes, it cannot be said that early experiences fully determine adult outcomes (Fraley & Roisman, 2019) as this would overplay the magnitude of influence. However, secure infant attachment is found to be associated with better relationships later in life, improved emotional regulation, fewer personality difficulties, improved social abilities and higher self-esteem. Insecure and disorganised infant attachments are associated with higher rates of adult mental health problems and physical health problems.

Attachment styles are more malleable earlier in life, but change is still possible during middle childhood and there is some evidence that some children may be genetically more responsive to help and support than others.

RECOMMENDED READING

Brumariu, L. E. & Kerns, K. A. (2022). Parent–child attachment in early and middle childhood. In P. K. Smith & C. H. Hart (Eds.), The Wiley-Blackwell handbook of childhood social development (pp. 425–442). John Wiley & Sons.

Ranson, K. E. & Urichuk, L. J. (2008). The effect of parent–child attachment relationships on child biopsychosocial outcomes: A review. Early Child Development and Care, 178(2): 129–152.

REFERENCES

Ainsworth, M. D. S. (1967). *Infancy in Uganda: Infant care and the growth of love*. John Hopkins University Press.

Ainsworth, M. D. S. (1990). Some considerations regarding theory and assessment relevant to attachments beyond infancy. In M. T. Greenberg, D. Cicchetti & E. M. Cummings (Eds). (1993). *Attachment in the preschool years: Theory, research, and intervention*. University of Chicago Press.

Bakermans-Kranenburg, M. J. & Van IJzendoorn, M. H. (2007). Research review: Genetic vulnerability or differential susceptibility in child development: The case of attachment. *Journal of child psychology and psychiatry*, 48 (12): 1160–1173.

Bakermans-Kranenburg, M. J. & Van IJzendoorn, M. H., (2016). Attachment, Parenting, and Genetics. In J. Cassidy & P. R. Shaver (Eds), *Handbook of attachment: Theory, research, and clinical applications* (3rd Ed., pp. 155–179). Guilford.

Belsky J. (1997). Variation in susceptibility to rearing influence: An evolutionary argument. *Psychological Inquiry*, 8: 182–186.

Belsky J. (2005). Differential susceptibility to rearing influence: An evolutionary hypothesis and some evidence. In Ellis B. & Bjorklund D. (Eds), *Origins of the social mind: Evolutionary psychology and child development* (pp. 139–163). Guilford.

Bernier, A., Beauchamp, M. H. & Cimon-Paquet, C. (2020). From early relationships to preacademic knowledge: A sociocognitive developmental cascade to school readiness. *Child Development*, 91(1): e134–e145.

Bohus, M., Stoffers-Winterling, J., Sharp, C., Krause-Utz, A., Schmahl, C. & Lieb, K. (2021). Borderline personality disorder. *The Lancet*, 398(10310): 1528–1540.

Boldt, L. J., Kochanska, G., Grekin, R. & Brock, R. L. (2016). Attachment in middle childhood: predictors, correlates, and implications for adaptation. *Attachment & Human Development*, 18 (2): 115–140.

Bowlby, J. (1969). Attachment and loss: volume I: attachment. In *Attachment and Loss: Volume I: Attachment* (pp. 1–401). The Hogarth Press and Institute of Psycho-analysis.

Bowlby, J. (1973). Attachment and loss: Volume II: Separation, anxiety and anger (pp. 1–429). London: The Hogarth Press and Institute of Psycho-analysis. Described in C. Fraley & P. R. Shaver (2008), *Attachment theory and its place in contemporary personality research.* In O. John & R. W. Robins (Eds) (2008). *Handbook of Personality: Theory and Research* (3rd Ed., pp. 518–541). Guilford.

Carlson, E. A., Egeland, B. & Sroufe, L. A. (2009). A prospective investigation of the development of borderline personality symptoms. *Development and Psychopathology*, 21(4): 1311–1334.

Center on the Developing Child at Harvard University. (2016). From best practices to breakthrough impacts: A science-based approach to building a more promising future for young children and families. www.developingchild.harvard.edu.

Coyne, J., Powell, B., Cooper, G. & Hoffman, K. (2019). The Circle of Security. In C. Zeanah (Ed.), *Handbook of infant mental health*, (4th Ed., pp. 500–513). Guilford.

Diamond, R. M., Brimhall, A. S. & Elliott, M. (2018). Attachment and relationship satisfaction among first married, remarried, and post-divorce relationships. *Journal of Family Therapy*, 40(Supplement 1): S111–S127.

Dozier, M. & Rutter, M. (2016). Challenges to the development of attachment relationships faced by young children in foster and adoptive care. In J. Cassidy & P. R. Shaver (Eds), *Handbook of attachment: Theory, research, and clinical applications* (3rd Ed., pp. 696–714). Guilford.

Farrell, A. K., Simpson, J. A., Carlson, E. A., Englund, M. M. & Sung, S. (2017). The impact of stress at different life stages on physical health and the buffering effects of maternal sensitivity. *Health Psychology*, 36(1): 35–44.

Fearon, R. P. & Roisman, G. I. (2017). Attachment theory: progress and future directions. *Current Opinion in Psychology*, 15: 131–136.

Fraley, R. C. & Roisman, G. I. (2019). The development of adult attachment styles: four lessons. *Current Opinion in Psychology*, 25: 26–30.

Gee, D. G. (2020). Caregiving influences on emotional learning and regulation: applying a sensitive period model. *Current Opinion in Behavioral Sciences*, 36: 177–184.

Gold, C. M. (2017). *The developmental science of early childhood: Clinical applications of infant mental health concepts from infancy through adolescence* (pp. 129–157). Norton.

Greenberg, M. T. & Marvin, R. S. (1982). Reactions of preschool children to an adult stranger: A behavioral systems approach. *Child Development*, 53(2): 481–490.

Groh, A. M., Roisman, G. I., Booth-LaForce, C., Fraley, R. C., Owen, M. T., Cox, M. J. & Burchinal, M. R. (2014). IV. Stability of attachment security from infancy to late adolescence. *Monographs of the Society for Research in Child Development*, 79(3): 51–66.

Kerns, K. A. & Brumariu, L. E. (2016). Attachment in Middle Childhood. In J. Cassidy & P. R. Shaver (Eds), *Handbook of attachment: Theory, research, and clinical applications* (3rd Ed., pp. 349–365). Guilford.

Kerns, K. A., Mathews, B. L., Koehn, A. J., Williams, C. T. & Siener-Ciesla, S. (2015). Assessing both safe haven and secure base support in parent–child relationships. *Attachment & Human Development*, 17(4): 337–353.

Marvin, R.S. (1977). An ethological-cognitive model for the attenuation of mother-child attachment behavior. In T. Alloway, P. Pliner & L. Krames (Eds) (1977), *Attachment Behavior. Advances in the study of communication and affect* (Vol. 3, pp. 25–60). Springer.

Marvin, R. S. (1997). Ethological and general systems perspectives on child–parent attachment during the toddler and preschool years. In N. L. Segal, G. E. Weisfeld & C. C. E. Weisfeld (1997). *Uniting psychology and biology: Integrative perspectives on human development.* American Psychological Association.

Marvin, R. S., Britner, P. A. & Russell, B. S. (2016). Normative development: The ontogeny of attachment in childhood. In J. Cassidy & P. R. Shaver (Eds). *Handbook of attachment: Theory, research, and clinical applications* (3rd Ed., pp. 273–290). Guilford.

McCrory, E., De Brito, S. A. & Viding, E. (2011). The impact of childhood maltreatment: a review of neurobiological and genetic factors. *Frontiers in Psychiatry*, 2: 48.

McCrory, E. J. & Viding, E. (2015). The theory of latent vulnerability: Reconceptualizing the link between childhood maltreatment and psychiatric disorder. *Development and Psychopathology*, 27(2), 493–505.

Pinquart, M., Feußner, C. & Ahnert, L. (2013). Meta-analytic evidence for stability in attachments from infancy to early adulthood. *Attachment & Human Development*, 15(2): 189–218.

Puig, J., Englund, M. M., Simpson, J. A. & Collins, W. A. (2013). Predicting adult physical illness from infant attachment: a prospective longitudinal study. *Health Psychology*, 32(4): 409–417.

Roisman, G. I., Booth-Laforce, C., Belsky, J., Burt, K. B. & Groh, A. M. (2013). Molecular-genetic correlates of infant attachment: A cautionary tale. *Attachment & Human Development*, 15(4): 384–406.

Roisman, G. I. & Fraley, R. C. (2008). A behavior-genetic study of parenting quality, infant attachment security, and their covariation in a nationally representative sample. *Developmental Psychology*, 44(3): 831–839.

Sawyer, S. M., Afifi, R. A., Bearinger, L. H., Blakemore, S. J., Dick, B., Ezeh, A. C. & Patton, G. C. (2012). Adolescence: a foundation for future health. *The Lancet*, 379 (9826): 1630–1640.

Sroufe, L. A., Egeland, B., Carlson, E. A. & Collins, W. A. (2005). *The development of the person: The Minnesota study of risk and adaptation from birth to adulthood*. Guilford.

Stovall-McClough, K. C. & Dozier, M. (2016). Attachment states of mind and psychopathology in adulthood. In J. Cassidy & P. R. Shaver (Eds), *Handbook of attachment: Theory, research, and clinical applications* (3rd Ed., pp. 715–738). Guilford.

Thompson, R. A. (2016). Early attachment and later development: Reframing the questions. In J. Cassidy & P. R. Shaver (Eds), *Handbook of attachment: Theory, research, and clinical applications* (3rd Ed., pp. 330–348). Guilford.

Williford, A. P., Carter, L. M. & Pianta, R. C. (2016). Attachment and school readiness. In J. Cassidy & P. R. Shaver (Eds). *Handbook of attachment: Theory, research, and clinical applications* (3rd Ed., pp. 966–982). Guilford.

Winnicott, D. W. (1953). Transitional objects and transitional phenomena – A study of the first not-me possession. *International Journal of Psycho-analysis*, 34: 89–97.

5

ATTACHMENT IN ADOLESCENCE

Professor Rudi Dallos

INTRODUCTION

This chapter focusses on the attachment needs of young people during adolescence. It takes the view that young people are involved in a network of attachment relationships through this period of their lives as they transition towards adulthood. The relationship between parents/carers and children is changing during adolescence with the potential for revision and growth of attachment experiences. For example, experiencing new levels of intimate relationships with friends and romantic relationships. This chapter will discuss how changes such as puberty and the growth of mental abilities offer new opportunities and challenges for young people.

To start with the important developments regarding sense of self and identity are described. This is followed by a consideration of the shift in attachment connections from parents to peers and the dilemmas and contradictions that parents and young people experience in negotiating independence. A family relational perspective is offered to illustrate how the changes in adolescence influence both the young person and their parents. Clinical examples are offered to illustrate how problems that adolescents experience need to be considered both within an individual but also within a family attachment framework.

CHANGES IN ADOLESCENCE

Adolescence can be a very turbulent time for many young people. Erikson (1968) suggested that the period is characterised by a

DOI: 10.4324/9780203703878-5

tension between 'identity and role confusion'. It involves moving from seeing oneself as a 'child' to starting to contemplate moving into the adult world. It can involve a range of challenges but also opportunities for the young person. There can be a sense of becoming more free, less bound by family rules, of experimentation but also anxieties and worries about friends, educations, interest, skills and so on. In Erikson's view, an adolescent's central questions are, "Who am I?" and "Who do I want to be?". He coined the term crisis to capture how these complex questions can coalesce to produce a state of anxiety and distress for the young person.

It has almost become an expectation, certainly in Western cultures where adolescents are allowed more freedom (Erikson, 1968; Allen & Land, 1999) that adolescence will be a turbulent and challenging period not just for the young person but their family and friends too. However, my clinical experience with young people and their families suggests that this common generalisation about young people may be an over-simplification (Shaw & Dallos, 2005). According to attachment theory, adolescents need to retain a sense of safety and security in order to be able to experiment, learn about themselves and develop their identity. Although adolescence can be an exciting period it can also be fraught with many challenges and dangers. I have seen many young people not able to experiment because they were anxious and concerned about their parents' problems and wellbeing or drawn into their conflicts.

IDENTITY DEVELOPMENT

The demands and challenges on adolescents to change can be seen as both personal and societal. First, there are significant and dramatic changes in their bodies such as the development of sexuality. This brings in new thoughts, feelings, needs, tensions and desires. Seeing changes in their bodies, growth of secondary sexual characteristics, body size, strength and so on can be exciting but also disconcerting. The onset of puberty marks these changes. There are differences between boys and girls (puberty typically starts earlier for girls) and also differences between children. For example, being one of the first in a class to develop breasts may be source of status for a girl but also starts to expose her to sexual attention or interest from other people earlier, and potentially dangerously so from inappropriate adults. This can be quite a challenge for a girl who, for example, is still only aged eleven or younger. Crittenden and Dallos (2009) describe this in terms of having a child's mind with an adult body.

Second, the challenges are also present in terms of societal expectations and demands. Young people are expected to start to form ideas about educational choices, jobs, developing skills and abilities. The demands for achievement become more acute and, in some areas, such as sports (gymnastics, football) or music, young people may be competing at top levels of the adult world despite still being in their teens.

EMOTIONAL DEVELOPMENT AND ATTACHMENT

In the previous chapters we have seen how attachment is a fundamental instinct that has evolved in order for children to gain the protection of their parents when exposed to dangers. Children develop differing attachment (self-protective) strategies in order to try to elicit this protection from their carers, but these can change as the child's cognitive, physical and emotional capacities develop. For example, as verbal skills develop, children become more able to express their needs, and differentiate between different aspects of their needs, using language. Children also become more able to consciously alter the expression of their needs and to deploy new strategies to influence their parents. For some children this involves learning to supress or hide how they feel for others. In some complex and dangerous family situations it may not be safe for children to express what they really feel, and they may have to resort to disguising their feelings or using forms of deception. Children compelled to use such strategies may become labelled as 'manipulative' rather than seen as trying to adapt as best they can to obtain their attachment needs. Children also become potentially more aware of their own needs, thoughts, intentions and those of others. This ability to "mentalize" (Chapter 2) and to see things from other's perspectives grows in adolescence but can also be displaced by earlier, more impulsive and self-centred thinking – sometimes to the exasperation of parents and others.

Children at various stages in their development show a tension between seeking the help and care from their parents that they need and seeking independence and autonomy. For example, the infant who wants to take the spoon from his father to feed himself, the toddler who starts to run or try to ride a bicycle or jump in the pool to learn to swim. During adolescence this tension between seeking care and demonstrating independence can become even more acute. Sometimes teenagers will respond to advice or attempts at support from parents by saying 'I am not a child anymore'. This might also be seen in the context of the cultural values that they should not be babyish and overly reliant on their parents.

In short, the core attachment process during adolescence can be seen as an attachment dilemma or bind:

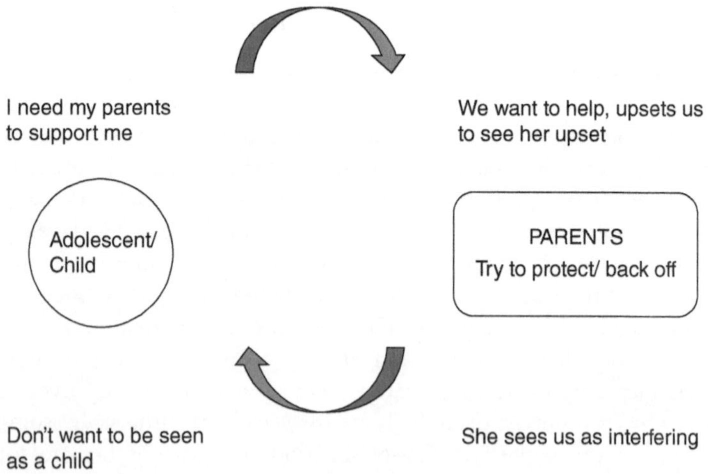

Figure 5.1 Adolescence attachment dilemma

The dilemma illustrated in Figure 5.1 above is a general attachment dynamic and need not in itself be problematic. The attachment-seeking bids from the young person are imbued with a layer of uncertainty and potential difficulty for both the young person and their parents/carers. However, it can become more problematic if the young person has already developed an insecure attachment pattern. Young people with a history of insecure attachment strategies are more likely to become stuck in such cycles with their parents, for example by withdrawing, which can leave them more vulnerable to dangers or at risk of continued escalating conflicts with parents. The latter can also prevent learning about effective conflict resolution, potentially leaving adolescents at a disadvantage to deal with their needs, from which further anxieties can emerge.

ADOLESCENCE HERALDS ATTACHMENT CHANGES IN THE FAMILY

As we have described in the earlier chapters, attachment can be seen as both something that is 'inside' the person and also a part of the relationships in a family. Family therapists have developed the concept of the family life cycle (McGoldrick & Carter, 2003; Dallos & Draper, 2015) to capture the idea that families need to continually change and adapt to shifting demands and circumstances. There are periods of time when these demands become greater, for example the birth of a child for a couple, a child leaving home, starting school, a divorce, bereavement and so on. In childhood, families need to develop different practical tasks, such as care for a child, or taking children to school. Adolescence also heralds change for the family attachment system. The adolescent's experience of relationships sets the family's mood music, with significant emotional resource being spent on the formation, sustenance and separations of friendship groups and romantic partners. Separations, transitions and explorations are commonplace through school trips, being a taxi service for adolescents when they go out with friends, venturing to night clubs and so on.

Notably, these "life moments" frequently involve physical or emotional separations or unions, and as such they necessarily involve re-organisation of attachment systems, including relationships in families (Dallos & Vetere, 2021). The frequency of meaningful relationship transitions mirrors that of very early childhood, but now in adolescence the focus is on expansion and transition of the attachment system, whereas before it was on security and familiarity. Adolescents need to develop different ways of relating. For example, they expect to have more autonomy, to be able to express differences of opinions to their parents and teachers, to wear the clothes they like and so on. Typically, adolescents may be turning to their friends and peers more for emotional support and guidance. While this can lead to parents feeling less central to their child and missing some of the intimacy they had with them, it is a healthy part of the individuation process. Their child's development of sexuality may also trigger feelings for their parents, for example they may feel threatened or anxious about their own intimacy. Parents who have focussed a lot of their emotions on their child may have become emotionally distant from one another. Their emotional communications may have been conducted through their child as the vehicle. This also more broadly relates to the concept of the "empty nest syndrome" (Dallos & Draper, 2015; McGoldrick & Carter, 2003) whereby an adolescence leaving home raises feelings of loss and a form of bereavement. In this example, it is further aggravated by marital anxieties for the parents of their future together. In some cases, the parents' story regarding a difficult marriage may be that they have stayed together 'for the sake of the children'. The prospect of the child now leaving may trigger anxieties and lead to contemplating separation or divorce. This can become a problematic attachment dynamic in families if it disrupts the ability of the parents to attend to their adolescent's attachment needs for safety and support.

The maturing of adolescent attachment patterns is likely influenced by both the parents' individual attachment styles (Chapter 8) and the quality of the parental couple relationship. In the shorter term, this might be because difficulties in the parental couple relationship reduce the parents' ability to meet the attachment needs of their adolescent, leading to greater attachment insecurity for the adolescent. In the longer term, this might be because the parents are role modelling relationship behaviours which either increase or decrease relationship security. Where parents have already separated, an adolescent may have more choice in how much they see their parents or even which one they will predominantly live with, and attachment styles may have some bearing on this dilemma.

In separated families, younger children tend not to be given as much choice in the arrangements regarding parental access. Now as adolescents they can challenge this and may even experience pressure from their parents to do so. Insecurity in attachment is likely to be part of the decision but becoming entangled in these disputes can also interfere with simultaneous attachment development in their own close friendships and romantic attachments.

A further complication can be that their child's romantic and sexual encounters may trigger emotions for their parents regarding their own adolescence experiences. This can lead parents to become emotionally over-involved with a child, for example, becoming very anxious about their friendships, sexual activities, or safety, which can have a negative impact on the young person. A consequence can be that the parents stay more focussed on themselves rather than the needs of their child. Sometimes adolescents feel safe enough to express this in a frequent expression of 'you are not listening to me'. However, in more complex situations they do not feel able to say this and a parent can convey a difficult and confusing message of "despite me trying to help you won't listen and change". Parents need to walk a fine line between offering advice and caution for their child and becoming embroiled in conflicts with them so that their young person feels that their parents are stifling their relationships and friendships.

The example below illustrates how the attachment patterns in families can influence how parents and adolescents manage these conflicts. Where stress or danger emerge, attachment patterns come into play as an instinctive mechanism to promote safety and ultimately survival. However, where formative attachment patterns have been insecure, especially for multiple members of the family, the emotional expressions of danger and safety may be compromised, leading to mental health and family dynamic difficulties. The case of David and his family below illustrates how a young person's attachment insecurities may become aggravated by conflictual attachment dynamics in the family.

CASE ILLUSTRATION: DAVID

David was a fifteen-year-old boy living with his mother, stepfather, and younger brother. He was reported by his mother to be suffering from anxiety, obsessive compulsive disorder and had previously had a period of elective mutism. He was a tall and handsome young man who was captain of the school football team and played rugby at county level. It was reported by his teachers that he was a bit of a 'heartthrob' at school, although he did not have a girlfriend. We were somewhat surprised by the report from his mother that he was extremely anxious at home, since he was clearly not anxious in some other contexts, especially demanding physical sports. It seemed as if the school environment, with its routines and distractions, were sufficient to contain David's feelings during the school day, but that the family system was either promoting a sense of emotional danger and/or unable to provide a sense of emotional safety and security. Attachment theory reminds us that attachment insecurity develops initially in the family system but, as with David, might not be so evident in how he is at school where he feels safer. In this case even when he was engaged in dangerous sporting activities.

In his individual sessions, David was able to feel safe and gradually able to talk with me about his anxieties and very much took responsibility for his own problems. He eventually mentioned that there was extreme conflict between the two sides of his family: his mother and stepfather and his biological father and new wife. In effect, the two families were at war and there had been a physical fight on the doorstep once when David was visiting his father. Both sets of parents complained about each other and demanded that David take sides. He explained that he never knew what was the 'right thing to say' to either set of parents when they criticised the other in front of him. In the presence of these significant emotional risks to his attachment relationships, it seemed as if David could not find a sense of safety and so had decided the best strategy in these circumstances was to say nothing - to become mute. Following some heated clinical sessions with the two sets of families together, they were also helped to feel emotionally safe enough to reflect that the sessions were helping them to realise the loyalty dilemmas they were putting David under. They agreed that they would not involve him in their complaints about each other and would try to have a more amicable relationship with each other. The core to this agreement was our invitation for them to try and put David's needs first and they agreed that they all shared a wish for David to get better, and how highly they all thought of him. This reduced David's sense of emotional danger, restoring his sense of emotional safety and focussed the adults on meeting his attachment needs. They also came to a realisation in one of the sessions that David becoming mute was perhaps related to him not knowing what to say. They discussed this in front of David and apologised to him for the distress their conflicts must have caused him and said they missed hearing him talk.

For David it seemed that gruelling and sometimes painful sporting activity had felt safer than in either of his two home situations. The distraction with these conflicts had meant that despite his good looks he had few close friendships, was very shy of girls and was seen as a bit 'odd' by his peers. Following the work with the two families, it also turned out that his mother was very closely attached to him and was jealous that she would lose him to girls "who were not good enough for him". His mother also suffered from anxiety, and her relationship with her husband was difficult.

Helping David to gain independence was a difficult task and required considerable reassurance for his mother that David would stay close to her for some time yet. As we will see in Chapter 8, parents' own attachment needs are often entangled with the needs of their child. In family work, sometimes parents need reassurance that their child will not emotionally abandon them, and the focus of the clinical work may need to shift to the parents' relationship and marital needs in order to permit their child to move towards independence.

ATTACHMENT AND SEXUALITY

As indicated at the start of the chapter, adolescence also involves important physical changes in their bodies and specifically sexuality. There is also the impact of a wide range of expectations relating to sexuality, such as starting to have boy/girlfriends, engaging in romantic and sexual explorations. However, these can be beset with dangers and contradictions. For example, despite expectations regarding sexual experimentation, there are also severe sanctions for transgressing the law, particularly in exposure to sexual relationships with adults. There is also likely to be encouragement or even pressure from peers and friends to become independent, stay out late, not be ruled by their parents and so on. All of these build the young person's sense of self but also represent possible dangers.

FIRST LOVE

An important and sometimes defining experience in adolescence can be the first experience of 'falling in love'. Bowlby (1965) described a close, trusting attachment relationship as like being in love, but in adolescence this has the added dimension of the first excitement of sexual attraction and intimacy. This can foster extremely powerful feelings, vividly captured in innumerable books, films and songs, not least Shakespeare's Romeo and Juliet. Shakespeare was preeminent in articulating how painful and damaging conflicts between young people's family systems can be, and in how the children's experiences of conflict between adults can be ignored, with tragic consequences.

First love is a cocktail of powerful emotions and strong cultural expectations. Young people often need but may not welcome the assistance of their parents to manage their feelings and again this is a delicate balance for parents. Interfere too much and your child may resent you for destroying this precious experience for them; stand by and see them suffer seemingly inevitably pain. When this goes badly for your child, for example if they experience being rejected by a boy/girlfriend, it can be extremely painful and crushing. The young person, their first exploration into the world of love having ended in tears, needs to retreat to their safe base, and hence can become very dependant again on their parents' support. If parents are not available during this time it can set a dangerous precedent of withdrawing from parents and seeking comfort through self-reliance. Where there is a history of attachment insecurity, self-reliance becomes more likely, as do the use of drink and/or drugs, depression and/or a withdrawal from future intimacy.

In addition, parents can be reminded of their own experiences and attachment pain to such an extent that it becomes difficult for them to help their child make sense of what has happened and learn from the experience. This paints a rather gloomy picture. On the other hand, adolescence offer opportunities for new activities, friendships and intimacies. If the young person is able to gain support from parents and carers or friends, there is also the possibility for re-organisation of attachment patterns. For example, propelled by feelings of sexual arousal, a young person who has developed a dismissing attachment orientation may take the risk of embarking on an intimate relationship. If this goes well it can also have a healing effect so that they are able to start to adopt a more trusting and secure attachment orientation – a more secure internal working model.

The combination of media encouragement for young people to move to sexual intimacy alongside legal sanctions can precipitate confusing and powerful feelings. Especially where children have not had secure attachment relationships there can be problems of 'inappropriate' activity becoming labelled as sexual offending in boys or lack of sexual morality in girls. Parents are extremely important in helping children to navigate this stage of sexual development. As an illustration of some of these issues we can think about Cindy, a young woman attending the out-patient department of an adolescent psychiatric unit. Cindy had experienced traumatic sexual events in her peer relationships at school and needed the assistance of her parents to help her to be safe, make sense of the experiences and to resume her friendships.

CASE ILLUSTRATION: CINDY

Cindy had been discovered by her parents and at school to be engaging in self harm and was showing indications of depression. Her parents said they did not really understand what the problems were and felt unable to help her. They also said that they had not noticed any deterioration in her mental health apart from being a little bit withdrawn from the family.

Cindy was fourteen years old and lived with her parents and younger brother. Her parents had been experiencing financial problems and had some difficulties in their marital relationship. Both parents had childhood experience of their own attachment needs not being adequately responded to. Cindy's paternal grandfather had been harsh with discipline and so her father had learnt to keep his feelings to himself and was now likewise emotionally distant from Cindy. Cindy's mother remembered that her parents had argued a lot and she had learnt to stay out of their way and kept her emotions to herself. She wanted to help Cindy but was also distracted and distressed by conflicts with Cindy's father and tended to draw Cindy onto her side against him.

In family therapy sessions, everyone in the family was helped to feel emotionally safe, for example by emphasising that the sessions were not about who was at fault or to blame. They were invited to talk about their relationships, feelings and understandings of Cindy's self-harm. Cindy's mother became tearful at times and apologised to Cindy that she had not realised that she was so unhappy. Both parents asked Cindy to try and explain what had caused her to be unhappy and said they did want to help her. They also reassured her with support from the therapist that they would not blame her whatever had happened or that she may have done.

Alongside the family session, I met with Cindy on her own and reassured her that whatever she said to me would be confidential. I would only share with her parents what she explicitly gave me permission to do. We discussed her life, friends, interests, as well as her concerns. As she became able to trust me, she hinted that school had been difficult for her and she eventually revealed that she had been repeatedly sexually molested by an older boy two years ago. She felt frightened and humiliated by the experience but had not told anybody apart from a friend who had told her to tell her mum and to tell her to get the school to do something about it. Cindy described that she had not wanted to do this because she felt it was her own responsibility and she should be grown up enough to do something about it herself. But she also said that she had not wanted to upset her parents and thought they would react so badly it might make things worse. She agreed that she now felt safe enough with our support to tell her parents about what had happened.

To some extent her fears were partly realised in the family sessions since the parents' initial response was somewhat accusatory 'well, why didn't you tell us?'. However, they did agree to support her, and her mother confided that she herself had experienced some difficult situations as a young woman and sympathised with Cindy. Her mother took time to talk with her, and her father offered to talk to the school. Cindy said that it was a bit too late now, but she clearly appreciated her parents' willingness to help. The family and Cindy reported that the self-harming actions stopped following the family sessions.

In Chapter 6, we will discuss the attachment patterns of adults and how these influence their own lives and also their ability to protect and nurture their own children. Both parents here had had challenging attachment experiences in their own childhoods. As a consequence, they may have been less able to tune in to Cindy's problems at school and they were also stressed and distracted by their own needs. It is important in therapy with young people like Cindy to help not just them but their parents to feel safe and in particular, for the parents not to feel blamed and a failure in relation to Cindy's problems. In this case, we spent time with Cindy on her own which signalled that we were acknowledging her emerging independence but also sessions with the family together. As indicated above, the core dilemma for Cindy was that she partly blamed herself for what had happened at school, felt she now should be adult enough to deal with it but desperately needed the support of her parents. Sensing that her parents were not available for her seemed to present a very difficult dilemma for her and she expressed this by inflicting pain on herself as a temporary distraction.

WHEN ATTACHMENT NEEDS ARE PERSISTENTLY UNMET

As stated earlier, the central issue for adolescents is the development of peer relationships, friendships, and romantic relationships but when they are distracted by the needs of their own parents this can be a more complex task. There are a number of complications and dangers; if they are not able to keep up with their peers, they may become singled out as different, odd, weird and be subject to bullying or ostracism. This can mean that they are thrown back to needing their parents which in turn can increase their isolation. Where parents are emotionally unavailable, through mental health issues, substance misuse, or their own life's demands, the young person may turn to other ways of seeking attachment comfort, such as drinking, alcoholism, self – harm, promiscuous sexual relationships and so on.

Where an insecurely attached baby grows up experiencing repeatedly unmet attachment needs during adolescence, the double dose effect can tip over into formal mental health difficulties. This can be a major contributing factor in a significant number of clinical conditions which emerge in adolescence, for example anorexia, self-harm, crime, violence and addictions.

SUMMARY

In this chapter we have considered that attachment in adolescence is a complex and at times contradictory process. The young person is moving between attachment systems of their family of origin and those of new relationships involving close friendships and sexual intimacy. This is not simply or predominantly a process of becoming independent from their family but of developing new dependencies and preparing to eventually form a family system of their own where they may eventually become parents themselves. Hence, adolescence involves a wish to establish independence, to separate parents and friendships, but to hold on to the bonds with parents if these continue to provide a secure base. Adolescence can therefore be seen as a transitional attachment stage which requires understanding and support from both the family and the new relational systems of friends and lovers. This sets the scene for adulthood, during which parents and romantic partners need to develop secure attachment relationships with each other and their own offspring.

REFERENCES

Allen, J. P. & Land, D. (1999). Attachment in adolescence. In J. Cassidy & P. R. Shaver (Eds), Handbook of attachment: Theory, research, and clinical applications (pp. 319–335). Guilford.

Bowlby, J. (1965). *Childcare and the growth of love* (2nd Ed.). Pelican Books.

Crittenden, P. M. & Dallos, R. (2009). All in the family: Integrating attachment and family systems theories. *Clinical Child Psychology and Psychiatry*, 14(3): 389–409.

Dallos, R. & Draper, R. (2015). *EBOOK: An Introduction to Family Therapy: Systemic Theory and Practice*. McGraw-Hill Education (UK).

Dallos, R. & Vetere, A. (2021). *Systemic therapy and attachment narratives: Applications in a range of clinical settings*. Routledge.

Erikson, E. H. (1968) *Identity: Youth and crisis*. New York: Norton.

McGoldrick, M. & Carter, B. (2003). *The family life cycle*. New York: Guilford.

Shaw, S. K. & Dallos, R. (2005). Attachment and adolescent depression: The impact of early attachment experiences. *Attachment & human development*, 7(4): 409–424.

6

MODELS OF ADULT ATTACHMENT

Professor Katherine Berry

INTRODUCTION

While we have focussed on childhood and adolescence up to this point, attachment theory is in fact a lifespan developmental theory because it can be used to understand relationships from childhood to old age. Bowlby (1979) famously argued that the theory was relevant "from the cradle to the grave" (p. 154). In this chapter, we cover theories and research applying attachment theory in adulthood relationships, including how attachment is understood and measured in the adult literature.

INTERNAL WORKING MODELS THROUGH ADULTHOOD

As discussed in previous chapters, early relationships with caregivers lead the person to develop "internal working models" of relationships which provide a template for future relationships. Internal working models are beliefs about the self, others and relationships with others (for example, "I am worthy of love and attention" or "I am unlovable", "other people can be trusted" or "other people let you down") and emotions associated with these beliefs such as contentment, sadness, anxiety and anger. These internal working models influence how people make sense of new relationship experiences, which in turn influences how they relate to other people and how people relate to them. For example, if a person mistrusts others and a friend does not turn up for a meeting as planned, the person may conclude that his friend's failure to turn up confirms his view that

DOI: 10.4324/9780203703878-6

other people let him down, rather than the possibility that his friend did not show, owing to circumstances beyond his control. As a result of the apparent confirmation of this belief, the person may decide to shun his friend in the future and not make it easy for the friend to explain himself or rekindle the relationship, thus pushing the friend away and further confirming the view that people let you down.

We typically think of attachment relationships as being important during infancy. However, according to attachment theory, adults also need attachment figures to provide a source of comfort and security during times of physical or emotional stress in the same way that infants and children do. For example, in the face of external stress, a person may seek out a sense of emotional sanctuary through his relationship with his spouse.

Mostly typically, people have tried to understand adult attachment in the context of romantic or couple relationships. However, adults may also have attachment relationships with their parents, and indeed as they get older and become more dependent, with their own children. Furthermore, as described in Chapter 1, internal working models provide a pattern for how adults approach caregiving in the context of parenting, providing a clear mechanism for the intergenerational transmission of attachment styles.

The main difference between attachment relationships in adulthood and attachment relationships in infancy is that in adulthood relationships people often alternate between being the attachment figure and the person in need of support, whereas in childhood the caregiver is always the attachment figure, and the child is always the recipient of the support. However, in some situations in childhood resulting from parental mental or physical health problems, the child may function as a caregiver in order to get their own attachment needs met. This is called parentification. For example, a child might take on caring responsibilities for an unwell parent because they facilitate the *child*'s need for closeness and affection, even though it may come at the cost of additional stress for that child.

DISTINGUISHING ATTACHMENT VERSUS OTHER SOCIAL RELATIONSHIPS

As attachment is relevant to relationships beyond infancy, it begs the question, can attachment relationships be distinguished from other types of social relationships? In both childhood and adulthood, the features of attachment relationships are defined as follows.

a A desire for close proximity to the attachment figure, particularly in times of physical or emotional stress.
b Evidence of distress following involuntary separation (although adults can tolerate much longer periods of separation than children or infants because they are more capable of mentally representing the absent attachment figures).
c Providing a "secure base" in both children and adults which enables the person to feel more confident to explore the world and try out new challenges. In this respect, the presence of a secure attachment relationship is a bit like knowing you have a safety net which can metaphorically catch you if you fall.

STABILITY OF ATTACHMENT STYLES

As discussed in Chapter 4, there is also the question of whether attachment patterns remain stable (i.e. stay the same) across the life-span. Attachment styles are thought to be stable over time because internal working models lead a person to think and behave in ways that are consistent with their pre-existing beliefs. This includes how they relate to others and expect others to relate to them. For example, a person whose internal working model is based on secure childhood attachments is more likely to anticipate other people will also be trustworthy, and to behave accordingly. Other people might include new partners or even health care professionals such as psychological therapists (see chapter 12). Nonetheless, Bowlby himself and later attachment theorists recognised that internal working models can be revised as a result of significant relationship experiences, particularly when there is a high degree of 'mismatch' between the pre-existing models and current experiences.

Research studies have found evidence of some stability, but not complete consistency in attachment styles, over timescales ranging from several months to thirty years (McConnell & Moss, 2011). For example, the strength of associations between childhood and adulthood attachment styles are modest (Fraley & Roisman, 2019). Some studies suggest that life events, including the loss or formation of relationships, or sexual or physical abuse are key factors in determining the stability of attachment style (Hamilton, 2000; Waters, Hamilton et al., 2000; Waters, Merrick et al., 2000). For example, studies which have measured changes in people's attachment patterns over time have found that people who have experienced abuse can move from having a secure to an insecure attachment style. Conversely, we know that people with insecure internal working models can develop a secure attachment pattern as a result of experiencing healthy relationships including a warm and loving spouse or even through experiencing psychological therapy (see Chapter 12 for a discussion of therapists as attachment figures).

One novel study used mathematical modelling techniques to test competing hypotheses about the influence of earlier internal working models on current relationships (Fraley, 2002). This suggested that earlier working models are not completely revised as a result of later life experiences, but that they continue to operate alongside newer models. In this respect, although a person may develop new ways of thinking, feeling and behaving in relationships, their former relationship experiences still influence their everyday experiences. In this situation, the "default" pattern of relationship behaviour might only emerge when a person is under stress, because that is when the attachment behaviour system is most strongly activated. For example, a person's way of relating to a spouse might change when they are under a lot of work stress or indeed the marriage itself is under stress.

There is also some evidence that life events may not be the only factors which influence the stability of working models, and some people may be more likely to change attachment patterns than others. For example, there is some evidence that individuals with more insecure attachment styles are more prone to change in their internal working model between different types of insecurity than individuals with secure attachment styles who are more likely to remain secure over time (Davila et al., 1997).

One further explanation for the finding of shifting attachment patterns is the finding, highlighted in previously chapters, that individuals have multiple attachment working models, which can become more or less dominant at different points in time. Many studies suggest that both children and adults have multiple attachment figures and different types and qualities of attachments in different relationships (e.g. Fraley & Davis, 1997; Trinke & Bartholomew, 1997; Doherty & Feeney, 2004). For example, adults might exhibit different attachment styles with each of their parents, which might be different again with their spouse. However, researchers are still trying to establish the way in which multiple models of attachment are organised, the strength and quality of relationships between working models in different attachment relationships, and whether different attachment representations are integrated into a generalised style.

Although it is accepted that people have different attachment relationships with different people, most adult attachment research has focused on measuring individuals' expectations about relationships in general, rather than relationships with specific others. There is limited research investigating associations between attachment patterns in different relationships, and associations between attachment styles and relationship specific attachment patterns. This lack of research is surprising given that attachment research in infancy focuses on measuring attachment in the context of specific relationship (for example, measuring the nature of the infant's attachment relationship to his attachment relationship with his mother separately to his attachment relationship with his father). The difference may be explained by the fact that the majority of measures of attachment styles in adulthood ask about attachment relationships in general as opposed to attachment relationships with one specific person. However, studies which have measured the nature of people's attachments to specific people in adulthood have found that people are more likely to have insecure attachment across lots of different relationships, whereas the secure pattern may vary across relationships (with some of the person's attachment relationships measuring secure and others insecure) (Ross & Spinner, 2001).

INDIVIDUAL DIFFERENCES IN ADULT ATTACHMENT

There are two approaches to attachment research in adulthood which developed independently from each other: the developmental psychology approach (commonly referred to as the narrative approach) and the social psychology approach (commonly referred to as the self-report approach). In the following section, we will describe different methods of assessing and conceptualising attachment within each approach and highlight similarities and differences. Table 6.1 compares how these different approaches describe the various attachment styles in adults.

NARRATIVE APPROACH

The narrative approach grew from the work of Mary Main and colleagues (referenced in Chapter 2). Main and colleagues developed the Adult Attachment Interview (AAI; Main & Goldwyn, 1984) to measure the way in which adults talk about the quality of their earlier attachment relationships, also known as "attachment states of mind". The AAI is a semi-structured interview that focuses on parent-child relationships during childhood. It involves twenty questions and takes around an hour to complete. Questions focus on earlier experiences of being parented, including asking people to identify five adjectives or words to describe each parent. Individuals are assigned to one of three primary categories: secure-autonomous, dismissing, or preoccupied, based on their descriptions of their relationships with parents, and the coherence of their narrative in terms of quality, quantity, relevance and manner. Individuals in the dismissing and preoccupied categories are deemed to be insecurely attached, while individuals in the autonomous category are deemed to be securely attached. The narrative of securely attached individuals is characterised as coherent in that their description and evaluation of attachment-related experiences makes sense (i.e., there are no inconsistencies), regardless of whether experiences were favourable or unfavourable. For example, a person with a secure attachment pattern may describe examples of feeling let down by a parent and report some reasonable upset in relation to these events. People with secure attachment may also be able to explain the reasons for their parent's behaviour. For example, the parent was not able to be as emotionally available as they should have been due to experiencing a particularly stressful time at work. Individuals who are classified as dismissing with respect to attachment minimise the significance of attachment-related experiences and their narrative is incoherent, with generalised representations of attachment history that are unsupported or contradicted. For example, individuals may describe their parent in global positive terms (for example, their mother was perfect), but report instances of neglect or negative interactions (such as their mother frequently beating or criticising them) and be unable to identify specific examples of their parent displaying the positive adjectives that they used to describe them. Individuals who are classified as being preoccupied with respect to attachment appear overwhelmed by attachment-related experiences and find it difficult to maintain focus or contain their responses to specific questions. For example, the person describes an early parental divorce in an extremely emotional state and keeps reverting to the topic despite the interviewer asking about different topics.

Adults can be assigned to a fourth category, termed unresolved/disoriented, if, when prompted about experiences of loss or abuse, there is evidence of disorganisation or disorientation when discussing these experiences. Evidence for an unresolved/disoriented response to questions includes: (i) lapses in speech, where the individual no longer appears appropriately aware of the interview context (e.g., silence mid-sentence, failing to finish the sentence, making no reference to the silence when resuming to speak); and (ii) lapses in reasoning (e.g., speaking of a deceased person as though they still currently relate to them).

The AAI measure has good reliability over time and between different raters, and good validity, meaning that its attachment classifications successfully predict longer term outcomes for individuals (Hesse, 2008). However, the AAI requires extensive training and is time consuming to administer and score.

The above method of scoring the AAI is referred to as the ABCD model. As described in Chapter 2, Pat Crittenden (2006) has developed an alternative approach to assessing and scoring the measure called the Dynamic-Maturational Model (DMM). The dynamic-maturational method differs from the Main and Goldwyn method in several ways, but most importantly, has an expanded array of attachment patterns, comprising six compulsive sub-patterns and six obsessive sub-patterns, plus combinations of these. According to Crittenden, the dynamic-maturation method is better able to identify people with psychological problems compared to the ABCD method because the DMM is based on research with clinical populations rather than the general population.

SELF-REPORT MEASURE APPROACH

Separate from the development of the AAI's interview-based method of assessing and classifying attachment, social psychologists began to assess attachment styles using self-report questionnaires. This approach was developed from the work of Hazan and Shaver (1987) who conceptualised romantic love as an attachment process and translated Ainsworth, Blehar, Waters and Wall's (1978) three categories from infancy (secure, ambivalent and avoidant attachment) into adult attachment styles. Several multi-item self-report questionnaires have since been developed by various research groups over the years, many of which are freely available on the internet.

One important development in the self-report tradition of attachment measurement was Bartholomew's (1990) attempt to integrate the AAI approach and the self-report approach. Bartholomew argued that Main and colleagues, and Hazan and Shaver, were measuring different types of attachment avoidance. Hazan and Shaver were measuring avoidance as a person's desire to present themselves as independent and not in need of other people, while Main and colleagues were measuring avoidance of being rejected by others and of being hurt. Bartholomew's (1990; 1997) model incorporates both types of avoidance labelled as dismissing-avoidant and fearful-avoidant and describes four attachment prototypes (secure, preoccupied, dismissing and fearful). These prototypes are described in terms of positive and negative beliefs about self and others. According to Bartholomew, secure individuals are characterised in terms of positive beliefs about the self (such as "I am worthy", "I am loveable") and positive beliefs about others (such as "Other people are trustworthy", "Other people care about me"). Securely attached individuals are hypothesised to be comfortable with both autonomy and intimacy and can use others as a source of support in times of distress. Preoccupied individuals are characterised by a negative belief about the self but positive beliefs about others. This attachment style is hypothesised to develop as a result of inconsistent parenting, typified by over intrusiveness and overt expressions of devotion, but also neglect. Individuals with preoccupied attachment styles are characterised as being highly focused on relationships, overly dependent on others, and are hypothesised to seek personal validation through gaining others' acceptance and approval.

Individuals with both fearful and dismissing attachment styles are characterised as having a negative belief about others as uncaring and unavailable, which develops as a result of consistent rejection from attachment figures, and which leads to subsequent avoidance of close relationships. However, according to Bartholomew's model, these individuals differ in terms of their own self-worth, with fearful individuals believing that they are unlovable and avoiding others, owing to a fear of rejection and dismissing individuals believing that they are self-reliant and invulnerable to the rejection of others. They are also hypothesised to differ in terms of their expressions of overt levels of distress, with people with fearful attachment displaying more distress than people with dismissing attachment.

Despite the popularity of Bartholomew's model of attachment, it has also been criticised. For example, some researchers have argued that attachment is better understood in terms of three as opposed to four categories. As described in Chapter 2, Main, Solomon and colleagues added a fourth attachment category for children who did not fit into Ainsworth's existing three categories of secure, avoidant or ambivalent. However, throughout childhood and indeed life, there is a constant striving for increased attachment organisation and security. Hence, some researchers have argued that by adulthood, individuals can be categorised into one of the three attachment styles, with "unresolved" as a supplementary classification if the nature of that conclusion is more tentative.

Bartholomew's model has also been criticised for excluding important individual differences in attachment. For example, the model can be criticised for characterising individual differences in attachment in terms of beliefs, and for neglecting differences in how people regulate and cope with difficult emotions. Bartholomew's depiction of individuals with preoccupied attachment style, in terms of a positive model of others, also contradicts empirical evidence, which suggests these individuals may have a negative view of others. For example, preoccupied attachment has been associated with hostile interpersonal styles and a lack of trust in others (Fraley & Shaver, 2000). The inconsistent nature of these individuals' hypothesised earlier attachment-related experiences would also seem to be more predictive of a negative as opposed to a positive view of others (Fraley & Shaver, 2000).

In attempt to address the above criticisms of Bartholomew's model, Fraley and Shaver (2000) developed an alternative model of adult attachment. Within this model, adult attachment is conceptualised in terms of two dimensions of attachment anxiety and attachment avoidance. Individuals can be scored on both dimensions. According to the model, one dimension or component of the attachment system involves monitoring the psychological proximity of the attachment figure and is related to individual differences in attachment anxiety. For example, individuals who are high in attachment anxiety are hypervigilant to attachment-relevant cues, as the attachment figure is inconsistently available; whereas individuals who are low in anxiety are less vigilant, as the attachment figure is perceived as being either available or irrelevant for personal safety. For example, individuals with high attachment anxiety might be always on the lookout for signs that their partner is not enjoying their company or is even being unfaithful. Conversely, individuals with low attachment anxiety may seem oblivious to their partner's reactions to them.

This model also proposes that the attachment system has a second component or dimension that is responsible for the regulation of attachment behaviour and is associated with individual differences in attachment avoidance. For example, to regulate attachment-related anxiety, individuals either withdraw and attempt to handle situations alone, or alternatively seek contact with the attachment figure.

This model has been ground-breaking because it moves us away from the idea that adult attachment is one continuum with four reasonable discrete categories, to now thinking about adult attachment as having two independent dimensions; an emotional dimension concerned with how much anxiety one feels and a more behaviour focussed dimension concerned with how one manages proximity.

CRITIQUE OF THE SELF-REPORT APPROACH

The self-report approach to measuring attachment has been criticised as there is evidence to suggest that individuals may lack insight into their motives and behaviour or may underreport symptoms of distress (Dozier & Lee, 1995). The criticism is particularly relevant in relation to dismissing attachment, as the positive self-evaluation in dismissing attachment has been hypothesised to represent a self-serving bias, as opposed to a positive working model of self (i.e., people are motivating to see themselves in a positive way and present this image to others even though they may not believe it deep down) (Bartholomew, 1997). However, this potential problem does not mean that measurement of attachment via self-report is not useful. Validated self-report measures can help us to unearth what people really believe when their behaviour and words might suggest otherwise. Nonetheless, self-report measures are limited by a person's own insight and so may need to be supplemented by additional tools which can help unearth unconscious processes.

Shaver and colleagues have pioneered the simultaneous investigation of both conscious and unconscious attachment processes. These authors have used both self-report measures of attachment (conscious processes) and experimental procedures from cognitive psychology (less-conscious processes) within the same study, and by doing so were able to provide empirical support for the defensive nature of dismissing attachment (e.g., Shaver & Mikulincer, 2005).

COMPARISON OF MODELS

As the above summary suggests, there are several different ways of conceptualising and measuring attachment during adulthood which can make it difficult to understand the literature and make comparisons between studies. While the measurement of attachment has become a highly sophisticated, albeit contested field, the application of such measures to routine clinical work and research studies is not unproblematic. Apart from the time and (sometimes) cost required for in-depth training, administration, scoring and interpretation, the research focus on classification may result in a failure to appreciate the complexity of attachment processes (Slade, 2008).

In order to provide a clearer picture of the attachment literature and different models of adult attachment, which is complex, we present the different models in Table 6.1. The table attempts to illustrate how the different categories of attachment style in adulthood developed by different theorists map onto each other, as well as categories of attachment categories commonly described in the childhood literature. The patterns described within each column are conceptually similar to each other, although not synonymous. Blank cells indicate that the attachment pattern is not represented within the system.

Table 6.1 Summary and comparison between different models of attachment

Authors associated with model or system of classifying attachment	*Method of assessing attachment*	*Attachment patterns identified**			
Ainsworth et al., (1978) Main & Solomon (1986)	Strange Situation in infancy	*Secure* Children feel confident that the attachment figure will be available, responsive and helpful in such a way that they are easily soothed by the caregiver in times of distress. They also use their caregiver as a safe base to explore their environment. The child will feel positive and loved as their caregiver will present as 'sensitive' to the child's needs.	*Ambivalent/ Resistant* Children will exaggerate their needs and expressions towards the attachment figure but will reject their attempts to engage and comfort. Children are unable to use caregivers as a secure base to explore novel surroundings. This is as a result of inconsistent responses from their caregiver at times of need, meaning the child is unable to develop feelings of attachment security.	*Avoidant* Children are very independent of the caregiver in both the physical sense, when exploring the environment, and emotionally. They will not seek help from the caregiver and inhibit their emotional needs. The caregiver often presents as insensitive and not responsive to their needs, owing to withdrawing at distressing times or not being available.	*Disorganised* Children appear afraid of their caregiver who presents in a manner that is confusing and unpredictable for the child, therefore not facilitating an 'organised' pattern of self-protection. Children may display behaviours such as overt displays of fear; contradictory behaviours or affects occurring simultaneously or sequentially; stereotypic, asymmetric, misdirected or jerky movements; or freezing and apparent dissociation.

Authors associated with model or system of classifying attachment	*Method of assessing attachment*	*Attachment patterns identified**				
Main & Goldwyn (1984)	Adult Attachment Interview in adulthood	*Autonomous* Individuals have a coherent and collaborative narrative when discussing earlier attachment experiences. They may have had positive or negative childhood experiences but hold an understanding perspective of their own and others' contributions to such experiences.	*Preoccupied* Individuals may appear overwhelmed, confused and preoccupied with details of past attachment experiences without taking an objective perspective. Their narratives in describing attachment experiences often seem long, incoherent and unable to maintain focus, while sometimes seeming vague or angry.		*Dismissing* The individual minimises or even fails to consider attachment experiences. When they actually provide details of such experiences, significant feelings are dismissed or are often short and generalised.	*Unresolved* The individual's narrative is disorganised when discussing and reasoning experiences concerning attachment loss or trauma. They may appear confused or unaware of the interview context by not completing sentences or changing to inappropriate tenses.
Hazan & Shaver (1987)	Self-report measure in adulthood (e.g. 3-item Relationship Questionnaire)	*Secure* These individuals describe themselves as being comfortable with intimacy and able to depend on their partners. They also report high self-confidence, self-esteem and trust in others.	Ambivalent/anxious: These individuals describe themselves as having a strong desire for closeness with and dependence on others. Their reported behaviour often consists of emotional highs and lows triggered by relationship experiences.	Avoidant: These individuals describe feeling uncomfortable being close to others and difficulty trusting others.		

Authors associated with model or system of classifying attachment	*Method of assessing attachment*	*Attachment patterns identified**			
Bartholomew (1990; 1997)	Self-report measures in adulthood (e.g. 4-item Relationship Questionnaire or Relationship Scales Questionnaire)	*Secure* These individuals report positive beliefs about the self and others, indicating a sense of worthiness and lovability. This includes an expectation that others are accepting and responsive in times of distress.	*Preoccupied* These individuals report negative beliefs about the self, but positive beliefs about others, indicating a sense of unworthiness but a positive evaluation of others. They report a tendency to strive for self-acceptance by gaining the acceptance of valued others.	*Dismissing* These individuals report positive beliefs about the self but negative beliefs about others, indicating a sense of self-worthiness with a negative disposition towards other people. They report a tendency to avoid close relationships, as they expect other people to be unavailable and insensitive.	*Fearful* These individuals report negative beliefs about the self and others, indicating a sense of unworthiness and an expectation that others will be untrustworthy and rejecting. They report a tendency to avoid close relationship to protect themselves from anticipated rejection by others.

Authors associated with model or system of classifying attachment	*Method of assessing attachment*	*Attachment patterns identified**			
Fraley & Shaver (2000)	Self-report measures in adulthood (e.g. Experiences of Close Relationships Scale)	*Secure:* Low levels of both attachment anxiety and avoidance. These individuals have a secure attachment and as such appropriate thresholds for detecting cues which signal the unavailability of the attachment figure and appropriately seek contact with attachment figures when needed.	*Preoccupied:* High levels of attachment anxiety, but low levels of attachment avoidance. These individuals have a predominantly anxious attachment style and as such low thresholds for detecting cues which signal the unavailability of the attachment figure. They will seek contact with attachment figures when stress is triggered.	*Dismissing:* High levels of attachment avoidance, but low levels of attachment anxiety. These individuals have a predominant avoidant attachment style and as such have high thresholds for detecting cues which signal the unavailability of the attachment figure. They will withdraw and attempt to cope with situations alone.	*Fearful:* High levels of both attachment anxiety and avoidance. These individuals have low thresholds for detecting cues which signal the unavailability of the attachment figure, but will withdraw and attempt to cope with situations alone.

Authors associated with model or system of classifying attachment	*Method of assessing attachment*	*Attachment patterns identified**				
Crittenden (2006))	Dynamic maturational method that can be applied to both the Strange Situation and the Adult Attachment Interview	*Secure and balanced* Relaxed, intimate and direct expression of feelings and desires. Able to negotiate conflict and disagreement	*Coercive* Maximises psychological involvement with the attachment figure, exaggerates problems and conflict. Can be threatening (resistant and punitive) and/or disarming (innocent and coy).	*Defended* Acts to reduce emotional involvement or confrontation. Limits opportunities for interaction in favour of exploration of the environment.	*Defended/coercive* Both defended or coercive behaviours appearing together or alternating	*Anxious/depressed* Sad/depressed or extreme panic/distress or staring

SUMMARY

In summary, attachment theory has been successfully applied to the understanding of close relationships in adulthood. Earlier attachment relationships in infancy can influence later attachment relationships in adulthood through the concept of internal working models. However, we know that it is also possible for attachment patterns to change over the life course. This is a positive finding as it means that those who have experienced hardships in earlier relationships can go on to develop secure attachment relationships in later life under the right circumstances. There are different models of adult attachment which describe slightly different types of attachment patterns and have different ways of measuring attachments. However, all models highlight the importance of secure attachment for psychological health and wellbeing in adulthood.

RECOMMENDED READING

Cassidy, J. & Shaver, P. (Eds). (2016). Handbook of attachment: Theory, research, and clinical applications (3rd Ed.). Guildford Press.

Mikulincer, M. & Shaver P. R. (2016). Attachment in adulthood: Structure, dynamics, and change. Guilford Press.

REFERENCES

Ainsworth, M. D. S., Blehar, M. C., Waters, E. & Wall, S. (1978). *Patterns of attachment: A psychological study of the Strange Situation*. Lawrence Erlbaum.

Bartholomew, K. (1990). Avoidance of intimacy: An attachment perspective. *Journal of Social and Personal Relationships*, 7: 147–178.

Bartholomew, K. (1997). Adult attachment processes: Individual and couple perspectives. *British Journal of Medical Psychology*, 70: 249–263.

Bowlby, J. (1979). *The making and breaking of affectional bonds*. Tavistock Publications.

Crittenden, P. M. (2006). A dynamic-maturational model of attachment. *Australian and New Zealand Journal of Family Therapy*, 27: 105–115.

Davila, J., Burge, D. & Hammen, C. (1997). Why does attachment style change? *Journal of Personality and Social Psychology*, 73: 826–838.

Doherty, N. A. & Feeney, J. A. (2004). The composition of attachment networks throughout the adult years. *Personal Relationships*, 11: 469–488.

Dozier, M. & Lee, S. (1995). Discrepancies between self- and other- report of psychiatric symptomatology: Effects of dismissing attachment strategies. *Development and Psychopathology*, 7: 217–226.

Fraley, R. C. (2002). Attachment stability from infancy to adulthood: Meta-analysis and dynamic modelling of developmental mechanisms. *Personality and Social Psychology Review*, 6: 123–151.

Fraley, R. C. & Davis, K. E. (1997). Attachment formation and transfer in young adults' close relationships and romantic relationships. *Personal Relationships*, 4: 131–144.

Fraley, R. C. & Roisman, G. I. (2019). The development of adult attachment styles: Four lessons. *Current Opinion in Psychology*, 25: 26–30.

Fraley, R. C. & Shaver, P. R. (2000). Adult romantic attachment: Theoretical developments, emerging controversies, and unanswered questions. *Review of General Psychology*, 4: 132–154.

Hamilton, C. E. (2000). Continuity and discontinuity of attachment from infancy through adolescence. *Child Development*, 71: 690–694.

Hazan, C. & Shaver, P. (1987). Romantic love conceptualised as an attachment process. *Journal of Personality and Social Psychology*, 52: 511–524.

Hesse, E. (2008). The Adult Attachment Interview: Protocol, method of analysis, and empirical studies. In J. Cassidy and P. R. Shaver (Eds), *Handbook of attachment: Theory, research, and clinical applications* (2nd Ed., pp. 552–598). Guildford Press.

Main, M. & Goldwyn, R. (1984) *Adult attachment rating and classification system*, Unpublished manuscript. Berkeley, CA:University of California at Berkeley.

McConnell, M., & Moss, E. (2011). Attachment across the life span: Factors that contribute to stability and change. *Australian Journal of Educational and Developmental Psychology*, 11: 60–77.

Ross, L. R. & Spinner, B. (2001). General and specific attachment representations in adulthood: Is there a relationship? *Journal of Social and Personal Relationships*, 18: 747–766.

Shaver, P. R. & Mikulincer, M. (2005). Attachment theory and research: Resurrection of the psychodynamic approach to personality. *Journal of Research in Personality*, 39: 22–45.

Slade, A. (2008). The implications of attachment theory and research for adult psychotherapy: research and clinical perspectives. In J. Cassidy & P. R. Shaver (Eds), *Handbook of Attachment: Theory, Research, and Clinical Applications* (2nd Ed., pp. 762–782). Guilford Press.

Trinke, S. J. & Bartholomew, K. (1997). Hierarchies of attachment relationships in young adults. *Journal of Social and Personal Relationships*, 14: 603–625.

Waters, E., Hamilton, C. E. & Weinfield, N. S. (2000). The stability of attachment security from infancy to adolescence and early adulthood. *Child Development*, 71: 678–683.

Waters, E., Merrick, S., Treboux, D., Crowell, J. & Albersheim, L. (2000). Attachment security in infancy and early adulthood: A twenty-year longitudinal study. *Child Development*, 71: 684–689.

7

ATTACHMENT THEORY AND ADULT MENTAL HEALTH

Professor Katherine Berry

INTRODUCTION

In this chapter, we outline how attachment theory can be used to help us understand the development of some mental health problems in adulthood. We also describe research investigating associations between attachment difficulties and adult mental health problems, as well providing a critique of this literature.

WHY SHOULD WE CONSIDER ATTACHMENT THEORY TO BETTER UNDERSTAND MENTAL HEALTH PROBLEMS?

We believe that attachment theory has a number of strengths in terms of developing our understanding of the cause and treatment of mental health problems. Firstly, mental health problems are often understood in terms of cognitive, social and emotional factors. Taking the common mental health problem of depression as an example: depression can be understood in terms of cognitive factors, such as negative beliefs about the self (e.g., "No one likes me", "I am useless"), social factors, such as social isolation and loneliness and emotional factors, such as feeling apathetic, unmotivated or very sad. As we will see later in the chapter, attachment theory describes different attachment styles in terms of each of these domains and as such provides a useful framework for thinking about how problems in each domain might develop and reinforce each other.

Secondly, attachment theory can be seen as less blaming towards individuals with mental health problems than traditional biological

DOI: 10.4324/9780203703878-7

or some other psychological approaches to understanding mental health problems, as the theory emphasises the social causes of mental distress rather than causes that are located within individuals themselves. A central idea is that behaviours which are maladaptive and lead to distress in the context of the adult's life once served to keep the child safe and helped him adapt to adverse earlier caregiving environments. By contrast, biological theories of mental health problems argue that people develop mental health problems, owing to disturbances in their brain chemistry. Cognitive theories (another type of psychological theory of mental health problems) argue that people develop mental health problems, owing to unhelpful thinking patterns. Both of these approaches can feel blaming towards the person with mental health problems themselves as they locate the problem within the person. In contrast, attachment theory argues that mental health problems result from problems in earlier caregiving experiences and are essentially related to ways in which the young person learnt to survive and get their needs met in this earlier environment. In this respect, insecure attachment styles are "survival strategies" to adapt to suboptimal caregiving environments but increase vulnerability to the development of mental health problems in later life. For example, if caregivers are overly harsh or critical, it is adaptive for the infant to learn to keep their distance and not display overt signs of distress. Although this strategy may help to keep them safe in infancy by avoiding punishment or criticism, in later life or in the context of more healthy relationships it may mean that they do not use the support of others to get their emotional needs met, increasing vulnerability to mental health problems. While attachment theory may be less blaming of individuals themselves for the development of their problems compared to some other theories, as we suggest later in the chapter, there is a danger that attachment theory can be misinterpreted as blaming parents or early caregivers for later problems. However, once one understands that there is intergenerational transmission of attachment patterns, the whole concept of blame becomes less of an issue.

Finally, as we highlight in Chapter 4 and in this chapter, there is lots of evidence from research studies to show that attachment difficulties are highly associated with mental health problems, meaning that it is hard to ignore the role of attachment theory in explaining the development of these problems.

HOW MIGHT ATTACHMENT STYLES INFLUENCE MENTAL HEALTH?

Insecure attachment per se is not pathological. Insecure attachment styles may be functional in terms of reducing the likelihood of caregiver maltreatment and infant distress. However, they are hypothesised to increase vulnerability to psychopathology and lead to worse outcomes following the onset of psychological difficulties. For example, insecure attachment styles typically involve negative beliefs about both the self and others, which have been repeatedly shown to increase vulnerability to, and the maintenance of, various forms of psychological distress (Beck, 2011). Behaviours associated with insecure attachment styles may also alienate others, thus reducing opportunities for protective interpersonal ties (Cutrona & Russell, 1987). Furthermore, insecure styles may be associated with less helpful methods of coping with stress, which have been implicated in the onset and course of psychological difficulties (Mikulincer & Shaver, 2019).

ASSOCIATIONS BETWEEN INSECURE ATTACHMENT STYLES AND MENTAL HEALTH PROBLEMS IN ADULTHOOD

Research has found that insecure attachment as a whole is over-represented in studies of people diagnosed with a mental health problem (Bakermans-Kranenburg & Van IJzendoorn, 2009). More specifically, insecure attachment has been found to be over-represented in those receiving mental health diagnoses, such as depression, anxiety, eating disorders, personality disorder and schizophrenia (Mikulincer & Shaver, 2012; Mikulincer & Shaver, 2016). Insecure attachment styles are characterised by negative beliefs about self and/or others, difficulties in forming relationships with others and difficulties in regulating emotion. All of these factors may place individuals at risk of developing mental health problems and mean that problems are more likely to persist once they develop. For example, someone with an avoidant attachment pattern is likely to hold negative beliefs about others, avoid help seeking and try to block out negative emotions. If this person were to experience a stressful life event, such as losing a job, he may blame others for the event, bottle-up negative feelings (possibly using alcohol to help numb emotions), not talked to loved ones about his feelings about the event and not seek support from other people to find a new job. Taken together these responses may increase the person's risk of developing symptoms of depression and may perpetuate feelings of low mood. Conversely, a person with a secure attachment style is likely to hold positive beliefs about the self and others, seek help and use adaptive coping strategies. If this person were to also lose his job, he may appreciate the range of different factors that could have led to the event, talk to his friends about his feelings of loss and possible anger, ask for support from former colleagues to identify a new job and use adaptive coping strategies such as exercise to help regulate low mood. Although the person may experience a dip in mood as a result of losing a job, these more helpful responses may minimise the potential impact of the event and may even help to resolve the stressor (i.e., help him to find a new job).

The majority of adult attachment research has focused on the associations between mental health and attachment insecurity *in general*, as opposed to *specific* types of attachment insecurity. However, there is some evidence to suggest that "unresolved attachment" assessed on the Adult Attachment Interview and "fearful attachment" assessed on self-report measures of attachment might be more important in leading to the development of mental health problems than other types of attachments.

George and West (1999) argue that as a result of traumatic experiences, individuals with "unresolved attachment" are sensitised to stress and develop disorganised (or incoherent) attachment patterns, which once triggered lead to intense emotional flooding and difficulty containing mental distress. Based on Bartholomew's (1990; 1997) theory of attachment presented in Chapter 6 on models of adult attachment, it could also be argued that fearful attachment styles increase vulnerability to mental distress, as these individuals have negative beliefs about the self and other people and are thus not protected by either a positive self-image or a belief that others are available to help.

In making sense of research looking at associations between different types of insecure attachment and mental distress, it is, however, important to remember that the degree to which people are likely to report distressing feelings is likely to be affected by attachment style. For example, people with a dismissing-avoidant attachment styles might not openly describe distressing symptoms or even be consciously aware of physiological distress so any association between dismissing attachment and distress would be hard to detect by studies that use self-report measures of mental health problems (Dozier & Lee, 1995).

EXAMINING THE LINKS BETWEEN ATTACHMENT CATEGORIES AND MENTAL HEALTH PROBLEMS

On a theoretical level, dismissing-avoidant attachment which is characterised by attempts to minimise attachments needs and distress, may be more likely to be associated with mental health problems that involve focusing on external issues to help distract from painful underlying feelings, such as forms of anxiety with high levels of avoidance and eating disorders. Conversely, preoccupied or anxious attachment styles, which are characterised by negative beliefs about the self and high levels of distress, may be more likely to be associated with mental health problems that are characterised by a higher level of preoccupation with one's own feelings, such as forms of depression with features of self-blame and self-depreciation and forms of anxiety with high levels of fear.

Despite theoretical links, empirical studies have not found evidence of consistent associations between specific types of insecure attachment and particular types of mental health problems (Mikulincer & Shaver, 2012). This might be related to differences in samples of participants studied, differences in measures used to assess mental health problems and the fact that different studies use different instruments to assess attachment styles. As outlined in the chapter on models of adult attachment (Chapter 6), there are two distinct research paradigms with different systems of classifying and measuring attachment which do not necessarily overlap and thus provide an additional complicating factor in trying to make sense of research findings.

Crittenden, who developed the Dynamic-Maturational Model of attachment, has also criticised procedures to diagnose mental health problems as these rely on symptoms clusters and tend not to address the cause of the problems. Crittenden argues that mental health problems with different symptoms may sometimes be functionally very similar in attachment terms. She favours a formulation-based approach to understanding psychopathology, which involves understanding the development of the person's attachment classification as opposed to one which conceptualises mental health problems in terms of different diagnoses based on symptoms (Crittenden, 1995).

A further problem with research into attachment style and mental health is that most studies measure attachment styles and mental health problems at the same point in time. This type of research is called cross-sectional research and is the most common type of research in psychology as it is relatively easier and less expensive to carry out than longitudinal research which involves following people up over time. However, when researchers use cross-sectional designs, it is not possible to say whether insecure attachment styles cause mental health problems. It is equally probable that the presence of mental health problems result in people being more likely to report attachment difficulties. For example, if a person is depressed and experiencing associated low mood and a negative thinking style, they may be more likely to describe relationship experiences more negatively on a questionnaire assessing attachment styles.

Ideally, we need studies which assess attachment styles in large groups of people prior to the development of mental health problems and then follow people up over time to see if those who were previously assessed as having insecure attachment difficulties are more likely to go on to develop mental health problems. Studies which follow people up over time in this way are called longitudinal studies. For example, one well known 30-year longitudinal study by Sroufe and colleagues that began in the 1970s set out to test whether attachment patterns in infancy predicted development (Sroufe et al., 2005). The so-called Minnesota study (also described in Chapter 4) involved a sample of more than 200 mothers and infants from Minnesota in the USA. The mothers were viewed as at moderate risk for parenting difficulties, owing to their experience of poverty. Participants engaged in frequent assessments of parenting, attachment and many other measures of functioning (e.g., measures of cognition, language and socio-emotional development), starting in infancy and continuing throughout school years and into adulthood. The study assessed participants in multiple domains (home, school, laboratory, and peer group) and included an assessment of developmental context (e.g., parent characteristics, family life stress, and social support), for purposes of statistical control and to provide factors that might influence continuity and change in child development. While variations in attachment did not relate consistently to every outcome assessed, they were related to many critical development functions, including social relatedness and emotional regulation. Most notably, disorganised attachment in infancy was related to numerous indicators of psychopathology in adolescence and adulthood.

A literature review by Stovall-McClough and Dozier (2016) which summarised findings from lots of studies of infant attachment and mental health problems in adulthood also highlighted the importance of disorganised attachment and in particular the role that this might play in predicting later symptoms of dissociation. Dissociation is the experience of feeling disconnected from yourself and the world around you and is common in mental health problems like Borderline Personality Disorder (also referred to as Emotionally Unstable Personality Disorder) and psychosis. Stovall-McClough and Dozier (2016) also concluded that resistant attachment was associated with anxiety disorders in adulthood.

Although longitudinal studies are considered as 'gold standard' in developmental research, they are notoriously difficult to carry out. For example, you need large samples of participants to ensure that at least some of the sample develop mental health problems. There is also a risk that people are "lost to follow up" meaning you cannot track them down to complete follow up assessments. Finally, even if you can demonstrate that insecure attachment is associated with the later development of mental health problems, it is still possible that other factors which are related both insecure attachment and mental health problems provide a better explanation of the relationship. Take the example of insecure anxious attachment styles and symptoms of depression; it is possible that both are related to being female meaning that women are more likely to report anxious attachment styles and depressive symptoms. It is therefore, possible that insecure anxious attachment and depression appear to be related simply because they are both related to being female. This so-called "third variable" problem is common in psychological research, and researchers need to ensure that they measure third variables so their significance can be explored using statistical analyses. However, it may not be possible to measure every 'third' variable that may potentially be important.

In making sense of the literature investigating associations between attachment and mental health problems, it is also important to remember that there is good evidence that not everyone diagnosed with a mental health problem has an insecure attachment style (Mickelson et al., 1997). This suggests that attachment theory does not in itself offer an adequate account of the complexity and subtlety of the development of mental health problems i.e. attachment theory alone does not explain all instances of mental health problems. There are also plenty of so-called 'healthy' people without mental health problems who would be classified as having insecure attachment styles on measures of attachment (Mickelson et al., 1997). Insecure attachment must therefore be seen as only one risk factor among many which results in diagnosable mental health problems.

Another problem within the attachment and mental health literature is that the majority of the research has focused on the role of insecure attachment in increasing vulnerability to problems. There is a relative lack of research investigating or conceptualising the role of secure attachments in promoting resilience to the development of mental health problems. However, in a review of thirty-three previous studies, Darling Rasmussen et al. (2019) found a weak to moderate, although statistically significant, correlation between secure attachment and resilience. The idea of resilience in this context means that those people with secure attachment patterns might be less likely to develop mental health problems when faced with stressful life events because they have the psychological resources to deal with stress in healthier ways, for example, turning to those close to them for support and regulating their own difficult feelings by trying to adopt a more healthy outlook or perspective on the situation, for example, by reminding themselves that things are likely to improve and that the problems are not their fault. In support of this theory, research suggests that individuals with secure attachment are able to confront life stressors without being overwhelmed, seek support in times of distress and use a more diverse range of strategies (Mikulincer et al., 2003; Mikulincer & Shaver, 2019; Collins & Feeney, 2000).

THE DANGERS OF BLAMING PARENTS: A CAUTIONARY NOTE

As we suggested that the beginning of the chapter, attachment theory may be less blaming of individuals themselves for their problems compared to other theories of mental health problems, but there is a danger that the theory could be used to blame parents and mothers in particular for the development of mental health problems. As we outlined earlier in the book, attachment theory was developed based on research by John Bowlby and Mary Ainsworth investigating mother-child relationships. In fact, because of biases in research, which reflect societal beliefs about mothers being the primary caregivers of children, most attachment research focusses on mothers, and we know less about the role of fathers in attachment relationships. The theory therefore has the potential to be "maternal blaming" if not applied with appropriate caution. This caution is especially important in mental health research, as earlier psychological theories of mental health problems highlighted the causal role of family interactions (and mothers in particular) in the development of severe mental health problems like schizophrenia (e.g., Bateson et al., 1956). These theories were met with a backlash of opposition in the 1970s from both relatives and biological psychiatrists. Until relatively recently the idea that families, or indeed environmental factors, might influence the development of severe mental health problems was a taboo subject. In investigating the potential role of earlier caregiving experiences in the development of later mental health problems, it is therefore important to avoid the concept of blame and consider the range of factors that influence the caregiving environment and parenting, such as the availability social support and economic resources, as well as the parents' own attachment histories.

SUMMARY

Adult attachment styles are rooted in early experiences of care and protection, but the strength of associations between childhood and adulthood attachment styles are modest (Fraley & Roisman, 2019). There is clear evidence that adults who are insecurely attached are more likely to have mental health difficulties of various kinds. Longitudinal studies which follow children up into adulthood are rare, but those that have measured childhood attachment and later adult mental health suggest insecure attachment is indeed a causal risk factor. However, we cannot yet say for certain which types of adult attachment pattern lead to which kinds of mental health problems.

Taken together, the body of research suggests that while attachment status influences the likelihood of mental health problems, it is not the only factor. In other words, attachment influences but does not determine mental health problems. This makes good evolutionary sense and is not inconsistent with Bowlby's original thinking. In evolutionary terms, attachment is a motivational system which promotes both improved longevity through proximity to a caregiver, but also flexibility to adapt to changing circumstances throughout life. Later life experiences such as bereavement, trauma, marriage, friendship, parenthood and therapy may influence the more changeable aspects of our attachment style while leaving the less changeable core or default pattern intact, although Fraley and Roisman (2019) suggest that change is more likely during childhood and adolescence than adulthood.

RECOMMENDED READING

Mikulincer, M. & Shaver, P. R. (2012). An attachment perspective on psychopathology. World Psychiatry: Official Journal of the World Psychiatric Association, 11(1): 11–15.

Danquah, A. & Berry, K. (2014). Attachment theory in adult mental health: A guide to clinical practice. Routledge.

REFERENCES

Bakermans-Kranenburg, M. J. & van IJzendoorn, M. H. (2009). The first 10,000 Adult Attachment Interviews: Distributions of adult attachment representations in clinical and non-clinical groups. *Attachment & Human development*, 11(3): 223–263.

Bartholomew, K. (1990). Avoidance of intimacy: An attachment perspective. *Journal of Social and Personal Relationships*, 7: 147–178.

Bartholomew, K. (1997). Adult attachment processes: Individual and couple perspectives. *British Journal of Medical Psychology*, 70: 249–263.

Bateson, G., Jackson, D. D., Haley, J. & Weakland, J. (1956). Toward a theory of schizophrenia. *Behavioral Science*, 1(4): 251–264.

Beck, J. S. (2011). *Cognitive behavior therapy: Basics and beyond* (2nd Ed.). Guilford Press.

Collins, N. L. & Feeney, B. C. (2000). A safe haven: An attachment theory perspective on support seeking and care giving in intimate relationships. *Journal of Personality and Social Psychology*, 78: 1053–1073.

Crittenden, P. M. (1995). *Attachment and psychopathology. In S. Goldberg, R. Muir and J. Kerr (Eds.) John Bowlby's attachment theory: Historical, clinical, and social significance* (pp. 367–406). Analytic Press.

Cutrona, C. E. & Russell, D. W. (1987). The provisions of social relationships and adaptation to stress. *Advances in Personal Relationships*, 1(1): 37–67.

Darling Rasmussen, P., Storebø, O. J., Løkkeholt, T., Voss, L. G., Shmueli-Goetz, Y., Bojesen, A. B. & Bilenberg, N. (2019). Attachment as a core feature of resilience: A systematic review and meta-analysis. *Psychological Reports*, 122(4): 1259–1296.

Dozier, M. & Lee, S. W. (1995). Discrepancies between self- and other-report of psychiatric symptomatology: Effects of dismissing attachment strategies. *Development and Psychopathology*, 7(1): 217–226.

Fraley, R. C. & Roisman, G. I. (2019). The development of adult attachment styles: Four lessons. *Current Opinion in Psychology*, 25: 26–30.

George, C. & West, M. (1999). Developmental vs. social personality models of adult attachment and mental ill health. *British Journal of Medical Psychology*, 72: 285–303.

Mickelson, K. D., Kessler, R. C. & Shaver, P. R., 1997. Adult attachment in a nationally representative sample. *Journal of Personality and Social Psychology, 73(5)*: 1092–1106.

Mikulincer, M. & Shaver P. R. (2016). *Attachment in adulthood: structure, dynamics, and change.* Guilford Press.

Mikulincer, M. & Shaver, P. R. (2012). An attachment perspective on psychopathology. *World Psychiatry: Official Journal of the World Psychiatric Association*, 11(1): 11–15.

Mikulincer, M. & Shaver, P. R. (2019). Attachment orientations and emotion regulation. *Current Opinion in Psychology*, 25: 6–10.

Mikulincer, M., Shaver, P. R. & Pereg, D. (2003). Attachment theory and affect regulation: The dynamics, development, and cognitive consequences of attachment-related strategies. *Motivation and Emotion*, 27: 77–102.

Sroufe, L.A., Egeland, B., Carlson, E. & Collins, W.A. (2005). The place of early attachment experiences in developmental context. In K. E. Grossmann, K. Grossmann, E. Waters (Eds). *The power of longitudinal attachment research: From infancy and childhood to adulthood* (pp. 48–70). Guilford Press.

Stovall-McClough, K. C. & Dozier, M. (2016). Attachment states of mind and psychopathology in adulthood. In J. Cassidy & P. R. Shaver. *Handbook of attachment: Theory, research, and clinical applications* (3rd Ed., pp. 715–738). Guilford Press.

8

ATTACHMENT THEORY AND PARENTING

Professor Rudi Dallos

INTRODUCTION

Attachment theory as we have seen in the previous chapters has focussed on the nature of the child's bonding to its parents as part of a fundamental instinct that helps to ensure the child's protection and safety. In this chapter the focus is how the parents similarly possess an instinctual system to provide this protection. However, as we saw in the earlier chapters there are significant differences in the patterns of security that infants develop, and this chapter looks at how this is shaped by differences in how parents respond to their infants. In contrast to exploration of the differences between children, differences in parenting have received relatively less attention. The pioneering work on parental sensitivity developed by Mary Ainsworth is described alongside descriptions of exciting developments in exploring parenting and the development of patterns of parent- child attachments.

THE PARENTAL CAREGIVING SYSTEM

A significant turning point for attachment theory occurred when Mary Ainsworth and colleagues (1978) showed that attachment 'insecurity' could be seen in intact families. While children might not have experienced significant physical separations, there appeared to be something in the nature of their relationships with their parents that generated insecurity in them. This inspired a large body of research exploring in more detail the nature of these family differences and how they influence a child's subsequent development, such as their

DOI: 10.4324/9780203703878-8

mental health, ability to form friendships and predictions for their adult life, such as choice of romantic partners.

However, how children's attachment patterns relate to differences in parenting has arguably received comparatively much less attention. Bowlby (1969) suggested there were two inter-related attachment systems: the child's proximity and comfort seeking system and a reciprocal parental care-giving system. Both had an evolutionary survival function to enable the processes of care-seeking and caregiving to occur. Understanding these parenting systems is important not just conceptually but also in clinical work with children, families and adults. The problems that a child experiences are often related to the nature of their relationships with parents or carers.

INTERNAL WORKING MODELS

Bowlby used concepts from cognitive neuroscience to suggest that attachment experiences through childhood become represented as a set of understandings and feelings. Bowlby (1969,1982) called this the child's "internal working model" (Chapter 1), implying that it is an active mental system which is able to hold representations of past experience and perform manipulations of these to help the child think about future events. The core purpose of the internal working model is to ensure the child's safety and protection and for the child to be able to develop a variety of behavioural and emotional strategies in order to ensure that this goal is met.

Bowlby conceptualised attachment as a goal–directed system based on feedback in which the child alters their strategies as necessary. Over time some consistent patterns are seen to develop, the well-known attachment styles or strategies. These have been called insecure or secure, but these terms somewhat confuse the fact that all of the strategies are an adaptation and are functional as the best fit the chid can develop in the circumstances of their family. However, these strategies may become problematic when applied to other relational systems outside of the family and in later life.

Parents were seen to employ these working models from their own childhoods in how they acted as parents towards their own children. In other words, Bowlby predicted that we tend to parent our children the way we were parented. There is some evidence to support these ideas in parents' attachment; patterns revealed in the Adult Attachment Interviews (Chapter 6) tend to match the patterns of their own children's attachment to them (Fonagy et al., 1991; Crittenden et al., 2014).

Relatively less is known about whether parents have similar or different working models for different children, although there is evidence to suggest that within families, attachment patterns can differ between parents and their different children (Cook, 2000). There may be various reasons for this, for example their children may have different temperaments and personalities, the family circumstances, stresses and demands may also change as different children are born which can influence how emotionally available parents are and the subsequent quality of the attachments with the children.

It is possible to explore parents' working models of their child through conversations with them rather than just observation as with infants. This has led to the development of a number of interview formats within which to explore parents' representations of their children and of their parenting. Two of these, the Experience of Parenting and the Meaning of the Child will be discussed later in the chapter.

There is now a substantial body of research inspired by the pioneering studies of Mary Ainsworth, especially based upon the Strange Situation Procedure (SSP). These studies propose that the different strategies adopted by young children to cope with the separation and then re-union with their parents (predominantly mothers) are causally related to differences in how the parents respond to their child's attachment requests. The SSP provided a substantial body of data about how infants responded to the separations and some observational data on how mothers differed in the way they acted before they left the child and also when they returned. Ainsworth (1978) supplemented her SSP studies with observations of mothers and infants in naturalistic situations. As well as Ainsworth's detailed observations of infants during the Strange Situation Procedure (Chapter 2), she developed a sophisticated framework for classifying parenting which was composed of four proposed dimensions: Sensitivity, Control, Availability and Rejection.

Importantly, these observations and their analysis included not only how the parent or carer *behaves* but also what might be their *perceptions* of the baby and herself. It is these perceptions of herself, her child and of their relationship that constitute the mother's 'internal working model'.

The interactions between the baby and mother were technically described as a goal-organised feedback system but can be more elegantly thought of as a 'dance' where there is a harmonious balance of co-ordinated movement, feelings and shared understanding between two equally contributing partners (Brazelton, 1975). Crittenden et al. (2017) have argued that some parenting programmes have overly focused on sensitivity as a behavioural approach that can be 'taught' to parents. This can unfortunately result in parents trying to enact the training in a mechanical way without awareness of their perceptions of the baby, themselves as parents or of their relationship. In Ainsworth's descriptions however, it was apparent that sensitivity involved the parent's ability to 'mentalize' – to be able to think about the baby's own mind, including their thoughts and feelings.

SENSITIVITY AND CONTROL

Sensitivity is perhaps the most widely known of Ainsworth's four dimensions of parenting and has been widely applied in parenting training interventions including in video feedback approaches (described in Chapter 10).

Ainsworth (1969) describes maternal sensitivity as:

> the mother's ability to perceive and to interpret accurately the signals and communications implicit in her infant's behaviour, and given this understanding, to respond to them appropriately and promptly. Thus, the mother's sensitivity has four essential components: (a) her awareness of the signals (b) an accurate interpretation of them (c) an appropriate response to them and (d) a prompt response to them.
>
> (Ainsworth, 1969, p. 1)

The sensitive mother is not only physically available to her child but also accurately perceives what the child needs. For example, being aware that slight mouth movements might not always signify that the child is hungry and might instead be a wish to play, a sign of discomfort and so on. The mother is able to think about the baby's needs with a sense of tentative curiosity as opposed to rapidly becoming over certain about what the child needs. She is, therefore, able to be flexible and tune in to the baby's signals and needs rather than becoming overly rigidly guided by her initial interpretation. Importantly, she is also able to differentiate her own needs from those of the child.

Ainsworth also observed that parents differed in the extent to which they were able to allow and nurture a sense of independence in the child, which she referred to as the control component. Parents able to facilitate independence can both initiate activity with the baby but also be led by the baby's invitations. A particular feature of this was the extent to which a parent intruded on the child's activities, for example cutting across what the baby was doing and introducing something the parent wants them to do. For some parents there appears to be a feeling of threat at the prospect of their child being autonomous so they disrupt or interfere with the child's activity and take over to control and direct it. The parent appears to be guided more by their own needs rather than the child's. An example of a controlling response might be where a parent repeatedly encourages a child to perform, such as 'come on, show us the little wriggle, a little dance'. The interaction or play can become more about the parents feeling good about themselves and showing to themselves and others what a good parent they are to have produced such a clever baby, than about whatever activity the baby was actually enjoying. Infants may learn that this pleases their parent and collaborate with this performative process but may also come to resent their parents for it.

AVAILABILITY AND REJECTION

Ainsworth's third component of parenting was how available or accessible the parent can be. Some parents may explicitly ignore or be unresponsive to the child's request for comfort or interaction, while others are more responsive and able to make their mind available for the child's communication and needs. This in turn linked to Ainsworth's fourth component which was whether the parent accepts or rejects the child's need. Both availability and rejection were seen to relate to the balance between the mother's positive and negative feelings about her baby. At the positive end a sense of love and acceptance which could overcome or defuse her frustrations, irritations and tiredness. In contrast, her negative feelings of resentment, irritation, or boredom, resulting in her withdrawal from or rejection of the baby. Ainsworth recognised that both positive and negative feelings were inevitable and needed to be acknowledged and tolerated. Also, that when tired, anxious and stressed mother's needed support from their partners and family in order to be able to manage conflicting feelings about their baby.

Ainsworth's (1978) detailed observations about attachment styles and the parenting dimensions she proposed have formed the basis for much of the subsequent research on attachment and parenting. This has produced much evidence that suggests that children's attachment strategies appear to be related to features of the ways parents respond to their child's attachment requests. For example, responding to the infant's cries, facial expressions and gestures which may signal needs for food, comfort, reassurance, comfort, attention and so on. Broadly, the body of research suggests the following:

Secure Children: Mothers of children who are classified as secure have been described as sensitive to their child's signals of distress, to respond rapidly and flexibly to provide reassurance, soothing and a sense of safety for their child (Ainsworth et al., 1978; Belsky et al., 1984; Egeland & Farber, 1984).

Avoidant: Mothers of infants classified as avoidant have been found to be slower in noticing their child's feelings, to respond minimally or to reject the child's requests. Parents in this group appeared to engage in what Bowlby (1969) termed 'de-activation', a defensive process whereby information about the child's needs is excluded from parental consciousness. In effect, they do not respond to the child's needs because they do not appear to have consciously noticed what the child was feeling. At mild levels the parent is somewhat emotionally disengaged and at extremes almost oblivious to what the child may be feeling.

Anxious/ambivalent: Mothers of children classified as anxious/ambivalent have been found to respond in a non-contingent way, sometimes responding and sometimes not, which escalates the child's distress rather than soothing them. George and Solomon (2008) suggested that this involved a defensive process of 'disconnection' in that the emotions a parent might experience, such as anger, frustration, or fear were not closely connected to the child's needs and feelings. The parents were driven more by their own needs and feelings than being able to tune in to their child's feelings and needs. As an example, a parent may almost exclusively focus on describing how anxious or upset 'they' feel when their child is not eating properly rather than being able to consider different reasons for why their child might not be eating.

Extreme – Disorganised: Children classified as 'disorganised' were often seen to have parents who themselves had been traumatised and were reacting to their child with extreme non-responsiveness, lack of sensitivity, and could be either frightening towards or frightened by the child. Parenting here could combine both de-activating and disconnected responses. For example, a parent might generally be emotionally disconnected from her child but certain actions could trigger memories of the parent's earlier traumas leading to disconnected emotional responses. For example, a mother who had experienced repeated domestic violence from her infant's father became aware, as a result of therapeutic support that she was emotionally reacting to her baby as if he was like his father. The mother had been emotionally withdrawn from the boy (de-activated) but also intermittently become fearful, anxious and angry with feelings that were disconnected from anything that he was doing.

Similarly, Jenny in the example below may appear to be responding to her young son , but this can be seen as 'disconnected' from what he is doing and being triggered by memories that his actions are evoking for her:

> When my son starts screaming it triggers those feelings of stress that I had when my mother used to scream (at me) ... that kind of brings it all back, it's sort of like triggering, which is why I think that I find it particularly stressful [...] there you know there's a link between the past and the present.
>
> (Dallos, 2022 "Jenny", personal clinical material)

Such responding by the mother can remain incomprehensible and highly confusing to the child since the intensity of the mother's response of fear and anxiety is not contingent on what he is actually doing.

THE TRANSMISSION GAP

Ainsworth's work inspired researchers to explore whether maternal sensitivity fully predicted observed attachment security in infants, but this produced somewhat disappointing findings (Belsky et al., 1984). That maternal sensitivity does not fully predict infant attachment security came to be known as the "transmission gap" (Van IJzendoorn, 1995). and it was suggested that a. the measure of sensitivity needed to be improved and b. that the mechanisms of sensitivity needed to be more closely examined and that an important aspect of this might be not just what the parents were observed to do but their representation or 'internal working model' of the child and their relationship. In the next section, I outline the Care Index (Crittenden, 2001, 2010) which attempts a more sensitive and relational observational approach, and the remainder of the chapter will look at parents' representations of the child.

AN OBSERVATIONAL APPROACH – THE CARE INDEX

The Care Index consists of a detailed observational measure of parental sensitivity for infants aged from birth to 15 months and toddlers from 16 to 48 months in which a parent and infant are asked to play together for about 5–7 minutes. It is inspired by Ainsworth's work but rather than employing all four of Ainsworth's categories which were seen to overlap it focusses on sensitivity as the over-riding dimension which incorporated the other dimensions. Briefly, she suggests that sensitivity subsumes the dimensions of controlling (over engagement) and unresponsive (under-engagement, lack of availability). In turn, both the controlling and unresponsive patterns can constitute a rejection or neglect of the baby – in the controlling patterns by coercing her to act as the mother wants, and in the unresponsive pattern by withdrawing from and neglecting the infant.

Crittenden's assessment model is based on the idea that parents show the above three main types of behaviour towards the child, which map onto Ainsworth's parenting components (*sensitivity, control and availability*). In turn, the infants were seen to respond with behaviours that are classified as:

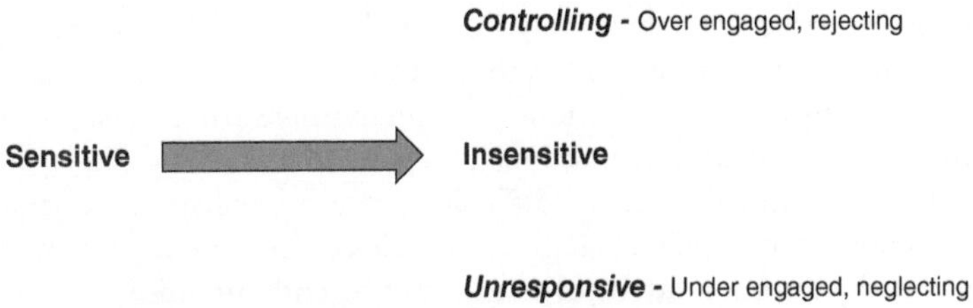

Figure 8.1 The Care Index: Two types of insensitivity

1 'co-operative' which matches sensitive parenting
2 'passive' in relation to unresponsive parents
3 'compulsive' (compliant) patterns in relation to controlling parenting.

Infants may attempt variations of these patterns by showing a 'difficult' pattern, in effect protests to resist control or to activate the parent's attention. The underlying concept of the model is that it focusses on the relationship rather than just what the parent or the child does (see Table 8.1).

Sensitivity is coded on a scale and reflects the extent to which there is synchrony or a smooth flow and connection in the parent-child relationship. In the controlling patterns, the parent attempts to assert their authority over the child to compel them to do what they want and may intrude on the child's attempts at autonomy. A developmental process is suggested in this model in that infants initially attempt a variety of responses towards the parent, but these are gradually shaped by the parent's responses and demands on the child. There may be a process whereby the child initially does not collaborate with the parent's control and shows 'difficult' behaviours in refusing the parent's demands. They may also attempt to

Table 8.1 The Care Index: parent and child interactional patterns

Parent	*Child*
Controlling	Compulsive/Passive or Difficult
Unresponsive	Compulsive/Passive or Difficult
Sensitive	Co-operative

passively withdraw which may not be allowed by the mother so that they are continuously stirred into acting the way that is required. In extreme situations, an unresponsive parent essentially 'tunes out' and is not emotionally available at all. Although the child may initially show 'difficult' protest behaviours, crying, wriggling or compulsive attempts to please the parent they may eventually abandon attempts to gain the parent's attention.

Care Index analysis is focussed on the relationship. Parent-child relationships range in degrees across the patterns, for example difficult behaviours and protest remain a part of the pattern so that it is not completely and unresponsive or controlling.

RUPTURE AND REPAIR

Rather than focussing on sensitivity as something a parent does or has, the CARE Index is a relational approach which focusses on the dynamic between the parent and child. Central to this is how 'ruptures' in their relationship are repaired. Ruptures refer to moments when the dance of interaction between them has fallen out of step, either through a misstep or one of the parties disengaging. For example, when the baby cries, wriggles in discomfort, turns away from the parent, what happens between them? Some parents show curiosity about the infant's state and initiate ways of soothing the child, for example, smiling, making soft sounds, gently soothing them and so on. Importantly, they continually monitor how the infant is responding to their actions so if what they are doing makes the baby more fretful, they may back off or try something else. In contrast, more controlling parents show irritation and try to coerce the infant to settle down. If what they try makes the baby more fretful, they are likely to do more of what they had been doing or do it more intensely rather than use feedback to adapt their responses. In turn, the infants may increase their display of discomfort and distress sometimes prompting potentially dangerous escalations. Parents using unresponsive strategies also do not respond to feedback from the baby, either appearing not to notice or withdrawing further from their baby. After a time, these infants appear to 'give up', offering little further to indicate distress or to invite their parent to engage with them.

FALSIFYING AFFECT – COMPULSIVITY

An innovative feature of the Care Index approach is the idea that the child may also disguise or distort their feelings in the interaction. In the examples above the infants experiencing a controlling and intrusive pattern of engagement from the parent may also develop what Crittenden (2006) terms a "compulsive" or fearful pattern in which they learn to supress their displays of distress. The infant may learn to stifle their cries, try to look away from their parent and show a sort of startled freezing when the parent physically intrudes by touching, poking or forcefully kissing or nuzzling their face into them. In contrast, older infants who experience unresponsive parenting may learn not just to inhibit their own emotions but to display 'false positive affect', pretending they are happy. They try to focus on their parents' needs and try to please them by looking happy and cheerful in order to maintain attention and emotional contact with their parents.

The Care Index has been employed in both research, child protection and clinical contexts. The assessment employs a rating of the extent to which the parent -child relationship appears to be 'at risk' by offering both an indication of the patterns between the child and parent and also the overall level of sensitivity. The assessment employs video recording of the interactions and this has also been employed to assist in clinical work with parents. This has overlap with the video-based interventions described in Chapter 10. Also, as a research tool it has been employed to explore the effectiveness of parenting interventions.

In the next section we move from looking at what parents do with their children to what underlies their attachment to them in terms of their understandings of themselves derived from their childhoods – their working models and how this shapes their views of their children and their relationships with them.

PARENTS' WORKING MODELS OF PARENTING

Rather than simply focussing on parents' externally observable behaviour, contemporary attachment approaches explore parents' internal working models, including perceptions of their child and their relationship. These approaches attempt to understand how parents' working models of their own childhood shape their views of their child and the relationship. The relationship a parent has with their child is current and shaped by day-to-day events in their lives together. This makes it more fluid unlike childhood representations of relationships with parents which over the span of time crystallise into characteristic patterns. This has presented a challenge for attachment researchers in that it is harder to undertake more 'objective', experimental research on perceptions and how they might reliably predict how parents' working models influence how they act and how their child will develop.

Two models of parents' representations of their children will be described: The first is George and Solomon's (2008) approach and the second a more recent development, Grey and Farnfield's (2017) Meaning of the Child model. Both use an in-depth interview with parents called the Parent Development Interview (PDI) to explore their 'working models'. The analysis is informed by the concepts used to explore defensive processes in the Adult Attachment Interview (George et al., 1985; Crittenden et al., 2014). The PDI is in two parts. The first explores the parent's own attachment history (times they were upset, separations, comfort and illness, losses and so on). The second part explores their relationship with their child, including how they view their child, times they got on well and times they did not, feelings about parenting, being separated from their child and so on (Slade, 2005).

George and Solomon (2008) have developed four dimensions of parents' representations of their child based on the analyses of parents' interviews; secure base, rejection, uncertainty and helplessness.

The ***secure base*** scale assesses the degree to which a mother's mental representation of caregiving reflect her commitment and ability to provide physical and psychological safety and protection for her child. A secure base representation is characterised by the mother's positive attitude towards caregiving and flexibility in how she thinks about herself, her child and their relationship. Secure base mothers could describe and give examples of their attempts to help the child cope with real and psychological threats, evaluating her strategies against her child's and her own needs and age-appropriate autonomy. Further, her memories and evaluations were straightforward, frank, and integrated into a balanced and undefended portrait of herself as the caregiver of this child.

The ***rejection*** scale assessed the degree to which the mother's mental representation of caregiving reflected unwillingness, in herself and in her child, to participate in the caregiving relationship. Unwillingness was revealed, in part, by negative evaluations of self and other (e.g., she considered herself a poor mother, the child was demanding, devious or manipulative). Further, the mother's descriptions of the relationship demonstrated her unwillingness to participate in a mutual and flexible relationship with the child. The rejecting mother emphasised her own perspective and needs and was unwilling to acknowledge and therefore to integrate the child's attachment needs. Finally, memories and descriptions were explored in a manner that attempted to dismiss, discount, or distance negative emotions.

The ***uncertainty*** scale assessed the degree to which a mother's mental representation of caregiving reflected questioning, doubt, confusion, or vacillation in regarding herself as a caregiver, the child and their relationship. Uncertainty was manifested when the mother was unable to describe herself clearly as a parent, uncertain about how to evaluate her attributes or contributions. The mother emphasised positive evaluations of the child (e.g., good, nice, polite, perfect child). However, she also described some of the child's negative qualities (e.g., unable to communicate clearly, emotional) but was unable to understand their origins. Finally, her descriptions and memories were often contradictory, or her opinions vacillated. Unable to integrate positive and negative thought, the mother was left questioning herself, the child and the relationship.

The ***helplessness*** scale assessed the degree to which a mother's mental representation of caregiving reflected her evaluations of self, child and their relationship as being out of control. Helplessness was manifested when the mother evaluated herself as helpless and out of control, lacking appropriate and effective strategies to handle the child or the situation. She described the child as being either out of control (often beyond help) or precociously in control. The former was reflected in descriptions of the child as wild, unruly, or unmanageable. The latter was reflected in descriptions of the child as having maturity, intellect, or powers that enabled the child to handle the situation without the mother's involvement. The descriptions suggested that the parents felt unable to change or alter the relationship with the child. Alternatively, there was an indication of a form of "role reversal" where the child was seen as having developmentally impossibly advanced mental skills to be able to manipulate and control the relationship. This appeared to be combined with a heightened emotional state of arousal and fear for the parent.

Table 8.2 below summarises George and Solomon's findings in terms of showing connections between how children respond in a separation situation (SSP), the parent's own attachment strategies and their predominant parenting model.

George and Solomon's (2008) findings confirm the body of attachment research suggesting that there is a causal link between parents' own attachment histories and how securely their child will be attached to them. They also reveal that the parent's own attachment histories are associated with the various parenting models in that a dismissing parental attachment orientation appears to lead parents to adopt a model of seeing themselves as needing to withdraw from and a wish to reject their child's attachment requests. Parents showing a pre-occupied attachment style appear to have a view of the child and their relationships characterised by uncertainty.

The helpless parenting model is the one which is associated with the most complex and extremely insecure patterns in children. This is particularly interesting because much of the disorganised attachment literature had previously focussed on parents who are frightening, emotionally abusive or neglecting. George and Solomon have produced subsequent research to show that the helpless parenting model, which may also be associated with bereavements,

Table 8.2 Parenting model and its relationship to infant security and parent attachment style

Parenting Model	*Parental Attachment Style: Adult Attachment Interview*	*Infant Security: Child in the Strange Situation SSP*
Secure	Balance	Secure
Rejecting	Dismissing	Avoidant
Uncertain	Pre-Occupied	Ambivalent
Helpless	Extreme/Unresolved	Disorganised

illness and childhood exposure to violence including domestic violence, is associated with complex/disorganised patterns in children (George and Solomon, 2008). This suggests that disorganised attachment is not always an indicator of child abuse; George and Solomon's work suggests it can also be a reflection of parents being overwhelmed by current stresses and past traumas.

MEANING OF THE CHILD

This approach to assessment develops the focus on exploring parents' conceptualisations of their child and their relationship with them. Importantly, it also suggests that parents develop unique sets of meanings, understandings and predictions regarding their different children. This heralds a change for attachment theory which has been interested in continuities in terms of how the parents own attachment histories shape their relationship with a child.

This model of understanding parents' representations of themselves, their child and their parenting role (Grey & Farnfield, 2017) also uses the PDI interview but allows the use of other narrative material, e.g., from clinical interviews. This approach, developed in the context of the authors' work in child protection and safeguarding contexts, aims to predict levels of risk indicated in the parents' working models of their child. They also argued that a parent may hold differing models in relation to different children in the family. This was based on the observation that some children in a family appeared to arouse more negative feelings in their parents than others and could therefore be greater targets for dangerous and abusive actions towards them from their parents. The approach is based on the Dynamic Maturational Model (Crittenden et al., 2014) of attachment which offers a greater differentiation of attachment strategies in parents and children and also regards all strategies as attempts at adaptation. Consequently, it does not employ a concept of 'disorganised' attachment and instead considers how children and parents form various types of attempts at adaptation and these develop and change in accordance with the child's maturing mental and physical abilities. For example, (as shown in Figure 8.2), as children grow they are more able to engage in tactics such as withdrawal from others, deception, disguising their true feelings, manipulation and so on.

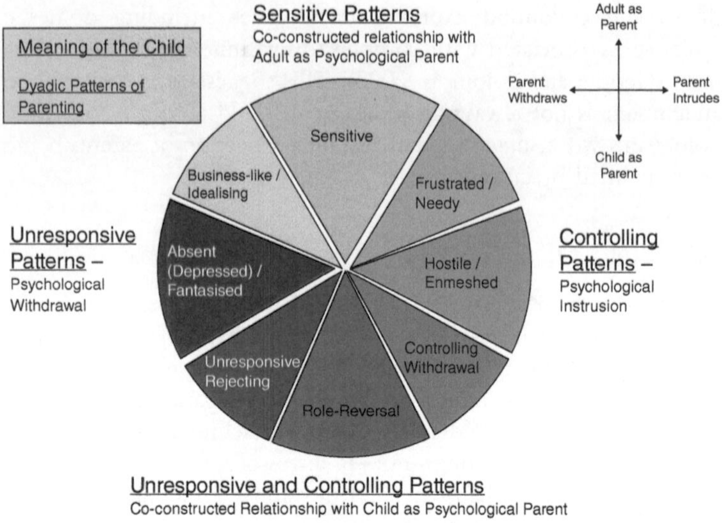

Figure 8.2 The Meaning of the Child Model (Grey and Farnfield 2017)

The central aim of the Meaning of the Child assessment is to map the meanings relating to the parent-child relationship dynamics in terms of two axes. These are shown in the pie chart and also in the four arrows summarising the overall dimensions:

Reciprocity and Mutuality: This is based on Ainsworth et al.'s (1978) concept of maternal sensitivity as sensitive, withdrawn or intrusive. This dimension consists of parents who at one extreme withdraw and disengage from the child and at the other intrude to shape the child to be how they want it to act and feel. At the extreme end this is driven primarily by their own rather than the child's needs.

Protection and Nurturance – this also relates to Ainsworth's conceptualisation of the availability of the parent but identifies the parent as being more concerned with protecting and nurturing themselves rather than their child (Crittenden, 2014). At the extreme this becomes a role-reversed relationship where the parent appears to be responsive to the child (often mistaken for sensitivity), but this functions to protect the parent more than the child. Instead, the child comes to look after the needs of the parent and sacrifices their own needs for protection as a result.

The various categories of sensitive, controlling, and unresponsive employed in the Meaning of the Child are summarised below:

SENSITIVE CAREGIVING

The concept of sensitive parenting can visually be summarised as both connection and independence between the parent and child (Figure 8.3). The mother is able both to empathise with her child's needs but is also able to acknowledge the child as separate from herself and to be curious about the child's feelings and needs and not confuse these with her own.

The emphasis of interviews with sensitive caregivers is a collaborative relationship between parent and child where the parent waits for the child's requests, listens to, and tries to understand their child. The parent is seen to engage in a collaborative conversation with the child and recognises and communicates back to the child that the child's request is acceptable and that they will respond positively to them. They are seen to engage in a 'dialogue' involving mutual actions and expression of a variety of emotions. The parent shows that they feel free to let the child contribute to, initiate and alter the directions of their interaction. In the Meaning of the Child interview, the parents are able to be free to explore openly and honestly their relationship with their child. The overall tone of such interviews is likely to be affectionate and positive, but the parent is also open to discussing and thinking about frustrations and problems. There is a clear sense of the parent knowing the child well, with reference to incidents and images that are personal

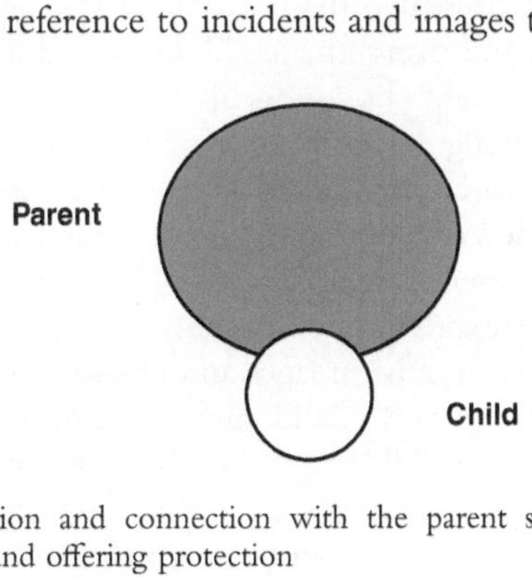

Figure 8.3 Separation and connection with the parent sensitive to child's needs and offering protection

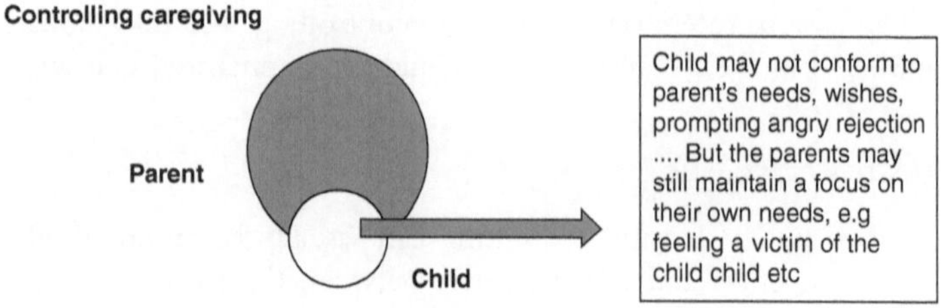

Figure 8.4 Child is not seen as separate but confused with parents own needs

to the relationship rather than generalisations or clichés from media, parenting manuals etc. Parents' stories about the child and their relationship are credible with appropriate feelings being expressed. The stories also indicate awareness of the child's mind including what they think, feel an awareness of and inclusion of their version of events.

The emphasis of interviews with controlling parents is that the parent is seeking to be dominant in the interaction and the creation of meanings with the child. The child is required to see things the parent's way and the child acting autonomously or offering different meanings to the parent is seen by the parent as a threat or that the child is seen as argumentative and difficult. The controlling parent responds to the threat they perceive from the child by attempting to make the relationship what they want or need it to be, rather than feeling secure enough to allow the relationship to develop in a way that respects the child's subjectivity and personality. The parent constructs the meaning of the child in such a way as to necessitate directing the child onto a different path from which he or she might choose on his or her own.

Parents employing a controlling pattern often perceive their child as wishing to control them or the child is seen to differ too much in their views or opinions to the parent. Problems in their relationships are often seen as caused by the child. This orientation can also involve expression of hostility towards the child this is often expressed in negative images and phrases, the child as 'nasty', 'selfish' being a 'cry baby', 'whinging', 'tantrum' and so on. The hostility towards the child might be disguised in humour or trivialising language, for example the child's fascinations with a game described as an "obsession", play as acting like a "little princess" and so on. Frequently, the child is seen as devious and manipulative often beyond what they are developmentally capable of. Such negative views of the child are often seen to be employed to justify the parents' negative views or punitive actions towards the child.

The controlling orientation to parenting can include a seemingly more positive but emotionally entangled stance. Here the parent appears to think more about the child but confuses their own needs and desires which are projected into the child. The parents can become angry or frustrated and express how anxious or distressed they are feeling about their child. This can sound like genuine concern for the child, but the parent is in fact more focussed on their own needs and feelings and is unable to separate these from what their child might actually be feeling. A variation of this is seen where the parent expresses a need for the child to help them feel better. For example, they might mention how sad or depressed they would be without the love, devotion and attention of their child. The parent in a sense invites others to help them to secure the affection they need from their child.

The overall orientation here is to withdraw from the demands of the child. One key way this can happen is that the parents constructs a story that is over idealistic about the child's competence, independence, abilities so that the parent is seen as unnecessary – "they don't really need me". In extreme cases the parent can appear to embrace a form of blaming themselves, such as "I have been so depressed that I cannot help him".

This can create a vacuum of care that the child must try to fill for themselves. The parent appears to fear the possible responsibility if they were fully available for their child. This can become a

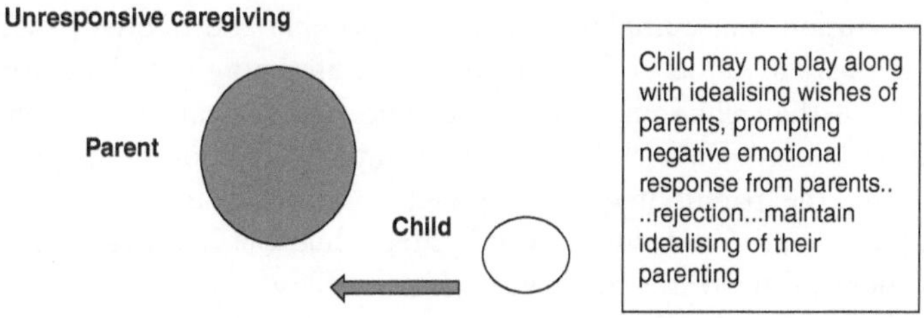

Figure 8.5 Child is separate, disengaged from the parent, needs not recognised

reciprocal process; as the child necessarily develops some self-sufficient strategies these confirm for the parent that they are not needed and legitimises their further withdrawal, leading to a striking absence of emotional involvement by the parent. The child and their relationship appear to be invisible to the parent, who is unable to recount images or specific events with their child that capture the uniqueness or intimacy of their relationship. At the extreme are depressed parents who have withdrawn to the extent of giving up on the relationship and perceive it as hopeless and beyond repair.

This pattern can also involve what might appear to be very positive views of the child in a form of idealisation of the child and his abilities. For example, he might be described as wonderful, a little angel or doing amazingly well in skills of various sorts without any assistance from the parent. The child can appear to be placed on a pedestal but at the same time this can imply that they need little protection or nurturance from the parents since they are already so perfect. This can leave the child at some risk if, for example, they are seen to have an awareness of danger and abilities to cope that are developmentally out of their range. The parent also imagines that the child understands complex issues without assistance from the parent as if by some magical process. A less extreme variation is where parents maintain some emotional distance from the child but do provide for their basic needs. This has a business-like quality of providing basic physical needs, tending to illnesses but without any show of affection, joy, fun or emotional care.

UNRESPONSIVE AND CONTROLLING CAREGIVING

An important aspect of the Meaning of the Child framework is its recognition that complex patterns are possible and frequent, with some parents using both controlling and unresponsive orientations towards their children. For parents who have a controlling orientation towards their child, if their attempts to control them appear to fail, the parent may consequently experience a sense of disappointment and failure towards their child. This can prompt a withdrawal from the child with some hostility and a view there is nothing they can do. In contrast, parents who adopt an unresponsive pattern may find that their child's expressions of distress or hostility do not conform to the ideal 'good child'. Parents' consequent hostility towards and rejection of the child can serve to maintain their distance and withdrawal.

A more complex version is where both orientations are employed and there can appear to be a connection with the child, but unlike the sensitive category, these relationships function to protect and even nurture *the parent*, rather than the child. The depiction therefore mirrors that of the sensitive parent, but the nature of the cooperation involved does not support the child's development. In effect, there is only room for the parent to be the needy one in the relationship.

The example below comes from our research using the PDI with parents with moderate autism. It is offered to illustrate some core aspects of the Meaning of the Child framework. The PDI provides a picture of the parent's own childhood attachment history as well as their understanding of their child and their relationship.

To illustrate the Meaning of the Child model an example is shared with permission from our research programme exploring a family-based intervention to assist families who had a child with a diagnosis of autism (McKenzie et al., 2022).

ANGELA AND ANDY

Angela has two children, and her younger son Andy (aged ten) has a diagnosis of moderate level autism. Angela was adopted when she was four years old, and her adoptive parents fostered a large number of very 'needy' children. Angela found this to be very difficult at times and described that she had received very little attention and care from her parents. She is divorced from Andy's father.

Angela's PDI interview indicated that she had a controlling and hostile orientation towards her son Andy. He was seen as a problematic child and many aspects of him were seen by her to be flawed. Angela also described him as very clever, e.g., he was learning Spanish, but overall, he was experienced by her as a burden. In some ways, this sense of having an unwanted person burdening her life appeared to resonate with the story of the unwanted and very needy foster children that had been in her life:

You either leave him alone and don't go near him or he's just in your face talking a load of crap.

Overall, Angela appeared to hold a negative view of Andy who, at times, she found frightening since he could become angry. She also found him irritating and his interest in cars boring. She felt she had to do a lot for him, that he was demanding, and she did not feel rewarded in her interactions with him nor connected with him:

That's bad isn't it really not being able to relate to your child, but I suppose if you ain't got it, then you don't realise what you've lost.

The PDI asks about times that the parent and child 'clicked'. Angela had no memories of them doing so:

Oh, we got him an Xbox 360 for his birthday, and I had to he was talking to me about his flipping Jurassic revolution thing about these blimming dinosaurs he'd made up yeah.

The diagnosis of autism features strongly in her description of him; she withdraws from him because of it but also sees him as responsible:

I was about two minutes late and he slapped me in the face in front of everybody and he got really angry that I was late and then when I told him when I tried telling him off you know it really hurt, I'm not kidding you it was full wallop I'll tell you that now I was so embarrassed.

She appeared at times to see Andy as dangerous and capable of humiliating her. In a disparaging way she drew on experiences from other members of her family to support her view of Andy as flawed and herself as a victim:

My sister had Andy once overnight she said never again yeah (laugh) so we don't tend to um because he's got quite a lot of little quirks and if you don't do them and if you don't do them with routine wise properly, he can cause so many problems.

Overall, Angela's working model of Andy and their relationship appeared to be he was hard work and this was due to his failing. An important feature of the MotC is that it attempts to link the parent working models of the child to their own histories. Here it did appear that Angela was angry about her childhood experiences of being neglected but had never expressed this to her parents describing her mother as:

> My mother's quite she's probably a better parent than me if I'm being honest with you, they fostered 400 kids in 35 years.

However, her supressed anger about this experience appeared to have become displaced to a sense of having to sacrifice her own needs and being burdened again but now with Andy, her own child.

DISCUSSION

Parents constitute the context in which a child develops and grows. How parents respond to their child's attachment needs and requests shapes the development of security in the child. Attachment theory predicts continuity over the generations, so that how we parent our children is shaped in turn by how we were parented. While it is important to recognise this cascade across the generations, there are also possibilities for change, including increased attachment security in subsequent generations.

One of the criticisms of attachment-based assessments of parenting is that they can appear somewhat pejorative and even blaming of parents. Terms like insecure, controlling, intrusive, unresponsive, withdrawing, rejecting can suggest a conflictual and negative relationship between parents and children. Given that broadly fifty percent of parents will fall into a classification of insecure in their own attachment strategies and are consequently likely to have unresponsive or controlling patterns towards their children, this is quite a pessimistic view of parenting.

John Byng-Hall (1998) offered an important contribution to attachment theory in emphasising that alongside the strategies we develop to manage our own attachment needs and which we apply to our parenting, we also develop intentions about what we wish to repeat or change from our own experiences. This allows us to see something about what lies behind what parents are seen to be doing and tells us about their understandings about their children and their parenting. For example, a parent classified as 'controlling' may be striving to be more available for their child than their parents had been for them. An 'unresponsive' parent might be trying to give their child more autonomy and emotional space than had been their experience of their emotionally suffocating parents (Dallos, 2019). This raises broader theoretical issues for attachment theory, with the need to give a greater focus to the more explicit choices that parents attempt to make, alongside a recognition of how these will also be shaped by the implicit emotional forces from their childhoods.

Finally, Bowlby and Ainsworth both described attachment as a relationship and this is captured clearly in the Care Index and Meaning of the Child approaches which emphasise that parents and children are mutually constructing their attachment relationship. Just as a child can feel controlled or ignored by their parent so too can a parent by their child. These experiences can be problematic, but they can also be opportunities for growth and change., In the case example at the beginning of this chapter, Jenny reflects on her son screaming at her and how it reminded her of her own mother screaming: 'there's a link between the past and the present'. Such insights provide opportunities for change and development, both at an individual level and across the generations.

SUMMARY

This chapter has offered an overview of the development of attachment between a child and its parents. As indicated at the start of the chapter this has been an area that has received much less attention than exploration of the patterns of attachment that develop in children. Ainsworth's pioneering ideas and research has been summarised and in particular her suggestion that 'sensitivity' that is shown by the parent towards the child's expression of its needs is central. Developments of the concept of sensitivity have been discussed and the MotC approach has been described to indicate that parent's sensitivity is a complex process and can vary for different children based on the meanings that the child hold for the parent. These meanings are in turn shaped by memories that are triggered from parents' own childhood attachment experiences. So, as in the other chapters in this book attachment can be seen as an evolving thread between our memories of past experiences and current dynamics between parents and children and the family system. The focus on parenting is also exciting and important since it has important implications in terms of helping children to be safe when parenting may become dangerous and also in assisting parents to manage to parent their children with affection and care when they themselves feel stressed and unsafe.

REFERENCES

Aber, J., Slade, A., Berger, B., Bresgi, I. & Kaplan, M. (1985). *The Parent Development Interview: Interview protocol.* Unpublished manuscript, Barnard College, Columbia University, New York, NY.

Ainsworth, M. D. S. (1969). Maternal care scales. Unpublished manuscript. Retrievable as Maternal Sensitivity Scales from www.psychology.sunysb.edu/attachment/measures/content/maternal%20sensitivity%20scales.pdf.

Ainsworth, M. D. S., Blehar, M. C., Waters, E. & Wall, S. (1978). *Patterns of attachment: Assessed in the Strange Situation & at Home.* Hillside. Lawrence Erlbaum.

Belsky, J. (2002). Developmental origins of attachment styles. *Attachment & human development*, 4(2): 166–170.

Belsky, J., Rovine, M. & Taylor, D. G. (1984). The Pennsylvania Infant and Family Development Project, III: The origins of individual differences in infant-mother attachment: Maternal and infant contributions. *Child development*: 718–728.

Bowlby, J. (1969). *Attachment and loss.* In Attachment. Penguin Books.

Bowlby, J. (1982). Attachment and loss: retrospect and prospect. *American Journal of Orthopsychiatry*, 52(4): 664–678.

Bowlby, J. (1988). *A secure base: Parent-child attachment and healthy human development.* Basic Books.

Byng-Hall, J. (1998). *Rewriting family scripts: Improvisation and systems change.* Guilford Press.

Cook, W. L. (2000). Understanding attachment security in family context. *Journal of personality and social psychology*, 78(2): 285.

Crittenden, P. M. (2001). CARE-Index infant and toddlers. Family Relations Institute: Miami, FL.

Crittenden, P. M. (2006). A dynamic-maturational model of attachment. *Australian and New Zealand Journal of Family Therapy*, 27: 105–115.

Crittenden, P. M. (2010). CARE-Index: Infants. Coding manual (Unpublished manuscript). Family Relationships Institute, Miami, FL.

Crittenden, P. M. (2017). *Raising parents: Attachment, representation, and treatment.* Routledge.

Crittenden, P. M., Dallos, R., Landini, A. & Kozlowska, K. (2014) *Attachment and Family Therapy*. McGraw-Hill Education (UK).

Dallos, R. (2003). Using Narrative and Attachment Theory in Systemic Family Therapy with Eating Disorders. *Clinical Child Psychology and Psychiatry*, 8(4): 521–537.

Dallos, R. (2019) *Don't blame the parents.* London and New York: McGraw-Hill Education.

Egeland, B. & Farber, E. A. (1984). Infant-mother attachment: Factors related to its development and changes over time. *Child development*: 753–771.

Fonagy, P., Steele, H. & Steele, M. (1991). Maternal representations of attachment during pregnancy predict the organization of infant-mother attachment at one year of age. *Child development*, 62(5): 891–905.

George, C., Kaplan, N. & Main, M. (1985). The Adult Attachment Interview. Unpublished manual, Department of Psychology, University of California at Berkeley, Berkeley, CA.

George, C. & Solomon, J. (2008). The caregiving system: A behavioral systems approach to parenting. In J. Cassidy & P. Shaver (Eds), *Handbook of attachment: Theory, research, and clinical applications* (Vol. 2, pp. 833–856). New York: Guilford Press.

Grey, B. and Farnfield, S. (2017) The Meaning of the Child Interview: A new procedure for assessing and understanding parent–child relationships of "at-risk" families. *Clinical Child Psychology and Psychiatry*, 22(2): 204–218.

McKenzie, R., Dallos, R., Vassallo, T., Myhill, C., Gude, A. & Bond, N. (2022). Family Experience of Safe: A New Intervention for Families of Children with a Diagnosis of Autism Spectrum Disorder. *Contemporary Family Therapy*, 44(2): 144–155.

Slade, A. (2005) Parental Reflective Functioning: An Introduction. *Attachment and Human Development*, 7: 769–782.

Solomon, J. & George, C. (2011) The Disorganized Attachment-Caregiving System. In J. Solomon & C. George (Eds), *Disorganized attachment and caregiving*. New York: Guilford Press, pp. 3–24.

Van IJzendoorn, M. (1995). Adult attachment representations, parental responsiveness, and infant attachment: A meta-analysis on the predictive validity of the Adult Attachment Interview. *Psychological Bulletin*, 117: 387–403.

9

BEREAVEMENT AND LOSS

ATTACHMENT AND FAMILY LIVES

Professor Rudi Dallos and
Professor Arlene Vetere

INTRODUCTION

An exploration of loss and bereavement was central to Bowlby's initial formulation of attachment theory. Although initially focussing on loss through the death of attachment figures he also described how the experience of grief could be similar to the ending of relationships, such as the culmination of a love affair, parting of close friends or the finality of divorce. He also regarded the emotional impacts of separations, for example for a child to be separated from her parents due to illness, removal into care and so on, as similar in many ways to the experience of a bereavement. In his studies with Robertson (Bretherton, 2006), Bowlby showed dramatically on film how young children appeared to experience the separation as a form of bereavement and showed similar patterns of fear, anger, shock, numbness and in many cases a form of depression. We can understand this especially for young children who do not yet have the mental capacity to reason that their parents will return and thus can experience this as an overwhelming sense of fear and abandonment. A parent may be immersed in the process of bonding with a new baby and at the same time having to deal with the grief of the loss of her own parent. Likewise, newlyweds may be attempting to cope with the deterioration in health and death of a parent alongside starting out on the path of a new marriage with memories of the euphoria of wedding celebrations. Attachment theory has perhaps had less to say about these complex family attachment

DOI: 10.4324/9780203703878-9

dynamics, but we can usefully consider them as representing 'attachment dilemmas'. We can easily see in both of these examples that they are prone to complex, mixed and ambivalent emotions.

ATTACHMENT, BEREAVEMENT AND THE FAMILY LIFE CYCLE

Grief is an essential and defining aspect of the attachment system, rooted in unavoidable biological processes of life and death. Bereavement is the act of losing someone through death while grief is the plethora of the thoughts, feelings, behaviours and emotions triggered by and associated with bereavement, the total personal experience. Mourning may be viewed as the process of grieving, often referred to as the bereavement journey. While grief and mourning are usually experienced powerfully by individuals, the process of grief and trajectories of mourning are systemically shaped by family values and traditions as well as by cultural expectations. It is interesting to note that typically in Western cultures we do not have a language for defining and talking about grief at family and community levels. Perhaps this reflects a tradition in Western psychology for locating, describing and explaining emotional processes as residing within the individual person.

A central concept in systemic family therapy has been that of the 'family life' cycle (McGoldrick & Carter, 2003). This suggests that families may proceed through various 'stages' or phases of their lives, such as the formation of a couple, arrival of children, divorce, lone parenting and/or stepfamily formation, children leaving home and death and bereavement.

In Figure 9.1, we can summarise some of the major changes that families may go through. Of course, there are many variations, e.g., not all couples decide to have children, nor do they divorce, some adults adopt children and/or live in stepfamilies. Some children do not leave home and some children live in residential homes or live between home and boarding school. Some people do not live as a couple, and some live in extended kin systems with parenting shared across and within the generations. These are important cultural variations, and the life cycle is not thought to be a linear progression but arguably we all hold stories and expectations about what 'normally' happens in our communities. In particular, we hope and expect that parents die after a rich and full life but when this happens unexpectedly or due to tragic circumstances, we may feel that our world has

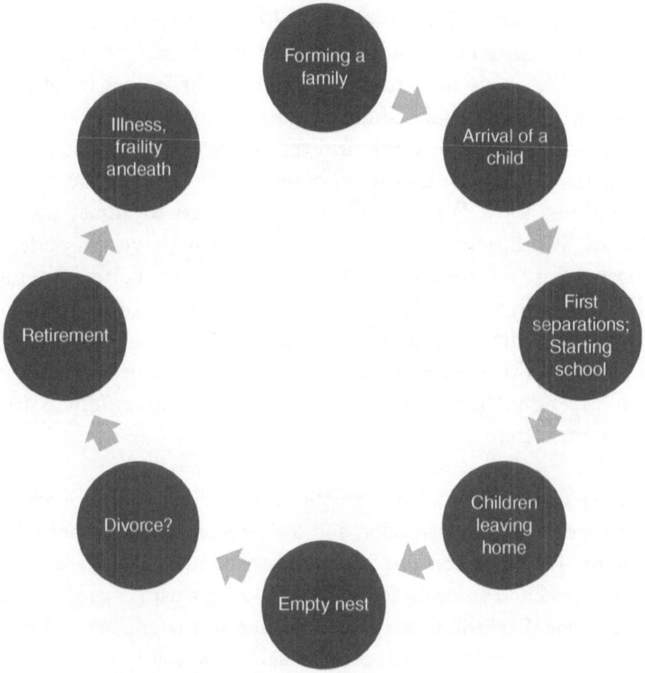

Figure 9.1 Major changes in family life

been unfairly swept away. Also, the stages may intersect, for example a child on the brink of leaving home and starting out in life as an adult may be impacted by the emotional impact of the death of a parent or grandparent. His own parents may be less emotionally able to support him in the struggles he is facing, leaving him to adopt a more self-reliant attachment strategy. In some cases, this can lead to a sense of growth and maturity and connectivity with supportive friends. In others, it may result in a turn towards self-medication through use of alcohol or drugs or becoming involved in abusive relationships.

These various stages have been described as representing significant challenges and opportunities for families which they attempt to navigate and resolve. In some cases, the demands of such transitions unfortunately appear to trigger major forms of distress and subsequent problems. For example, depression in women might be associated with the birth of a child, mental health problems such as anorexia with adolescence and psychotic disorders with leaving home.

Family life cycle transitions require major re-organisations of family attachment relationships where revision of attachment relationships may lead to growth and the development of more secure and balanced patterns. Likewise, bereavement can also be a time of great sadness for a family and imposes a need to adjust the hierarchy of attachment relationships. This may have the effect of strengthening attachment relationships as the family members together celebrate the life of the person who has died but equally may leave family members struggling with their own grief in complex ways that impede the maintenance of attachment bonds.

Bowlby noted how closely inter-woven bereavement is to the attachment system:

> Many of the most intense emotions arise during the formation, the maintenance, the disruption and the renewal of attachment relationships. The formation of a bond is described as falling in love, maintaining a bond as loving someone, and losing a partner as grieving over someone. Similarly, threat of loss arouses anxiety, and actual loss gives rise to sorrow; whilst each of these situations is likely to arouse anger. The unchallenged maintenance of a bond is experienced as a source of security and the renewal of a bond as source of joy.
>
> (Bowlby, 1980, p. 40)

Bowlby's quote includes the very important point that loss involves not just sorrow but also anger. This is often the less acceptable aspect of loss and the bereaved may entertain feelings of anger towards the person who has died: for example, why did they not look after their health better; how could they have taken risks leading to such an accident; or more existentially a sense of spiritual or religious betrayal, "How can a merciful God allow someone so young and talented to be taken?"

One of the most significant attachment features of bereavement is that we lose the very person we have learnt to turn to for comfort when we desperately need comfort to cope with their loss. We frequently try to turn to other figures at these times. In families, complex changes may happen such as a parent who has lost their spouse turning to their children for comfort, or to friends

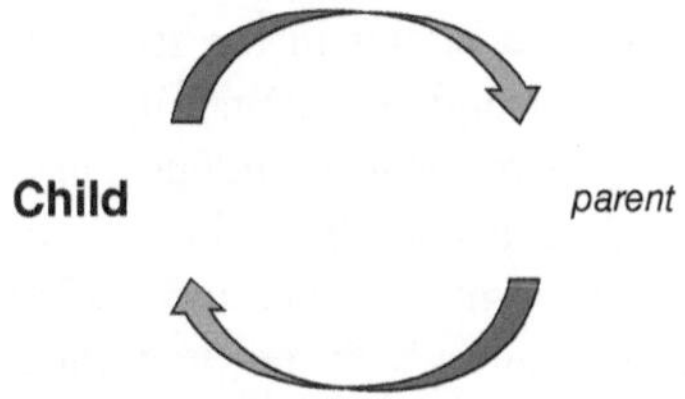

Figure 9.2 The Child's sense of the parent as diminishing in availability

or extended family. The response to the bereavement – the mourning - therefore is shaped by a range of relational processes. Each member of the family influences each other in how the mourning happens, for example whether there is a shared position of being stoical, being emotionally expressive, taking roles in comforting each other and so on.

For a young child who loses a parent, especially a key attachment figure such as their mother, this can be a bewildering and extremely lonely experience. In Figure 9.2, graphically the deceased parent is starting to disappear in terms of being present as the attachment figure who had been able to look after and comfort the child. They no longer have the person who they could routinely count on to take care of them and have to turn to others. Complex feelings may also be involved, for example, intersecting developmentally with a child's understanding of causation such that they believe they are somehow to blame for what has happened. This can be compounded by the reactions of the remaining parents who may also be struggling to remain an attachment figure for their child while attempting to deal with their own grief for their partner. Jenny and Alison are a mother and daughter whom Rudi Dallos worked with that illustrates some of the attachment dynamics and dilemmas that may occur when in relation to an unexpected bereavement experienced by a child and her family. Case details shared with permission.

JENNY AND ALISON: PUTTING A BRAVE FACE ON LOSS

Alison came to see us because she was extremely concerned and anxious about her seven-year-old daughter Jenny. She described that Jenny seemed to have become morbidly curious about death, noticing dead animals and insects in the street, being fascinated by news items about death and accidents, and seeking out pictures related to death in papers. Alison told us she was very confused about what to do. We asked about her circumstances, and she described that she was living on her own with Jenny and mentioned in passing that Jenny's father had died six months previously. This was totally unexpected since he was in his thirties and a fit and active fire-fighter. We asked her about this loss and explored the sequence of events that had followed.

Alison described that she wanted to protect Jenny from the sadness and did not want to burden her by showing her own feelings of loss. She was trying to put a brave face on things. Jenny

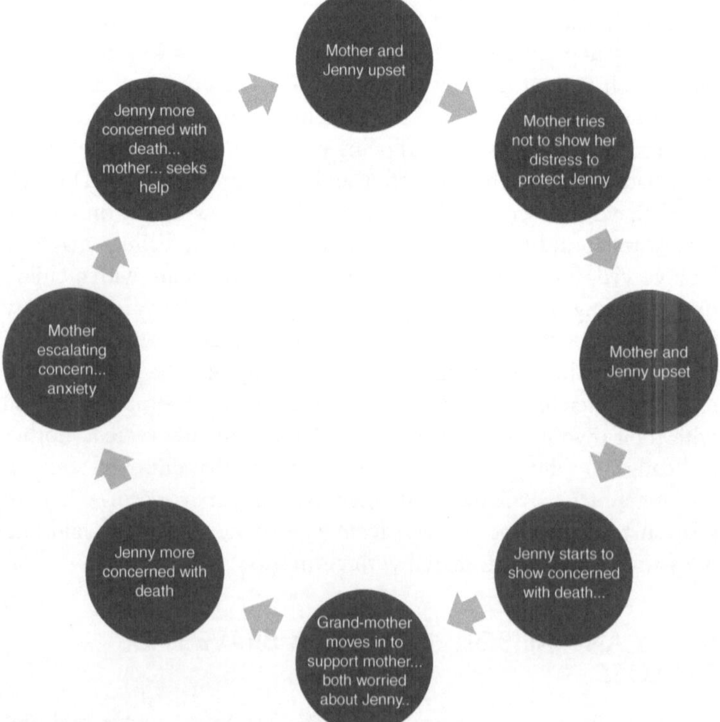

Figure 9.3 Jenny and Alison: Putting a brave face on the loss

did not express her grief through tears but was becoming increasingly interested in death. Alison was confused about what was best and talked with her mother who agreed that protecting Jenny from her mother's grief was the best thing to do and kindly moved in temporarily to support her daughter. However, instead of decreasing Jenny's fascination with death it instead increased to what was becoming seen as a morbid obsession. We discussed with Alison her ideas about how best to cope with grief and she described that she had thought about being more open, perhaps together looking at pictures of Jenny's Dad, talking about him with Jenny and crying with her but was not sure if it was the best thing to do. As we discussed this she began to cry and apologised to us for doing so. We reassured her and stated that we had seen many families each coping differently with their loss; there is no prescribed right way but sometimes sharing the grief with a child could be helpful.

Alison returned with Jenny a few weeks later and reported that things were much better; they had talked about their loss, looked at pictures and shared a cry and warm cuddle together. Jenny was invited to talk about what she remembered about her father, and she emphasised that he was brave, funny and had been kind to her. We asked her to tell us about his continuing presence in her mind, for example how he might want Jenny to remember him, and she described that sometimes he might want to hear that she was sad and missed him but also that he might be pleased that sometimes she was able to forget her sense of loss and be a happy girl enjoying her life. She said she was sure her father would want her to be happy.

(We will talk later in the chapter about 'continuing bonds' and contemporary views of loss which suggest that coping with grief is not simply moving on but conserving and elaborating upon an attachment connection with the person who has died.)

We also discussed with Alison how her preferred attachment strategy was to minimise distress, to be self– reliant and not burden others with her feelings. This made sense in the systemic context of a family narrative that identified with the lifestyle of the father being a firefighter. Danger was ever-present and Alison learned there was a need to de-activate arousal, anxiety and fear in order for her partner to do such a risky job and for the family to manage their daily anxieties. However, although functional on a day-to-day basis this strategy perhaps was less functional in coping with grief.

We suggest that this example illustrates how loss can temporarily destabilise a family into increasingly insecure and anxious attachment responses. It invites us to consider what is the meaning of tears in the context of loss. Surely, they are best understood as an honest and open message conveying the yearning and pining that envelop mourning a deceased loved one. The wish for parents to protect their children is born out of good intent yet it creates a double jeopardy; a grieving parent may struggle to provide the care and comfort to meet their own bereaved children's attachment needs.

Historically, cultural discourses may be misguided in placing an embargo on the expression of strong and genuine emotions associated with grief. Furthermore, what we have come to understand as avoidant scripts may well have been passed down through generations that were heavily influenced by the post war culture at least in the UK, shaped by the unbearable loss of two generations of predominantly young men. Indeed, for all cultures there will be a prevailing discourse about the acceptable expressions of grief (Walter, 1999).

As we write this chapter our personal experiences are triggered, and this is perhaps a key feature of an attachment-oriented way of working with bereavement. For Arlene – my father was killed in a motor accident when I was eleven years old. I watched my mother turn her face to the wall in her shock and her pain. Somehow it left no room for my experience of loss as I tried to assist my much younger brother adapt to our changed circumstances. My mother's dismissing strategies did not help her at this time, forged as they were during her experience of evacuation and disconnection during World War II. She seemed helpless to cope for nearly two years and when she slowly emerged back into some kind of existence, she turned to me for listening and support. The dynamics in our family were changed irrevocably with the sudden death of my father. In my example, we see that bereavement is as much a systemic relational process of family reorganisation as it is a personal experience. I am now seventy-two years old, and I continue to talk with my father and I imagine his responses. I have two sons and two grandsons, and I wish my father had met them. My memories of my father provide an enduring source of comfort as I hold him in mind, using all my memory systems: procedural and sensory in embodied memories of playing; semantic in memories of his ideas and stories of travel; and episodic and integrative in how I story our continuing relationship – our continuing bonds (Neimeyer, 2000).

BEREAVEMENT AND CONTINUITY OF ATTACHMENT

There have been many theories of bereavement and mourning, perhaps among the most influential have been the 'stage theories (Murray-Parkes, 2002) which influenced by Freud's (1917) ideas consider grief as going through a number of stages towards a resolution. This suggest that eventually we 'get over' the person we have lost and become able to 'move on'. This view has dominated theories of grief such that clinical diagnoses have been developed around what constitutes normal as opposes to abnormal or pathological grief (DSM 5, Prigerson et al., 2021). From a personal reflection we may experience that such theories do not really capture what many of us experience. As Irving Yalom and his wife, Marion Yalom write in their joint book 'A Matter of Death and Life' (2021), as she is dying with cancer, that they face death as we all do and with wonderful openness they explore their questions of intimacy, love and grief. After her death, Irving Yalom continues with their writing in this book and tells us that… 'life is not the same without her, cannot be the same without her and yet their love lives on to help him live without her' (Yalom & Yalom, 2021).

In understanding bereavement and loss, we need to understand the bonds we hold with each other – how they weave and interweave over time with our learning, development, and experience. These bonds can be both fluid and stable; broken and healed; intense and faded; strengthened and weakened; kind and cruel; hopeful and despairing; and above all else, they can be life affirming. In writing this chapter we shall use an attachment narrative informed approach to explore a relational appreciation and understanding of love, dying, death and survival. We do not pathologise grief and grieving, but we do recognise that sometimes those who survive the death of a loved one struggle with the challenge of picking up the pieces of what was a shared life. In every instance of bereavement and loss a huge adjustment is needed to manage the transition into the future. For example, Arlene Vetere (AV) met a family at the request of a social worker who was concerned about the wellbeing of two siblings, whose brother had committed suicide at the age of fourteen. The two parents had continued to set his place at the meal table many months after his death. It transpired that this was both to honour their son and his memory i.e., his 'place' in the family, but also it reflected their joint struggle to understand, assimilate and make sense of how and why their son died. Neither parent had realised the impact on their other two children of continually setting his place at the table and nor had they been able to orient well to the developmental needs of these two children in their own grieving process. The two children in their turn had protected the parents by not saying how upsetting it was to have to sit at the dinner table with the constant reminder of the empty place setting. The two children spoke with their school counsellor about their grief and their feeling of disconnection from their parents which led to the referral to us. We were able to assist them in creating a gentle, sad and reflective space where feelings of guilt, misery, anger and suffering could be seen and heard in such a way that the parents and the two children could begin to name, illuminate and expand their feelings and understandings in a careful and titrated way over many months to come. In such a context it is often hard for children to express pleasure and joy at other happenings in their lives, for fear of upsetting their parents. As our discussions, and our use of reflective silences, proceeded it became easier for all family members to speak of both ordinary matters and happenings and gradually for hope to find its place in this family again.

CONTINUING BONDS

There has been a significant change in the revelation through research that healthy grieving may be characterised more by remembrance than forgetting and this is central to the concept of continuing bonds (Klass et al., 2006). The concept of continuing bonds suggests that our attachment connections do not simply cease after a person has died but that we continue an emotional connection with the deceased person in our daily lives even when we have accepted the reality of their death. Young people also establish continuing bonds both as an active choice to keep memories of the deceased person alive but also at a more unconscious emotional level (Clabburn et al., 2021). Hence, the attachment bond can be seen not as severed but rather transformed through memories of conversations, events we have engaged in and now imagined conversations with the deceased. However, these may differ between people consistent with the nature of the type of attachment relationship they had with their loved one while they were alive. For some people their attachment relationship was characterised by a minimisation of emotional expression and was task oriented. Similarly, their way of coping with the loss may be to distract themselves and to try not to think about the person and their loss. This may also form a family pattern where there is an implicit agreement 'not to talk' about or mention the person for a shared fear that people will become upset. This was similar to Alison and Jenny's family.

In another example, we can see how protection of self and others we care for often lies at the heart of not speaking about the person who died. The protection may originate from times of unbearable agony and suffering. When AV returned to the UK from Canada, fourteen months after the death of her father, she met with her paternal grandmother and aunt and proudly showed them her treasured colour photograph of her father. Her grandmother cried in dismay, saying 'take it away', and her aunt rushed to reassure and comfort her own mother, leaving AV bewildered, confused and hurt. No one spoke to AV, no one explained. Now of course, AV can understand what happened, but still holds a deep and embodied memory of that experience that has guided her in her work with bereaved family members to notice the unsaid and the "not to be spoken" aspects of the experience of grief.

In other families, the expressions of emotions may be continuous and over-whelming. Turning to each other and responding to each other's distress can maintain the emotional state even with a sense that anyone who is not showing distress is perhaps being disloyal, insensitive or uncaring.

SILENCE AROUND A DEATH – SUZY

In the following example from AV's work (shared with permission), we see how a family and community were silent around the death by suicide of a father and husband who was temporarily admitted to a local psychiatric hospital. There was also an apparent somatising response for the child in the family.

A paediatrician asked for consultation regarding Suzy, a ten-year-old girl who had stopped walking. She no longer attended school and her mother used a large stroller to help her get about. Suzy complained of extreme pain in her knees. The paediatrician had exhausted all tests and explanations and before referring her to a surgeon to physically open her knees referred her to a paediatrician to assess her mental state, including her family and emotional circumstances. The paediatrician's letter told of the death by suicide of the father who had hung himself one year ago. Apparently, the mother did not like to speak about it and told the paediatrician that Suzy did not know how her father had died. When the mother and daughter arrived, Suzy insisted on standing up from the stroller and walking to a chair, a process that took her nearly 40 minutes. Suzy's posture as she stood was striking; she hung her head from her neck. It seemed possible that she was confused about how her father had died but had perhaps picked up signs from her mother that something traumatic had happened. Also, that she was communicating some of this distress and confusion through her body.

A decision was made to meet next time with the mother alone to discuss her husband's death and it emerged that she was trying to protect the daughter from knowing what had happened to her father. Bowlby (2012) had similarly described how parents may attempt, with good intentions to distort and hide the truth from children in such traumatic situations. He also described how this could lead to convoluted layers of misunderstandings and confusions with the result that the attachment dynamics become distorted, and a sense of mistrust and unreality can prevail.

The example of Suzy demonstrates how attachment needs are communicated in both explicit (verbal) and implicit (non-verbal) ways. In this case, gradually the mother started to close the gap between verbal and non-verbal communicational levels by agreeing to speak with Suzy about the father, initially using photographs. She also asked Suzy if she wanted a photo of her father by her bedside, which she did. As the process of fond remembering began, the girl wanted to use the stroller less and less and within a few months she was walking normally and attending school. AV stayed in touch for a few more meetings to assist with the re-integration back into school, which went well due to the sensitivity of the staff and the community of children around the girl.

DUAL PROCESSING – A BALANCE OF ATTACHMENT STRATEGIES AND COPING WITH LOSS

Dual processing theory of bereavement suggests that grieving needs to utilise both the hyper and de-activating features of attachment responses (Stroebe & Schut, 2010). This concept connects with the concepts of distancing and proximity seeking discussed in earlier chapters. However, it relates more broadly to the emotional processes that are activated in attachment dynamics. De-activation relates to physiological processes leading to shutting down our feelings and expression of emotions. In contrast, hyper – activation refers to the reverse of this process whereby emotions are increasingly felt and expressed (Mikulincer et al., 2003). It may be necessary to supress emotions so we can manage the demands and practicalities of life but also at other times to experience the emotions and sadness. More broadly this also defines so called 'secure' attachment which is not a different attachment process to 'insecure' patterns but rather that we are free to be able to choose to employ both de-activating and hyper-activating strategies in a balanced way rather than becoming constrained to only one. However, this balance may alter over time and people may use hyper or de-activating strategies less or more at different times. This does not happen independently of other relationships; a significant attachment dilemma might be allowing ourselves to make new connections without fear of disloyally to the deceased person. AV: "When my beloved husband Graham died sixteen years ago, I thought my life had ended. I was fifty- five. I was still a mother, a grandmother, a sister, a friend and a worker, but as a woman, it was over. Or so I thought. Three years later I met Paul. Paul's previous couple relationship had ended in disappointment over six years ago. His sense of loss led him to 'give up' any hope of a future relationship and to be fearful of hurt. Paradoxically, I found I preferred the comfort of my known grief to the uncertainty and anxiety of waking anew to the emotions of a new relationship. Different experiences of loss, and yet hesitation and withdrawal as protective defences were experienced by both of us. It was with the help and encouragement of friends and family that we both found the courage and persistence to face the 'waking up' of new life, and new hope. We are both grateful for their love and belief in not only us, as people, but in the possibility that love springs anew.

Bowlby's attachment theory is an integrative, developmental theory of the social regulation of emotions in family systems. As we have seen in the other chapters in this book it began as a theory of child development but has been elaborated to include the study adult and couple relationships (Shaver & Mikulincer, 2007). Specifically, in bereavement through the death of a loved one, we walk with the dead. What is it that helps us turn towards those who are living, to walk again with them (Dallos & Vetere, 2021)? Many theories have been put forward to explain the process of grieving and recovery; dual process theories (Worden, 2018), developmental theories (Parkes, 2002) and stage theories (Kübler-Ross, 1969). The theoretical challenge is to integrate the powerful personal experience of dealing with loss while recognising the generalisable aspects of the process, both to illuminate and to provide signposts when we feel there is no end to our agony.

Attachment theory conceives the strategies we employ as 'self-protective' in giving us ways to manage our arousal regulation and seek and offer support and comfort. As much as we wish not to pathologise experiences of grief, bereavement and loss, there is also the risk of minimising and/or mis-diagnosing the pain and timeline of grief. In our clinical work, we meet many bereaved parents and partners who fear they are going mad as they live the roller coaster of shock, turmoil, distress, sadness, numbness, flat affect, irritation and irritability, sleeplessness, yearning, hyper-vigilance and the long haul of putting life back together.

Arguably, still relatively little contemporary attachment-based knowledge is widely shared in our society about grief. An important example of this is that it is 'normal' to feel the effects for two to five years rather than it being an indication of lack of resolution or 'morbid grief' (Parkes, 2002). Similarly, the concept of 'moving on' can suggest pressure for people to resolve their grief and even to blame themselves for being 'weak'. They can find it helpful to instead think of 'recovery' and prefer to think that they will always remember, even though the pain of remembering loss lessens as new life and new relationships develop. For many, remembering can become a source of pleasure and comfort. Arlene - for example, my best friend died recently, and her husband came to have dinner with us. We spent the evening in joyful reminiscing about their years together and our conjoint friendships. At the end of the evening, he said how uplifting it had been to speak so much of her without this being seen as the 'ramblings of a sad old man'. His fear of being seen to talk too much of his wife can be seen to be rooted in what Irving Yalom (Yalom & Yalom, 2021; Yalom & Lieberman, 1991) calls our existential fear of death and dying, i.e., the reminder of the inevitability of death for us and those we love, our ultimate aloneness and for some, the absence of any obvious meaning or sense to life. The above example of my best friend's husband illustrates a marriage featuring a sense of security and balance in their attachment relationships in which their partnership functioned as a safe haven and a secure base, and likewise it now feels safe to reminisce about their life together.

We also meet those whose partnerships were characterised more by the dismissal of emotion and those whose manner of relating encompassed more preoccupied strategies in those inevitable difficult and conflictual relational moments. Both dismissing and preoccupied attachment strategies seem to predict more difficulty in adjustment following bereavement through death and divorce. Difficulties can include somatising responses for those who have learned to self-protectively dismiss and distort sensation and physiological feedback; and for those who remain preoccupied with the experience of loss, constant physiological arousal, and exhaustion. As with therapeutic work with people who are still alive, we can assist by helping to develop more secure and balanced narratives regarding the person who has died as a way helping people and families to manage the loss.

SUMMARY

We have attempted to illustrate how bereavement is a fundamental aspect of attachment theory in that it represents one of the most significant separations in our lives. It is also a separation that is irreparable in the sense that the deceased person cannot return to meet our attachment needs. It also represents a fundamental attachment dilemma in that the very person we need to help us with dealing with this enormous emotional loss is not unavailable. As such it can represent a powerful sense of loneliness and of vulnerability. When the loss is that of a parent for a young child, this is also a great source of danger since they are no longer able to protect and nurture them. At the same time, bereavement is an inevitable part of life and attachment theory can help us to understand and hopefully assist us to deal with the impacts of the loss. We have seen in this chapter how the different ways of managing our attachment needs that we have acquired from our childhoods come into play in how we attempt to cope with bereavement. Also, we have seen how this can be seen as a relational process. Family members comfort each other, and different families do this differently according to the attachment patterns that they have developed. Finally, bereavement is a continuing process in that our bonds with the deceased person continue through our shared memories within our families and friendship groups.

We hope, that in writing this chapter, with our weave of personal and other accounts of death and grieving, that deep listening and assistance with processing both the experience of loss and making meaning of the loss is central to continuing learning and development.

REFERENCES

Bowlby, J. (2012, reprint). *A secure base*. Routledge.

Bretherton, I. (2006). The roots and growing points of attachment theory. In *Attachment across the life cycle* (pp. 17–40). Routledge.

Clabburn, O., Knighting, K., Jack, B. A. & O'Brien, M. R. (2021). Continuing bonds with children and bereaved young people: a narrative review. *OMEGA-Journal of Death and Dying*, 83(3): 371–389.

Dallos, R. & Vetere, A. (2021). *Systemic therapy and attachment narratives: Applications in a range of clinical settings*. Routledge.

Freud, S. (1917). *Mourning and melancholia*. Standard Edition, Vol. 14: pp. 243–258.

Freud, S. ([1917]1984) 'On mourning and melancholia'. *In The Theory of Psychoanalysis, Volume 11: On Metapsychology*. New York and London: Penguin, pp. 245–268.

Klass, D. (2006). Continuing conversation about continuing bonds. *Death studies*, 30(9): 843–858.

Kübler-Ross, E. (1969). *On death and dying: What the dying have to teach doctors, nurses, clergy and their own families*. Routledge.

McGoldrick, M. & Carter, B. (2003). *The family life cycle*. Guilford.

Mikulincer, M., Shaver, P. R. & Pereg, D. (2003). Attachment theory and affect regulation: The dynamics, development, and cognitive consequences of attachment-related strategies. *Motivation and emotion*, 27(2): 77–102.

Neimeyer, R. A. (2000). Searching for the meaning of meaning: Grief therapy and the process of reconstruction. *Death studies*, 24(6): 541–558.

Parkes, C. M. (2002). Grief: Lessons from the past, visions for the future. *Death studies*, 26(5): 367–385.

Prigerson, H. G., Boelen, P. A., Xu, J., Smith, K. V. & Maciejewski, P. K. (2021). Validation of the new DSM-5-TR criteria for prolonged grief disorder and the PG-13-Revised (PG-13-R) scale. *World Psychiatry*, 20(1): 96–106.

Shaver, P. R. & Mikulincer, M. (2007). Adult Attachment Strategies and the Regulation of Emotion. In J. J. Gross (Ed.), *Handbook of emotion regulation* (pp. 446–465). Guilford Press.

Stroebe, M. & Schut, H. (2010). The dual process model of coping with bereavement: A decade on. *OMEGA-Journal of Death and Dying*, 61(4): 273–289.

Walter, T. (1999). *On bereavement*. McGraw-Hill Education (UK).

Worden, J. W. (2018). *Grief counselling and grief therapy: A handbook for the mental health practitioner*. Springer.

Yalom, I. D. & Lieberman, M. A. (1991). Bereavement and heightened existential awareness. *Psychiatry*, 54(4): 334–345.

Yalom, I. D. & Yalom, M. (2021) *A Matter of Death and Life: Love, loss and what matters in the end*. Piatkus.

10

ATTACHMENT INTERVENTIONS IN THE EARLIEST YEARS

Dr Ruth O'Shaughnessy

INTRODUCTION

In earlier chapters, we read about the importance of attachment during the first few years of life as the foundation for future wellbeing. There is a wealth of evidence to demonstrate the benefits during early life, the so-called "first 1,001 days", of attuned responsive relationships with primary caregivers (usually parents) (Leadsome, Field, Burstow & Lucas, 2013; Wave Trust, 2015; Department for Health and Social Care, 2021). This chapter will outline the contribution of attachment theory research to practice with a focus on how the theory has been used to inform parenting interventions designed to enhance the parent-infant relationships. We will present the current evidence base for some attachment-informed interventions and describe a case example to illustrate the process of working with parents and their babies in clinical practice.

A BRIEF OVERVIEW OF ATTACHMENT AND INFANT MENTAL HEALTH IN THE UK

Infant mental health refers to the social and emotional wellbeing of an infant as a reflection of the caregiving environment. Infant mental health develops in response to the quality of care and relationships within which the child experiences. Infant mental health is therefore a field of study which focusses on parent-child and family relationships and their impact on the formative development of the brain and mind in the first few years of life. Basic principles

DOI: 10.4324/9780203703878-10

of infant mental health involve consideration of the parent(s), the child, and their relationship together; while keeping in mind the rapid and formative development of the brain and mind in the first years of life (Clinton, Feller & Williams, 2016). While interest in the emotional life of infants and young children in the context of their early relationships can be traced back to the work of John Bowlby (see Chapter 1), Mary Ainsworth (see Chapter 2), and Donald Winnicott (Winnicott, 1971) in the UK, the discipline of infant mental health emerged in the post-war USA with the work of Selma Fraiberg and colleagues. Fraiberg, Adelson & Shapiro (1975) introduced the metaphor "ghosts in the nursery" to describe how negative experiences from a parent's past can influence the ability to form a warm and attuned relationship with his or her child. The model of intervention developed from this work focussed on scaffolding a parent to reflect on their childhood history and the connection between past relationships and their new, developing relationship with their child (later complemented by Lieberman et al's (2005) concept "angels in the nursery").

The essential task of the first year of life is to attach (Bowlby, 1958). Babies are born absolutely dependent on their parents for physical care (without which they would die) and for the emotional care needed for neurobiological, mental and psychological development. An abundance of research (e.g., Sroufe, Egeland, Carlson & Collins, 2009) shows that "good enough" parenting plays a vital role in human development, allowing:

> .....the child to develop in the most optimal way, with emotional well-being, capacity to form and maintain relationships, healthy brain and language development leading onto cognitive development, school readiness and lifelong learning. Such children contribute to the establishment of a caring, nurturing, proactive and creative society.
>
> (Wave Trust, 2015, p. 6)

The phrase "good enough mother" was first coined in 1953 by Donald Winnicott, a British paediatrician and psychoanalyst. Through observations of hundreds of babies and their mothers, he came to realise that babies and children actually benefit when their mothers sometimes fail them in manageable ways and are imperfect (Winnicott, 1953). Most parents are "good enough" – able to provide a safe home, comfort their babies when distressed and support their explorations through play and positive regard.

However, as we've seen in previous chapters, a parent's ability to provide responsive parenting does not exist in a vacuum; historical factors such as unresolved trauma interact with their current circumstances, such as mental health difficulties or socio-economic stress, to influence parenting. Where a baby is at risk of not receiving "good enough" care, early intervention to support parenting and the attachment relationship can lead to more adaptive development and prevent poor outcomes.

INFANT MENTAL HEALTH

Infant mental health is receiving greater attention around the globe as witnessed by the establishment of the international, annual Infant Mental Health Week in 2016 and the rapid expansion of state, regional and national associations of infant mental health. The Nurturing Care Framework, created by UNICEF, the World Health Organisation and the World Bank in 2018, drew attention to the economic and health benefits for nations which invested in the social and emotional needs of babies (World Health Organization, 2018). In the United Kingdom, the Labour government of 1997–2010 was the first to prioritise the promotion of infant mental health and early intervention in the UK. Their flagship "Sure Start" initiative (Department for Education and Employment, 1999) was a place-based programme to deliver services and support to families living in the most disadvantaged areas based on the Early Head Start initiative in the U.S. (Administration for Children and Families, 2002). With an emphasis on community-driven initiatives and a reluctance to prescribe protocols, innovation was possible and gave rise to the development of innovative parent-infant interventions in the UK (see Barlow and Svanberg, 2009).

In 2014, in response to a global upsurge in research about infancy, (see Department for Health and Social Care, 2021, for summary), a cross-party manifesto "The 1001 Critical Days" was published, highlighting the importance of acting early to enhance the outcomes for children (Leadsome et al., 2014). An "All Party Parliamentary Group" for Conception to Age Two – First 1001 Days was established in 2019. What this means in practice is that politicians from across the political spectrum come together around a shared passion and agree to collaborate for the greater good: to ensure that every baby gets the best possible start in life through supporting better relationships between babies and their caregivers (Department for Health and Social Care, 2021).

In the UK, there has been investment in the establishment of specialist perinatal mental health services for new mothers and their babies (NHS England, 2019), including Mother and Baby Units for those mothers (and babies) experiencing the highest levels of mental distress and risk. The Better Start programme (funded by the National Lottery, 2015–25) has focussed on promoting good infant development (0–3 years) in five areas of England, while the Family Hub programme (Department for Health and Social Care, 2021) aims to ensure that families have access to the high-quality early interventions including evidence-based parenting programmes. However, despite these recent investments, infants remain the most overlooked sector of society in terms of both policy and practice (Parent Infant Foundation, 2019) with a disproportionate lack of investment in services to support early relationships and infant mental health.

PARENT-INFANT INTERVENTIONS – SUMMARY OF EVIDENCE AND KEY ISSUES

The positive long-term developmental outcomes associated with secure infant-parent attachment relationships provide an excellent rationale for implementing attachment-based interventions early in life. Parenting interventions for infants with less-than-optimal early relationships have been developed to primarily achieve two things: promote secure attachment and reduce risk of attachment disorganisation. These interventions have been largely directed towards enhancing caregiver sensitivity at a *behavioural level* (Ainsworth, Bell & Stayton, 1974) and a *representational level* (Meins, Fernyhough, Fradley & Tuckey, 2001; Fonagy, Steele, Moran, Steele & Higgitt, 1991; Slade, 2006). Behavioural level interventions aim to help parents become more sensitive to infant cues and representational level interventions aim to change parents' cognitive representations of how they were cared for by their own parents. Most of the available interventions fall into one of these two categories while others combine the two approaches (Egeland, 2019).

Having established that attachment behaviour is a significant predictor of a child's later psychological functioning (Sroufe et al., 2009), researchers began to focus on the antecedents (or precursors) of attachment. Specifically, *sensitive responsiveness* on the part of the parent was shown to be significantly associated with infant attachment security and therefore better social and emotional outcomes for babies. Thus, most attachment–based interventions have focussed on improving caregiver sensitivity (Ainsworth et al., 1974) supporting parents to 'pick up' on their baby's unique way of communicating (body movements, facial expressions, vocalisations etc) and to respond promptly, accurately, and sensitively (see Chapters 2 and 11).

Overall, research reviews have demonstrated good evidence for how to improve caregiver sensitivity and promote secure attachment (Bakermans-Kranemburg, van IJzendoorn & Juffer, 2003; Wright et al., 2015; 2017). In their seminal meta-analysis of seventy published studies, Bakermans-Kranemburg, van IJzendoorn & Juffer (2003) showed that the most effective attachment-based interventions to improve parental sensitivity and promote secure infant attachment had the following characteristics:

- A clear focus on behavioural training or education for caregiver sensitivity
- The use of video-feedback as the primary change mechanism
- A brief intervention model (less than 5 sessions are as effective as 5–16 sessions)
- Starting when the infant is age six months old or more

These results are encouraging, and in particular demonstrate effectiveness of brief, video-feedback interventions for relatively low-risk parents and their babies (Bakermans-Kranenburg, van IJzendoorn & Juffer, 2003). Based on their findings, it appears that attachment-based interventions that focus on enhancing sensitivity at a *behavioural level* are likely to work with parents who are motivated to learn new ways of responding to and being with their baby. For high-risk parents and babies (for example, parents with a history of trauma or adversity, families living in challenging poverty and disadvantage, parents with complex needs including learning difficulties and autistic spectrum conditions), more comprehensive interventions are necessary and include a focus on changing caregiver sensitivity at a *representational level* (Egeland, 2019). As described in greater detail below, a review of studies by O'Hara et al. (2019) showed that there is moderate evidence that video feedback improves sensitivity in parents of children who are at risk for insecure or disorganised attachment outcomes due to a range of difficulties, and that more research is needed to understand the impact of video feedback on attachment security.

Attachment theorists such as Ainsworth initially concentrated on understanding and measuring observable behaviours (such as eye-contact, smiling, play, separation-reunions), specifically in the interactions between parent and infant. The next leap forward in attachment theory focussed on trying to understand the underlying parental state of mind and its impact on the attachment status of their children. (In)secure parental representations of attachment (how parents recall and make sense of their own childhood and experience of being parented) are associated with caregiver (in)sensitivity and (in)secure attachment relationships. Therefore, interventions directed at the *representational level*, broadly aim to enhance parental capacity to reflect on their childhood experiences and the connection between past relationship and their new, developing relationship with their baby. Such interventions are based on the "transmission model" of attachment, which assumes that parents' ability to understand and respond appropriately to their child's behaviour is influenced by their childhood experiences (how they were parented) and their current internal working models (the 'lens' or 'blueprint' through which they see relationships). Specifically, the transmission model assumes that unresolved childhood adversity or "ghosts in the nursery" (Fraiberg et al., 1975) can cause parents to misunderstand their infant's cues and communications. For example, a mother who has been raised by unresponsive parents might now herself misinterpret her baby's crying as a personal rebuff or rejection, rather than a sign of hunger or physical discomfort. Interventions which encourage reflection and change at a representational level tend to be directed towards 'high-risk' parent-infant relationships.

SPOTLIGHT ON VIDEO FEEDBACK AS A MECHANISM TO ENHANCE CAREGIVER SENSITIVITY

Video feedback as a therapeutic intervention to enhance sensitivity was first developed in the Netherlands. A first attempt at enhancing parental sensitivity through watching actors model sensitive parenting was ineffective (Lambermon and van IJendoorn, 1989). The clinician-researchers hypothesised that parents "may not identify with the specific model of a parent-child dyad on the videotape, and they remain focussed on superficial differences in outlook and appearances of the dyad involved compared with their own situation" (p. 13). In other words, parents struggled to relate to the 'ideal parenting' interactions presented to them on a video recording. The clinicians instead started to record video-clips of parents with their babies as a '*mirror of their own daily interactions*' to enhance sensitivity, and they started to see better outcomes. The Netherlands group called their model 'Video-feedback to Promote Positive Parenting' or 'VIPP' and developed further variations including VIPP-SD (Video-feedback intervention to promote Positive Parenting and Sensitive Discipline). More recently, other video feedback approaches have been developed including Video Interaction Guidance (Kennedy et al., 2011).

Video-feedback has become increasingly common in parent-infant and perinatal mental health practice in the UK and abroad (see Barlow & Svanberg, 2009, for examples). Procedures used by different video-feedback models are similar. Typically, a short videotape of the parent and baby interacting is taken and used in the subsequent session to facilitate a discussion between the parent and the clinician / facilitator. The parent can watch what unfolds in their relationship with their baby from a different vantage point – with a 'third eye' – enabling new understandings to emerge about their relationship. Generally, the approach to guided feedback is to illustrate positive, reciprocal interactions between the parent and baby; acknowledging the parent as the expert on their own child; and supporting reflective discussion on the parents' own history of being parented. Next, we will briefly outline one of the most well-known video feedback interventions in the UK – Video Interaction Guidance (Kennedy et al., 2011).

AN EXAMPLE OF ATTACHMENT-BASED INTERVENTION: VIDEO INTERACTION GUIDANCE

WHAT IS VIDEO INTERACTION GUIDANCE?

Video Interaction Guidance (VIG) is a brief intervention through which a trained and supervised practitioner records and then collaboratively reviews video clips of a parent with their child. The focus of the video recording is on moments of connection, often play interactions, which are used to enhance communication within relationships. VIG can be used with any age group and is increasingly used with parents and infants in the perinatal period. VIG works in a respectful and collaborative way with parents by selecting video clips of "better than usual" communication as the basis of reflective dialogue about how to develop the relationship further. VIG emphasises that change can be achieved more effectively and in a more empowering way in the context of a 'coaching' relationship between a practitioner and parent, which is collaborative rather than prescriptive, empowering rather than deskilling, and expresses respect for strengths and potential. This process of helping parents in a strengths-based way mirrors attachment theory: learning and exploration are most likely to occur without anxiety, fear or defensiveness when the learner feels calm, safe and connected. A parent being able to stand back and look at their relationship on screen and actually observe communication can be empowering. The visual impact of the process can be significant, and parents are often quite moved by what they see.

WHAT HAPPENS IN A VIG SESSION?

VIG takes place in the context of a supportive existing relationship between an appropriately trained, qualified, and supervised practitioner and a parent. When a parent first meets with a VIG practitioner (or "guider"), together they set some goals for change known as "the helping question". Examples of helping questions include: "I want to understand my baby better" or "I want to support my baby's development". The guider helps the parent to frame their helping question in a positive light, so an initial request of "I want my baby to listen to me" or "I want my baby to cry less" might be adapted to "I want me and my baby to get along better" (Celebi, 2014).

At the second session, the guider records a short video (five to ten minutes) of the parent and baby interacting (e.g. playing, feeding). The video is taken in the parent's venue of choice, the place where they feel most relaxed, often the family home.

The VIG practitioner edits the film using principles of "attuned guidance" (see Table 10.1), meaning they look for moments when

Table 10.1 Principles of attuned interactions and guidance

Being attentive	Looking interested with friendly posture Giving time and space for other Turning towards Wondering about what they are doing, thinking, or feeling Enjoying watching the other
Encouraging initiatives	Waiting Listening actively Showing emotional warmth through interaction Naming positively what you see, think or feel Using friendly and / or playful intonation as appropriate Saying what you are doing Looking for initiatives
Receiving initiatives	Showing you have heard, noticed the other's initiative Receiving with body language Being friendly and/or playful as appropriate Returning eye-contact, smiling, nodding in response Receiving what the other is saying or doing with words Repeating/using the other's words of phrases
Developing attuned interactions	Receiving and then responding Checking the other is understanding you Waiting attentively for your turn Having fun Giving a second (and further) turn on same topic Giving and taking short turns Contributing to interaction / activity equally Co-operating – helping each other
Guiding	Scaffolding Extending, building on the other's response Judging the amount of support required and adjusting Giving information when needed Providing help when needed Offering choices that the other can understand Making suggestion that the other can follow
Deepening discussion	Supporting with goal-setting Sharing viewpoints Collaborative discussion and problem – solving Naming difference of opinion Investigating the intentions behind words Naing contradictions / conflicts (real or potential) Reaching new shared understandings Managing conflict (back to being attentive and receiving initiatives with the aim of restoring attuned interactions)

Reproduced with permission from Kennedy, H., Landor, M. and Todd, L. (2011). *Video Interaction Guidance: A relationship-based intervention to promote attunement, empathy and well-being*. Jessica Kingsley Publishers.

the parent shows responsiveness to infant's initiatives (e.g. infant vocalisation, eye contact). The practitioner edits three to four short (ten to thirty seconds) "successful moments of connection" to produce a short film focusing on strength-based examples of communication. These show the parent responding in an attuned way to the infant's action or initiative using a combination of non-verbal and verbal responses.

The next appointment is called the "shared review" where the parent and practitioner look at the edited clips together. The parent and practitioner shared review of behaviour quickly develops into exploring feelings, thoughts, hopes and intentions. The reflective discussion supports the parent to identify and take ownership of what they are doing well and helps them set further goals. Essentially, parents are supported to 'pick up' on their baby's unique way of communicating and to respond sensitively – the ultimate goal of the intervention being to improve parental sensitivity as this helps facilitate attachment security (Bakermans-Kranemburg, van IJzendoorn & Juffer, 2003; Wright et al., 2015; 2017).

VIG progresses with alternating videoing then reviewing sessions until the parent and guider agree that the therapeutic goals have been met. In line with the evidence base, a brief intervention model (fewer than five sessions are as effective as five to sixteen sessions) is generally used. Throughout filming and feedback sessions, parents can be supported to become more sensitive to infant communication and aware of how they themselves can respond in a positive way (see Figure 10.1).

CASE ILLUSTRATION – VIDEO INTERACTION GUIDANCE

Ellie (aged twenty-six) was referred by her health visitor to the specialist perinatal mental health service during late pregnancy with concerns around antenatal depression. Her baby Maisie was now five months old. Ellie and her partner Mikey (Maisie's dad) have been together for four years and have lived together for three of these. Ellie and Mikey describe themselves as having a good relationship and are both motivated to provide Maisie with a different experience of growing up than their own.

Ellie has not had contact with her father since she was five years old. She describes a difficult relationship with her mother who struggled with alcoholism and subsequently died of liver failure when Ellie was nineteen years old. Ellie accessed Child and Adolescent Mental Health Services 'on and off' but is unable to recall these episodes in any detail and is unsure about whether they helped with her 'feeling low and feeling bad'.

During the initial assessment, Ellie shares that she is worried that she won't love her baby and that her baby won't love her. She feels unsure about becoming a mother and whether she will be able to manage. These feelings become amplified in the postnatal period and Ellie starts to avoid Maisie, asking Mikey to feed, change, and comfort her. Ellie works with a clinical psychologist who is a trained VIG practitioner who normalises Ellie's thoughts and feelings, before introducing VIG as an intervention option:

BOX 10.1

"We know that lots of parents don't feel able to talk about how they really might be feeling because they can feel bad about how they are feeling – or are worried that others will think they are a bad parent. Thank you for telling me that you are worried about whether you can parent Maisie and be her mum. Every mum feels doubt, worry, and other tricky feelings towards their baby – this is normal.

There are lots of ways that we can help, if this is something you feel ready for and want. Sometimes we take short videos of mums with their babies and watch these together. This is called Video Interaction Guidance – it focusses on the strengths between you and your baby – sometimes these moments can be hard to see in the busy-ness of life.

We can take a short video clip of you playing with your baby, this will be edited, and then you have a 'shared review' – a space where you can watch and talk about the best moments between you and your baby. It's a great way to see a developing bond – especially if you are worried about bonding and how you feel about your baby".

Ellie agrees to try VIG with the recording in the family home. Prior to videotaping, they spent time working out their goals and formulating the "helping question". Ellie's initial goals of "I want to be a good mum", "I want to feel a bond with Maisie" and "I want Maisie to love me back" were reframed into a single helping question of "I want to explore moments when Maisie and I are getting to know each other better".

Ellie chose playing with Maisie in a bouncy chair and using some of Maisie's favourite toys including shakers, changing a nappy and bottle-feeding as everyday moments that could be videotaped. Using VIG principles of attunement, the VIG practitioner identified 'successful' moments (ten to thirty seconds) of connection where Ellie has left space for and then received Maisie's initiative in a sensitive or joyful way (Kennedy et al., 2011):

BOX 10.2

Maisie is sitting in her bouncy chair, safely strapped in and with a cross-bar of light-up toys surrounding her. She is holding a small egg-shaped shaker in both hands and is focussed on this. Ellie is sitting quietly on the ground opposite Maisie. She reaches out and clicks open the cross-bar, moving it to the side of the bouncy chair. Maisie looks up at Ellie and smiles. She starts to bounce and shake the shaker. Ellie smiles and says 'is that better?'

The practitioner opens the shared review session by asking Ellie what she notices in this short clip? The conversation is focussed on the video and trying to understand what Maisie is communicating. A range of open questions are used to support reflective dialogue 'Does she like that 'What do you think she is trying to say here? 'What do you think this smile means?' Other questions like 'What happened before she smiled?' enabled Ellie to understand what she did that preceded her daughter's smile and what happened next – opening up conversations about sequences of behaviour between them that led to moments of connection and attunement.

Ellie and her practitioner complete three VIG cycles, with conversations focussed on identifying strengths and moments of connection in their relationship. The reflective dialogue helps Ellie to name and take ownership of what she does well and builds confidence in her role as a mother to Maisie. Ellie starts to make links between her own childhood and her experience of being parented, for example, she started to wonder about her own experience of feeling rejected and unimportant as a child and how she felt rejected every time Ellie cried, leading her to avoid contact. Through the process of shared reviews and reflective conversations, Ellie starts to make sense of her "ghosts in the nursery":

BOX 10.3

The practitioner supports exploration of Ellie's childhood history and relationship with her parents, particularly her mother who was her primary caregiver:

Can you tell me a bit about your mum?
Can you choose three words that describe your relationship with your mum?
How were you played with as a young child?
When you were upset, what happened? How were you comforted?
Who else was important to you when you were growing up? (family, teacher, friends)
How do you think what happened with your mum, affects your relationship with Maisie?
What do you hope Maisie will learn from being parented by you?

In this case illustration, Ellie was helped to bring her parental representations of attachment into conscious thought so that she could reflect on them and the links between her experiences of being parented and of parenting (see Chapter 8). Helping parents to see themselves, their child, and their relationship with their child in a different way can increase parental sensitivity and enhance attachment security (Bakermans-Kranenburg, van IJzendoorn & Juffer, 2003; Wright et al., 2015; 2017). VIG is one of a number of attachment-based interventions to do this, in this case using video clips to provide a different perspective on what's happening both behaviourally (observable) and representationally (in the mind). The intervention itself is unlikely to be the only therapeutic ingredient here; we learnt in earlier chapters that feeling safe and secure are pre-requisites to exploration and learning. Ellie was helped to feel safe, calm and connected through the skill of the VIG practitioner, and this is likely to have helped Ellie to explore her own thoughts and feelings and reflect on them more easily. As a result, Ellie learned how to be more sensitive to Maisie's communications, strengthening attachment security between them. Furthermore, Ellie is in a supportive relationship with her Maisie's father Mikey. For many women, their partner is key in the identification of their perinatal distress and significantly supports the woman in seeking professional help (Antoniou et al., 2021). The high quality and quantity of prenatal support from the partner can contribute not only to the improvement of the health of the mother, but also of the infant during the postpartum period (Stapleton et al., 2012).

SUMMARY

The growing awareness of the importance of attachment over the last five decades has led to welcome innovations in clinical interventions. This is an exciting time in the field of perinatal and infant mental health, with the emerging evidence for attachment-based interventions developing apace, alongside growing consensus that early intervention is key to promoting life chances for vulnerable families and giving children the best start in life. Video feedback interventions are a popular choice among a wide range of individual and group approaches which seek to improve parental sensitivity and reflective functioning. These in turn are hypothesised to increase attachment security and reduce attachment disorganisation. Evidence to date shows that video feedback improves parental sensitivity but that more research is needed to understand the impact of video feedback on attachment security.

RECOMMENDED READING

Barlow, J. & Svanberg, P. O. (Eds). (2009). Keeping the baby in mind: Infant mental health in practice. Routledge.

Daws, D. & de Rementeria, A. (2015). Finding your way with your baby: the emotional life of parents and their babies. Routledge.

Leach, P. (2017). Transforming infant wellbeing: Research, policy, and practice for the first 1001 critical days. Routledge.

REFERENCES

Administration for Children and Families. (2002). *Making a difference in the lives of infants and toddlers and their families: The impact of Early Head Start.* Washington, DC: US Department of Health and Human Services.

Ainsworth, M., Bell, S. & Stayton, D. (1974). Infant-mother attachment and social development. In M. P. Richards (Ed.), *The introduction of the child into a social world* (pp. 99–135). Cambridge University Press.

Antoniou, E., Stamoulou, P., Tzanoulinou, M. D. & Orovou, E. (2021). Perinatal mental health: The role and the effect of the partner: A systematic review. *Healthcare (Basel)*, 9(11): 1572.

Balbernie, R. (2008). *An infant mental health service: the importance of the early years and evidence-based practice.* Child Psychotherapy Trust.

Bakermans-Kranenburg, M. J., van IJzendoorn, M. H. & Juffer, F. (2003). Less is more: Meta-analyses of sensitivity and attachment interventions in early childhood. *Psychological Bulletin*, 129(2): 195–215.

Barlow, J. & Svanberg, P. O. (Eds) (2009). *Keeping the baby in mind: Infant mental health in practice.* Routledge.

Celebi, M. (2014). How video interaction can promote attuned parenting. *Journal of Health Visiting, 2(2)*: 1–7.

Clinton, J., Feller, A. F. & Williams, R. C. (2016). The importance of infant mental health. Paediatrics & Child Health, 21(5): 239–241.

Department for Education and Employment. (1999). *Sure Start: a guide for trailblazers*. ERIC Clearinghouse.

Department for Health and Social Care. (2021). *The best start in life: a vision for the 1,001 critical days.* Retrieved from www.gov.uk/government/publications/the-best-start-for-life-a-vision-for-the-1001-critical-days. Accessed 1 July 2022.

Egeland, B. (2019). Attachment-based intervention and prevention programs for young children. In R. E. Tremblay, M. Boivin & R. Peters (Eds), *Encyclopedia on Early Childhood Development.* www.child-encyclopedia.com/attachment/according-experts/attachment-based-intervention-and-prevention-programs-young-children. Accessed 1 July 2022.

Egeland, B. & Erickson, M. (2004). Lessons from STEEPTM: Linking theory, research, and practice for the well-being of infants and parents. In A. Sameroff, S.McDonough & K. Rosenblum (Eds), *Treating parent-infant relationship problems* (pp. 213–242). Guilford Press.

Fonagy, P., Steele, M., Moran, G., Steele, H. & Higgitt, A. (1991). The capacity for understanding mental states: The reflective self in parent and child and its significance for security of attachment. *Infant Mental Health Journal*, 13: 200–216.

Fraiberg, S., Adelson, E. & Shapiro, V. (1975). Ghosts in the nursery: A psychoanalytical approach to the problems of impaired infant-mother relationships. *Journal of the American Academy of Child and Adolescent Psychiatry*, 14(3): 387–421.

Kennedy, H., Landor, M. & Todd, L. (2011). *Video Interaction Guidance: A relationship-based intervention to promote attunement, empathy and well-being.* Jessica Kingsley Publishers.

Lambermon, M. W. E. & van IJzendoorn, M. H. (1989). Influencing mother-infant interaction through videotaped or written instruction: Evaluation of a parent education program. *Early Childhood Research Quarterly*, 4(4): 449–458.

Leadsom, A., Field, F., Burstow, P. & Lucas, C. (2013). *1001 Critical Days: The Importance of the Conception to Age Two Period.* www.andrealeadsom.com/downloads/1001cdmanifesto.pdf Accessed 1st July2022. Accessed on 13 August 2022.

Leadsom, A., Field, F., Burstow, P. & Lucas, C. (2014). The 1001 critical days. The importance of the conception to age two periods–a cross-party manifesto. London: Office of Andrea Leadsom MP.

Lieberman, A. F., Padrón, E., Van Horn, P., & Harris, W. W. (2005). Angels in the nursery: The intergenerational transmission of benevolent parental influences. Infant mental health journal, 26(6), 504–520. https://doi.org/10.1002/imhj.20071

Lieberman, A. F., Weston, D. R. & Pawl, J. H. (1991). Preventive intervention and outcome with anxiously attached dyads. *Child Development*, 62(1): 199–209.

Meins, E., Fernyhough, C, Fradley, E. & Tuckey, M. (2001). Rethinking maternal sensitivity: mother's comments on infants' mental processes predict security of attachment at 12 months. *Journal of Child Psychology and Psychiatry and Allied Disciplines, 42(5)*: 637–648.

NHS England. (2019). The NHS Long Term Plan. Retrieved from NHS Long Term Plan » The NHS Long Term Plan Accessed on 1 July 2020.

O'Hara, L., Smith, E. R., Barlow, J., Livingstone, N., Herath, N. I., Wei, Y. & Macdonald, G. (2019). Video feedback for parental sensitivity and attachment security in children under five years. *Cochrane Database of Systematic Reviews*, 11: 1.

Parent Infant Foundation. (2019). *Rare Jewels Report: specialised parent–infant teams in the UK.* Retrieved from Resources for Professionals – Parent-Infant Foundation (parentinfantfoundation.org.uk) Accessed on 1 July 2022.

Slade, A. (2006). Parental Reflective Functioning. *Psychoanalytic Inquiry*, 26: 640–657.

Sroufe, L. A., Egeland, B., Carlson, E. A. & Collins, W. A. (2009). *The development of the person: The Minnesota study of risk and adaptation from birth to adulthood.* Guilford Press.

Stapleton, L. R. T., Schetter, C. D., Westling, E., Rini, C., Glynn, L. M., Hobel, C. J. & Sandman, C. A. (2012). Perceived partner support in pregnancy predicts lower maternal and infant distress. *Journal of Family Psychology*, 26: 453–463.

Toth, S. L., Rogosch, F. A., Manly, J. T. & Cicchetti, D. (2006). The efficacy of toddler-parent psychotherapy to reorganize attachment in the young offspring of mothers with major depressive disorder: A randomized preventive trial. *Journal of Consulting and Clinical Psychology*, 74(6): 1006–1016.

Wave Trust. (2015). *Building Great Britons: Perinatal Inquiry – Evidence Session on the First 1001 Days*. London, UK: APPG, Conception to Age 2.

Winnicott, D. W. (1953). Transitional objects and transitional phenomena; a study of the first not-me possession. *International Journal of Psychoanalysis, 34 (2)*, 89–97.

Winnicott, D. W. (1971). *Playing and reality*. Tavistock Publications.

World Health Organization. (2018). Nurturing care for early childhood development: a framework for helping children survive and thrive to transform health and human potential. World Health Organization. https://apps.who.int/iris/handle/10665/272603. Accessed on 13 August 2022.

Wright, B. et al. (2015). Clinical effectiveness and cost-effectiveness of parenting interventions for children with severe attachment problems: a systematic review and meta-analysis. *Health Technology Assessment*, 19(52): 1–347.

Wright, B., Hackney, L., Hughes, E., Barry, M., Glaser, D. & Prior, V. (2017). Decreasing rates of disorganised attachment in infants and young children, who are at risk of developing, or who already have disorganised attachment. A systematic review and meta-analysis of early parenting interventions. *PLOS ONE*, 12(7): 1–20.

11

ATTACHMENT INTERVENTIONS FOR CHILDREN IN CARE

Dr Ruth O'Shaughnessy

INTRODUCTION

Children in care, often referred to as Looked After Children, are a group of children who have been taken into local authority care for a variety of reasons, the most common being to protect them from (further) abuse or neglect. Many children in care are either at risk of direct harm from an immediate family member, or an assessment has concluded that their family cannot adequately protect the child from harm. Many children in care have experienced relationship difficulties with their parent(s)/carer(s), some since they were born.

Since early life attachment patterns are determined by caregiver sensitivity (see Chapter 2) and the experience of relationships in situations of high stress, it is no surprise therefore, that children in care have higher rates of insecure and disorganised attachment patterns (Vasileva & Petermann, 2018). Insecure and disorganised attachment patterns in childhood are in turn associated with a range of poor outcomes (see Chapter 4) including higher rates of school exclusion, poorer exam results and increased likelihood of diagnosis of mental health, emotional and behavioural difficulties (Cocker & Scott, 2006). These difficulties then put the child at even greater disadvantage, compounding the effects of their attachment difficulties.

Starting with an explanation of some attachment strategies frequently seen in children in care, this chapter will then focus on the practical and clinical applications of attachment theory in this context. We will outline how attachment-related trauma can present in the day-to-day lives of children in care, with a focus on

DOI: 10.4324/9780203703878-11

strategies that children learn to keep themselves safe from further harm. Then, we will focus on attachment-informed professional consultation as an intervention model, followed by a summary of evidence-based interventions for carers, children and young people. We use case illustrations of the clinical applications of attachment theory to illuminate key points.

ATTACHMENT IN THE LIVES OF CHILDREN IN CARE

The odds are stacked against children in care. Most children placed in the care of a local authority have been abused (physical, emotional or sexual) or neglected (Cocker and Scott, 2006). All forms of child maltreatment are associated with a wide range of negative outcomes (Gilgoff, Singh, Koita, Gentile & Marques, 2020). However, once in care, the relationship they develop with their carers (foster carers or residential carers) also plays a significant role in their development and life outcomes. Chambers, Howell, Madge and Ollie (2002) comment that:

> the physical and mental health problems of children in care and leaving care may be deeply rooted in their pre-care experiences and circumstances, the very factors which led to their coming into care - but the worrying issue for care providers is the evidence that the period 'in care' can actually exacerbate rather than reduce existing problems and can even create new dangers.
>
> (p. 34)

In an ideal world, children who are removed from the care of their biological parents would be placed with and remain with 'sensitively responsive' and culturally competent foster carers who are well supported through regular training and supervision. In this context, the foster carer's mind becomes the child's permanent 'secure base' from which they can make sense of and recover from trauma, building resilience throughout childhood and into adulthood. Sadly, children in care have multiple placements far too often, with each move creating new transitions to be managed and new challenges to be faced. Chambers et al. (2002) refer to these as "new dangers" which can include many things such as increased anxiety about whether this placement will last, whether they are

Table 11.1 Attachment strategies for coping with maltreatment

Attachment strategy	*Description*	*Caregiving context*
Compulsive control	Highly controlling behaviour, take control of interactions, games, relationships	Unpredictable caregiving, permissive, frightening
Compulsive caregiving	Role reverse, child 'looks after' parent to elicit parental response or attention	Neglect, parental mental illness e.g., depression
Compulsive compliance	Highly compliant behaviour, learn to do exactly what parent wants and reduce risk of punishment or harm	Harsh, punishing, overt abuse including sexual abuse

lovable or worthy of care, increased shame and sense of badness, and increased difficulty in trusting the motivation of others. Children in care might therefore be living in "a persistent state of fear" (Perry, 1998), chronically physiologically aroused (see Chapter 3) and hypersensitive to responses from adults. For example, a child who was beaten by a violent and alcoholic father or a punitive and aggressive mother might be hypersensitive to a foster carer's frown or look of disapproval. A seemingly benign response from an adult carer can trigger a 'fight-flight' response (see Chapter 3) in a traumatised child. Furthermore, children develop a range of self-protective "attachment strategies" for coping with child abuse and neglect and reduce the likelihood of immediate harm. These are summarised and described in the table below and the case illustrations that follow.

CASE ILLUSTRATION 1: MARKO

Marko is a four-year-old boy, born to an asylum-seeking mother, Precious. When she was seven months pregnant with Marko, Precious fled Uganda to escape community and sexual violence. Marko had been conceived by rape during a brief period of captivity. Upon arrival in the UK, Precious and Marko were dispersed to a block of mixed-sex bedsits in Manchester. Precious's mental health rapidly deteriorated – she rarely left her bedsit spending weeks inside with the curtains closed. Professionals grew concerned when they noticed that Marko was left in his cot in a corner of the bedsit with blankets covering the cot. He was unresponsive and seemed vacant. A female neighbour reported that she heard Precious shouting for long periods late at night, though never heard Marko crying. At eighteen months old, Marko was taken into emergency local authority care and placed with a white foster carer, Mary. Over several months, Marko began to socially respond to Mary for example turning towards her and making eye-contact, with improvements noted in his speech and language skills and gross motor skills.

Soon Marko joined a nursery and at this point his behaviour began to rapidly deteriorate at home and in nursery. Marko would go into unpredictable rages and adults found his behaviour bizarre and puzzling. They noticed that he often seemed 'spaced out' for long periods. Mary began to feel helpless and angry in the face of Marko's violent behaviour which, despite her best efforts, continued to escalate. Mary began to wonder if Marko was 'mentally ill like his mother', or whether this was part of him being 'an African boy'. At nursery, his keyworker reported that Marko was unable to follow rules and did not seem motivated by rewards charts or the usual behaviour management strategies. He would seek proximity to the nursery workers, but then upon contact, would lash out. Nursery staff became wary of Marko, noticing that they found it hard to keep a calm and friendly face when he arrived each morning.

BOX 11.1

Aggression is one of a number of challenging behaviours commonly seen in children who have experienced early neglect and abuse. For example, children with insecure and disorganised attachment patterns may try to increase their own sense of safety by employing controlling or rigid 'ways of being' in relationships. Controlling behaviour in children in care can often be an attempt to control and make safe a scary world. Even things that they might be looking forward to, like a holiday, visit to the park, or other 'treat', can be overwhelming for children for whom unpredictability has previously meant danger, and who therefore feel the need to be in charge of every minute.

At age six, Marko is on his third foster placement and is now in primary school. Although Marko continues to have aggressive outbursts, these are increasingly observed in the context of things not "going his way". He does not have any close friends, preferring to play alone. Every break time, he enjoys small world play, acting out 'search and rescue' scenes with whatever plastic figures are available. When approached by other curious children, Marko punches or screams until they leave. Occasionally Marko will allow one particular child, John, to join in. John is a quiet child who complies with Marko's rules for "search and rescue" (John is always the victim, Marko the rescuer). Marko struggles with changes in daily routine, for example, the introduction of a baking activity on a Friday afternoon saw Marko become increasingly aggressive and unable to participate. Marko's teacher begins to wonder about a referral for an assessment of autistic spectrum disorder.

CASE ILLUSTRATION 2: ELSIE

Elsie, aged seven, lives at home with her mother, who is severely depressed and uses heroin. Elsie has a younger brother, Ethan (aged two), whose cot was placed beside her bed from when he was just a few months old. Elsie learned quickly to comfort Ethan when he cried at night, taking him into her bed and cuddling him. Each morning she would change his nappy and get him toast and milk. Elsie also learned to wake her mother in the morning, who would walk the pair to school at the end of the road. At school, Elsie is called the "mother hen", often the first to help another child who is upset or left out of a game. Elsie is popular in school, with the teachers describing her as helpful and caring to everyone.

BOX 11.2

Another attachment strategy which can typically evolve in children in care is called "compulsive caregiving" or "parentification" (West, 1991; White, Gibson & Wastell, 2019). This is when the child is preoccupied by the importance of giving care in relationships, rather than receiving it. Compulsive caregiving is typically seen in children who are neglected (including emotional neglect). They learn to attend to what their parent(s) need by reversing their roles, thereby reducing the risk of neglect for themselves.

Elsie and Ethan are eventually taken into local authority care following the discovery of bruises on Elsie's back at a school swimming lesson. Elsie discloses that her mum's boyfriend, Jimmy, (Ethan's father) hits her and locks them in a room. Jimmy is alcoholic and has a violent and unpredictable temper. He lashes out when the children are playing, when Ethan is crying, or if there are toys left out of place. Elsie learns to keep the house tidy, and to keep quiet when Jimmy is in the house. She is acutely aware of the emotional states of others, always working hard to ensure that everyone stays in a good mood at home.

BOX 11.3

Children who have experienced harsh parenting learn to do exactly what their parents want, even before they ask. These children use "compulsive compliance" as an attachment strategy to protect them from their parents' anger and punishments, thereby keeping themselves safe from harm (Crittenden & DiLalla, 1988).

INTERVENTIONS WITH CHILDREN IN CARE AND THEIR CARERS

In Chapter 2 we heard about the importance of parents being able to reflect on their own and their child's behaviour, thoughts, and feelings, make sense of these, and respond sensitively to the child. Similarly, sensitive caregiving is a significant factor in the development of and the quality of the attachment relationship for children in foster care and residential care (Quiroga & Hamilton-Giachritsis, 2016). Abuse and neglect in the foster or adoptive caregivers' own childhoods are related to higher rates of insecure attachment patterns for children in their care (Cole, 2005). In one study, Wilson

(2006) found that challenging child behaviours can activate psychological self defence mechanisms in foster carers which interfered with their ability to provide sensitive parenting. Another study (Stovall & Dozier, 2000) showed how easy it is for foster carers to be pulled into the attachment 'dance' of the infants in their care. For example, if the infant had an avoidant attachment, the foster carer tended to stay at a distance. When the infant had an anxious-ambivalent pattern the foster carers tended to be frustrated or irritated because of their inability to comfort the child, demonstrating that the state of mind and sensitive responsiveness of the foster carers is crucial for the security of the foster child.

Taken together, this research suggests that careful evaluation of caregivers using an attachment framework is vital when recruiting foster carers. It also suggests that individual therapy for the child in care may not be the only, or indeed the most effective, approach. For foster carers, interventions can be offered to enhance their sensitivity, capacity to reflect on (or mentalize) their own experiences and the relationship with their foster child.

Below we describe a range of attachment informed interventions for children in care. First, we describe two key approaches to enhancing foster carer sensitivity and reflectivity; attachment informed therapeutic consultation and group work. Then, we describe individual work with children in care.

ATTACHMENT-INFORMED THERAPEUTIC CONSULTATION

Professional consultation is a therapeutic intervention and an effective alternative to working individually with traumatised children. It can involve working with the professional network (e.g., social worker, teacher, school nurse) with the foster carer at the heart, or working with the foster carer alone. Therapeutic consultation is usually delivered by an appropriately trained and qualified mental health professional such as a clinical psychologist, psychotherapist or mental health practitioner in a local Child and Adolescent Mental Health Service (CAMHS) or Therapeutic Social Work team. Therapeutic consultation can be brief or longer-term and is often one component of the overall treatment plan (see group and direct interventions below).

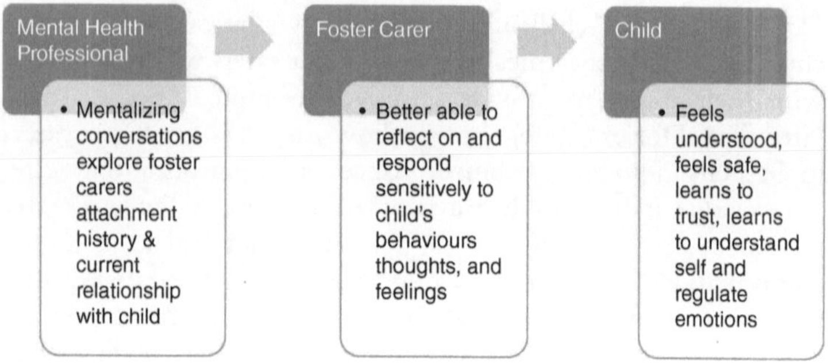

Figure 11.1 Model of therapeutic consultation

The aim of therapeutic consultation is to enhance the foster carer's ability to reflect upon or mentalize what is going on in their relationship with the child. As we know from Chapter 2, the capacity to mentalize is a core antecedent of attachment security. During consultation, increased ability to mentalize is achieved through regular, reflective conversations in which the foster carer can make links between their own attachment history and their current relationship with the child, in the context of a safe relationship with an appropriately qualified mental health professional (Figure 11.1). Elements of a safe relationship or "secure base" relationship include an attitude of playfulness, acceptance, curiosity, and empathy (Golding & Hughes, 2012).

Table 11.2 Examples of questions that promote reflection about the foster carers' attachment history (adapted from Main et al., 1985)

Can you describe your relationship with your mother / father from as far back as you can remember?
Can you think of three words that describes your relationship with your mother/father? Then I'd like to ask you why you chose them.
When you were upset as a child, what happened?
Did you ever feel rejected as a child? What happened?
When you were ill or hurt yourself as a child, what happened?
Why do you think your parents acted as they did when you were a child?
Is there anything in particular that you think you learned as a result of your childhood?

Table 11.3 Examples of questions that promote reflection on the here-and-now relationship between the foster carer and the child

What happens in your mind when [child] is melting down? What are you thinking and feeling?
What do you think is going on in [young person's] mind when she leaves the house suddenly?
I can see that when [child] ignores you, that you feel rejected by this. Is that a feeling you have felt before in other relationships?
I know that when [young person] calls you fat and useless, that you feel really angry and hurt. What do you think is going on in his mind when he says things like this?

ATTACHMENT-FOCUSED GROUP INTERVENTIONS FOR FOSTER CARERS

Overall, there is good evidence that group-based foster parent programmes are an effective way to reduce difficult behaviours and improve the relationship between the foster carer and the child (Golding & Picken, 2004). In addition to therapeutic consultation described above, group-based programmes tend to be offered as a first line of intervention to families parenting a child in their foster care. The Nurturing Attachments Training Resource (Golding, 2017) is a manualised eighteen-week group-work programme that is designed to provide guidance to any parent or carer of a child who has experienced trauma and has attachment difficulties. The programme is based on attachment theory, an understanding of relationship development and the impact of trauma on children's attachment security. This programme uses a "House Model of Parenting" which has a focus on providing secure foundations with close attention given to the parent-child relationship. The aim is to help children experience increased security by reducing fear and increasing trust. In particular, parents are encouraged to understand thoughts and feelings underlying a child's behaviour (mentalisation), providing emotional connection alongside positive behavioural support.

The Nurturing Attachments group programme provides a coherent set of ideas to therapeutically parent the children in a way that nurtures security of attachment and therefore resilience and emotional growth (Golding, 2017). Practical suggestions are offered to the group but these are grounded in theory so that parents can develop a deeper understanding about what they are trying to achieve.

One key element of the programme, known as "PACE" is borrowed from Daniel Hughes' Dyadic Developmental Psychotherapy (Hughes et al., 2019). PACE is an acronym for Playfulness, Acceptance, Curiosity and Empathy and is a way of thinking, feeling, communicating and behaving that aims to help the child feel safe (see Table 11.4). The concept is based upon how parents connect with their very young infants. With PACE, a traumatised child can start to think about him or herself and his or her needs, and to allow others to see a more authentic version of him or herself too.

Table 11.4 PACE model (from Hughes et al., 2019)

Playfulness	**An open, ready, calm, relaxed and engaged attitude:** When children laugh and giggle, they become less defensive and more reflective. Playfulness can help keep it all in perspective... It can also diffuse a difficult or tense situation when the parent has a touch of playfulness in his or her discipline.
Acceptance	**Unconditionally accepting a child makes them feel secure, safe and loved:** Actively communicating to the child that you accept their wishes, feelings, thoughts, urges, motives and perceptions that are underneath the outward behaviour. It is about accepting, without judgment or evaluation, his or her inner life. The child's inner life simply 'is'; it is not right or wrong.
Curiosity	**Without judgement children become aware of their inner life:** Curiosity involves a quiet, accepting tone that conveys a simple desire to understand the child: "What do you think was going on? What do you think that was about?"
Empathy	**A sense of compassion for the child and her feelings:** The adult will stay with the child emotionally, providing comfort and support... The adult is also communicating strength, love and commitment, with confidence that sharing the child's distress will not be too much. Together they will get through it.

ATTACHMENT-FOCUSED DIRECT-WORK INTERVENTIONS WITH CHILDREN IN CARE

There are many individual and dyadic psychological interventions which may be helpful to children and young people in care. However, a narrow focus on individual therapy as the 'solution' can lead to an expectation that children can or should adjust to a world for which they are ill-equipped. The therapy becomes a way of making children 'fit' (Golding, Courtney and Foulkes, 2006). Individual therapy also runs the risk of giving children the message that they are responsible for their own recovery and that they must achieve this in the confines of a therapy room with a mental health professional. Indeed, individual therapy is not always indicated, and when it is, may rely on first equipping the adults in the child's life to understand and contain their distress.

Therapy with children who have experienced abuse and neglect should always be considered one component of a multi-level treatment plan that takes into account the multiple systems within which children are embedded (e.g., home, school). There is no 'one size fits all' and intervention planning should be guided by a shared understanding or formulation of the child's unique needs, history, culture, and circumstances. Guidance produced in the UK by the National Institute for Health and Care Excellence in 2015 also recognises limitations of the evidence base for attachment-informed interventions for children and young people in care, stating that:

> various interventions are currently used to help address attachment difficulties that may be clinically effective, but without good quality evidence they cannot be considered by NICE.
>
> (National Institute for Clinical Excellence, 2015, p. 40)

However, a well-timed individual or dyadic psychological intervention can be effective in supporting children's recovery from relational trauma. For example, the UK's Social Care Institute of Clinical Excellence produced a practitioner guide for interventions for children who have experienced abuse and neglect (Social Care Institute for Clinical Excellence, 2018). This summary document provides an overview of evidence-based interventions that may be effective when working with children and young people who have experienced physical abuse, emotional abuse, or neglect. It includes information about the types of therapy that are appropriate for different age groups and describes the aims of each therapy. For example, for young children and their foster carers, Attachment and Bio-behavioural Catch-up aims to help the caregiver to think about and understand the child's behaviour (mentalize), respond positively to the child's feelings, and regulate their own feelings (Bernard et al., 2012).

Another example is the Multidimensional Treatment Foster Care programme which is delivered to foster carers and children over nine to twelve months and aims to increase the child's secure behaviour and decrease resistant and avoidant attachment behaviours (Fisher & Gilliam, 2012). This is achieved by helping the carer to provide responsive behaviour management, sensitive limit setting and close supervision of the child. The children also attend therapeutic playgroup sessions where behavioural, social, and developmental progress is observed and addressed. The theory behind this intervention is that multiple psychological interventions will produce a benefit over and above that which might be achieved by a single intervention alone.

Despite the many studies involving the treatment of children and young people in care, most report placement stability and behavioural change as key outcomes, and few studies have investigated attachment status as a specific outcome (National Institute for Clinical Excellence, 2015). Further research into the efficacy and effectiveness of attachment-focussed interventions for children in care is needed. Clinicians seeking to address attachment difficulties in children and young people in care need to take a whole systems approach, underpinned by a shared understanding of the child's strengths, needs and culture, and always with a focus on helping the caregivers to hold the child's 'mind in mind'. The next case illustration describes a multi-level intervention for Tommy (age six) and key adults in his life including his foster carers, his social worker, and his keyworker.

CASE ILLUSTRATION 3: TOMI

Tomi is a six-year-old boy, placed with local authority foster carers at age three. Tomi is the youngest of seven siblings removed from their biological parents on an emergency Care Order, owing to severe neglect and physical abuse. The siblings are all placed in separate local authority placements, owing to the degree of inter-sibling violence. Tomi was referred to his local Child and Adolescent Mental health Service (CAMHS) service within six months of his foster placement (aged three and a half), as a result of concerns about violence and extreme distress at home and in nursery. Tomi presents with a range of social and emotional difficulties; seems unable to focus and is rarely still, uninterested in play and preferring to break objects in the house, has sleep difficulties, and has regular behavioral outbursts described as extreme and prolonged. His foster carers, Joe and Kirsty, are finding it extremely difficult to care for Tomi and are concerned about the risk of placement breakdown. They are exhausted and feel useless, unable to comfort Tomi or make any difference to his quality of life. Kirsty is starting to feel frightened of Tomi.

Joe and Kirsty attend an initial consultation with a clinical psychologist in CAMHS. They are given the opportunity to talk about the impact of caring for Tomi on themselves and their relationship together. They describe high levels of stress and increasing tension in their marriage, recognising this as a potential impact on Tomi. The preliminary plan agreed is a series of weekly therapeutic consultations with the primary goal to prevent placement breakdown. Eight therapeutic consultations were completed with the following issues explored using an attachment- informed / mentalization-based approach:

- Reflective conversations together with Joe, Kirsty, their social worker and Tomi's social worker to hear the detail of Tomi's life history and family context.
- Reflective conversations together with Joe, Kirsty, their social worker and Tomi's social worker to build a knowledge of psychological and neurobiological theory which can help carers to understand the impact of neglect and abuse on the developing brain, body, mind, and relationships.
- Tomi's nursery worker also joins these consultations, enabling the key adults in Tomi's life to develop a shared understanding of his needs, viewed through a different lens and allowing a more compassionate interpretation of his behaviour to emerge.

- Reflective conversations with Joe and Kirsty to enhance their understanding of their relationship with Tomi and identify issues from their own life histories which might be impacting the relationship.

Over the course of therapeutic consultation, Joe and Kirsty build trust (a "secure base") in their relationship with their psychologist. They feel understood, safe and contained and are eventually able to talk about the things that are most difficult. Notably, Kirsty is able to reflect on her own childhood where she experienced violence in her relationship with her mother who was alcoholic. Kirsty begins to recognise that Tomi is a trigger for her own traumatic memories. Making connections between past and present means that Kirsty can start to relate to Tomi differently, remembering that he is a small and frightened child (and not the scary adult she experienced as a small child herself). The couple gain a better understanding about the impact of trauma on Tomi and on their relationship together. In a parallel to attachment theory, the therapist's ability to help Kirsty and Joe feel emotionally safe through sensitive and reflective conversations, afforded them the confidence over time take part in a therapeutic group with other foster carers.

Joe and Kirsty attend a 'Nurturing Attachments' group over a period of six months. With support from the facilitators and other foster carers, Joe and Kirsty use the programme to gain greater insight into the function of Tomi's behaviours (e.g., the feelings, thoughts and experiencing from the past that might be driving his current behaviours) and are able to identity more sensitive strategies and ways of responding. They also feel more confident and equipped to advocate for Tomi within the school setting and work closely with school staff to ensure he is well-supported.

SUMMARY

Children in care are at heightened risk of having experienced both insecure or disorganised attachment patterns and additional trauma, such as direct child abuse and neglect, witnessing traumatic events or feeling frequently frightened. As such, their attachment needs are often unmet, their resilience is often compromised, and their behaviour is frequently focused on increasing their sense of control and self-protection. They need sensitive, reflective adoptive or foster carers to help them recover and heal. Attachment difficulties, child abuse and neglect are over-represented in foster carers too, so they may need professional help and support to reflect on what they bring to their new attachment relationship with the child in their care. Individual therapy for children in care might be helpful to address trauma, including the trauma of being separated from previous attachment figures, but increasing attachment security requires their caregivers to create the right relationship context, so effective treatment necessarily includes them. Therapeutic principles from parent-child work, such as increasing parental sensitivity and reflective functioning, have also proven effective when applied to foster/adoptive carer-child relationships.

RECOMMENDED READING

Golding, K. & Hughes, D. (2012). Creating loving attachments: Parenting with PACE to nurture confidence and security in the troubled child. Jessica Kingsley Publishers.

REFERENCES

Bernard, K., Dozier, M., Bick, J., Lewis-Morrarty, E., Lindhiem, O. & Carlson, E. (2012). Enhancing attachment organization among maltreated infants: Results of a randomized clinical trial. *Child Development*, 83: 623–636.

Chambers, H., Howell, S., Madge, N. & Ollie, H. (2002). *Healthy care: Building an evidence base for promoting the health and well-being of looked after children and young people.* National Children's Bureau.

Cocker, C. & Scott, S. (2006). Improving the mental and emotional well-being of looked after children: connecting research, policy and practice. *Journal of the Royal Society for the Promotion of Health*, 126(1):18–23.

Cole, S. (2005). Infants in foster care: Relational and environmental factors affecting attachment. *Journal of Reproductive and Infant Psychology*, 23(1): 43–61.

Crittenden, P. M. & DiLalla, D. L. (1988). Compulsive compliance: The development of an inhibitory coping strategy in infancy. *Journal of Abnormal Child Psychology*, 16: 585–599.

Fisher, P. A. & Gilliam, K. S. (2012). Multidimensional Treatment Foster Care: An alternative to residential treatment for high risk children and adolescents. *Intervencion Psicosocial*, 21(2): 195–203.

Gilgoff, R., Singh, L., Koita, K., Gentile, B. & Marques, S. S. (2020). Adverse childhood experiences, outcomes, and interventions. *Pediatric Clinics of North America*, 67(2): 259–273.

Golding, K. (2017). *Nurturing Attachments training resource: Running parenting groups for adoptive parents and foster or kinship carers*. Jessica Kingsley Publishers.

Golding, K, Courtney, A. & Foulkes, J. (2006). Opening the door: how can therapy help the child and young person living in foster or adoptive homes? In K. Golding, H. Dent, R. Nissimm & L. Stott. *Thinking psychologically about children who are looked after and adopted: space for reflection*. Wiley & Sons.

Golding, K. & Hughes, D. (2012). *Creating loving attachments: Parenting with PACE to nurture confidence and security in the troubled child*. Jessica Kingsley Publishers.

Golding, K. & Picken, W. (2004). Group work for foster carers caring for children with complex problems. *Adoption & Fostering, 28*(1): 25–37.

Hughes, D., Golding, K. & Hudson, J. (2019). *Healing relational trauma with attachment-focused interventions: Dyadic Developmental Psychotherapy with children and families*. W.W. Norton and Co.

Main, M., Kaplan, N. and Cassidy, J. (1985). Security in infancy, childhood, and adulthood: A move to the level of representation. *Monographs of the Society for Research in Child Development*, 50(1–2): 66–104.

National Institute for Clinical Excellence. (2015). Children's attachment: Attachment in children and young people who are adopted from care, in care or at high risk of going into care. Available at: www.nice.org.uk/guidance/ng26 Accessed 19 July 2022.

Perry, B. (1998). Homeostasis, stress, trauma and adaptation: a neurodevelopmental view of childhood trauma. *Child and Adolescent Psychiatric Clinics*, 7(1): 33–51.

Quiroga, G. & Hamilton-Giachritsis, C. (2016). Attachment styles in children living in alternative care: a systematic review of the literature. *Child and Youth Care Forum*, 45(4): 625–653.

Social Care Institute of Clinical Excellence. (2018). *Therapeutic interventions after abuse and neglect: A quick guide for practitioners and managers supporting children, young people, and families*. Retrieved from Therapeutic interventions after abuse and neglect. Accessed on 19 July 2022.

Stovall-McClough, C. & Dozier, M. (2000). The development of attachment in new relationships: Single subject analyses for 10 foster infants. *Development and Psychopathology*, 12: 133–156.

Vasileva, M. & Petermann, F. (2018). Attachment, development, and mental health in abused and neglected preschool children in foster care: A meta-analysis. *Trauma, Violence, & Abuse*, 19(4): 443–458.

West, M. (1991). Parentification of the child: a case study of Bowlby's compulsive care-giving attachment pattern. *American Journal of Psychotherapy*, 45 (3): 425–431.

White, S., Gibson, M. & Wastell, D. (2019). Child protection and disorganised attachment: A critical commentary. *Children and Youth Services Review*, 105: 104415.

Wilson, K. (2006). Can foster carers help children resolve their emotional and behavioural difficulties? *Clinical Child Psychology and Psychiatry*, 11(4): 495–511.

12

ATTACHMENT IN ADULT PSYCHOTHERAPY

Professor Katherine Berry

INTRODUCTION

In this chapter, we describe how attachment theory can be used to guide therapy for adults with mental health problems and outline relevant evidence. We then present a case example to illustrate an attachment-based therapy for adults in practice.

WHY IS ATTACHMENT THEORY IMPORTANT IN THERAPY WITH ADULTS?

As we outlined in previous chapters, insecure attachment styles can have an adverse effect on adjustment in later relationships and can increase vulnerability to mental health problems. John Bowlby, the founder of attachment theory, argued that the relationship between a client and therapist can be thought of in terms of an attachment relationship and that effective therapy in adulthood can repair early attachment failures by bringing about what he termed "earned security" (Bowlby, 1977). Since Bowlby's seminal paper in 1977, which summarised the clinical implications of attachment theory, authors associated with a range of different models of therapy have developed these ideas further to describe how attachment theory can inform therapy with adults with mental health needs. Within the literature, there are two ways in which attachment theory has been applied to inform therapy for adults. The first is referred to as attachment-based therapies; specific types

DOI: 10.4324/9780203703878-12

of therapy that use attachment theory as a central guiding principle and specifically aim to help people work through previous attachment difficulties and develop more secure attachment patterns going forward. Jeremy Holmes's brief-attachment-based therapy is a good example of this type of therapy. The second is referred to as attachment-informed therapies where ideas from attachment theory can be used to complement or enrich other therapeutic approaches, such as Cognitive Behavioural Therapy or Psychodyamic therapy targeting a range of mental health needs regardless of whether or not the client has an insecure attachment pattern.

In this chapter, we summarise the ways in which ideas from attachment theory have been used across the literature describing both attachment-based and attachment-informed therapies. These concepts are organised into six key themes that were identified from a review of the literature describing attachment theory in the context of therapy for adults with mental health needs (Berry & Danquah, 2016). The six key themes are: i) helping clients develop more secure attachment working models; ii) the importance of the therapeutic relationship and creating a secure base; iii) understanding and processing relationship experiences; iv) therapists' own attachment histories; v) separation and endings in therapy; and vi) working with different attachment styles.

KEY THEMES

HELPING CLIENTS DEVELOP MORE SECURE ATTACHMENT WORKING MODELS

According to Bowlby (1977), the major goal of therapy should be to help the client move from insecure to more secure attachment working models by providing a "corrective emotional experience." However, this might not always be the goal of therapy if the client already has a secure attachment style. In such cases, ideas from attachment theory can still be useful in terms of making sure that the client has a secure base within the therapeutic relationship to bring about other changes in their lives, such as improvement in mental health problems and/or achievement of broader life goals.

In support of the theory that therapy can result in clients changing from insecure to secure attachment patterns, a review of studies examining change in attachment status following therapy found good evidence that this can happen even following relatively short courses of therapy. However, the researchers that carried out the review concluded that there wasn't enough evidence in the literature to determine what it is about therapy that leads to change in attachment patterns (Taylor et al., 2015a). A smaller number of studies in the review also suggested a significant relationship between change in attachment styles and symptom change, suggesting that improvements in attachment security might lead to improvements in mental health problems (Taylor et al., 2015a).

IMPORTANCE OF THE THERAPEUTIC RELATIONSHIP AND CREATING A SECURE BASE

According to Bowlby, it is the relationship between the client and the therapist itself (termed the therapeutic relationship) that is a key factor in promoting change in therapy. In attachment theory terms, the therapeutic relationship provides a "secure base" for the client. This "secure base" not only provides the so-called "corrective emotional experience" for insecurely attached clients who have a history of neglectful, unpredictable or abusive relationships, but also provides a platform from which to accomplish the potentially anxiety-provoking and exploratory work of therapy, akin to the secure base provided by a caregiver as the infant explores and learns about the world around them (Bowlby, 1977). In the case of therapy, the secure base enables the client to think and talk about potentially upsetting life events and associated emotions.

The role the therapist plays in providing a secure base raises the question of whether the therapeutic relationship can truly be considered an attachment relationship. Mallinckrodt (2010) addresses this issue by outlining the key characteristics of attachment relationships (Figure 12.1) and presenting empirical evidence to evaluate whether these criteria are met in the context of therapeutic relationships.

Mallinckrodt concludes that some clients: (i) seek proximity through emotional connection and regular meetings; (ii) rely upon their therapist as a safe haven when feeling threatened; (iii) gain a sense of felt security from their therapist, who serves as a secure base for psychological exploration; and (iv) experience separation anxiety when anticipating loss of their therapist. He also concluded

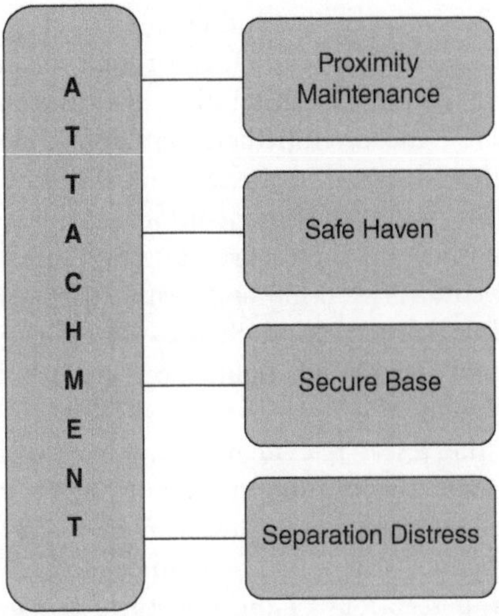

Figure 12.1 Criteria that define an attachment relationship

that some clients view their therapist as stronger and wiser than them although this criterion is more typical of attachment relationships in infancy as opposed to adult-adult relationships. Mallinckrodt (2010) cautions that not all psychotherapy relationships will meet the criteria for attachment relationships, although he argues that in order to help the client develop more secure attachment working models it is essential that these characteristics are present.

Within the literature, certain therapist qualities are seen as being necessary for the establishment of a secure attachment relationship and there is some overlap between these qualities and those of a sensitive and responsive caregiver in infancy that facilities the development of a secure attachment relationship between the caregiver and infant. These qualities include verbal and non-verbal communication that is attuned, sensitive and responsive to the other person's needs. The therapist qualities that lead to the establishment of a secure base can also be likened to the therapeutic "core conditions" outlined in Roger's theory of person-centred counselling. According to Rogers (1965) therapists should demonstrate three key conditions: i) congruence with the client (meaning that they are genuine and enable the client to experience who they really are and the full range of their feelings); ii) unconditional positive regard (meaning that the therapist accepts the client as they are); and c) empathetic understanding (meaning the therapist tries to understand how the client is feeling). However, as we outline below, in an attachment-informed therapy the therapist also needs to go beyond these core conditions and use the development of a secure relationship as a platform to carry out attachment-related therapeutic tasks, such as exploring the impact of past experiences with attachment figures on current functioning in relationships (Wallin, 2007).

In terms of the research evidence, it is well established that a positive therapeutic relationship is a key factor in determining good outcomes in therapy (e.g., Martin et al., 2000) and some more recent evidence that secure attachment to therapists is related to both clients' perceptions of the quality of therapeutic relationships and a greater reduction in client distress over time (Taylor et al., 2015b). Given well-established findings that caregivers' attachment style can influence their caregiving ability (for example in foster carers, see Chapter 11), it is also not surprising that there is also some emerging evidence of associations between therapists' own attachment styles and the quality of therapeutic relationships they are able to develop with clients, with securely therapists developing more positive therapeutic relationships with clients (Degnan et al., 2016).

UNDERSTANDING AND PROCESSING RELATIONSHIP EXPERIENCES

One of the key tasks of an attachment-informed therapy is to explore perceived separation and loss experiences with past and current attachment figures. This material can be elicited using standardised attachment measures, such as the Adult Attachment Interview described in Chapter 6. It can also be gleaned from general questions about the client's history (for example, how did early caregivers respond to the client's distress, how did the family talk about emotions, were there any breakdowns in relationships when you were growing up and how did they experience these events), or the therapist paying attention to how the client makes him or her feel (sometimes called transference). For example, therapists may find it hard to warm to and get close to clients with avoidant attachment patterns and may feel overwhelmed by the emotional reactivity of clients with anxious attachment styles.

In describing attachment experiences, it is subsequently important to help the client understand how their past experiences influence their current behaviour, symptoms, and relationships, including the therapeutic relationship. In terms of the therapeutic relationship, clients should also be encouraged to evaluate how their perceptions of the therapist fit with the reality. For example, clients with anxious attachment styles might interpret the therapist's late arrival at a session as meaning that the therapist does not care as much about them as other clients, whereas the late arrival might actually reflect a pressing risk issue that the therapist had to deal with in relation to another client or other circumstances beyond their control. Once a secure base has been established in therapy, the therapist might also share with the client how his/her interpersonal style makes the therapist feel and query whether it has the same impact on other people in the client's life. For example, a client with an avoidant attachment style might be hard to get to know and inadvertently push other people including the therapist away.

In helping clients develop an understanding of their past, therapists support them to try out new styles of relating with other people in their lives to help build up alternative and more fulfilling relationship experiences. For example, the client who typically avoids relationships, owing to a fear of being let down by others, should be encouraged to test out developing closer relationships and relying on other people for support when needed.

Attachment-informed therapies also highlight the importance of helping the client understand that his or her insecure attachment patterns or other maladaptive behaviours were functional in the context of earlier relationships, although they may lead to disruptions in later relationships. For example, avoidance may have kept the child emotionally safe in the context of an abusive or critical earlier caregiver, but it in the context of later more psychologically healthy relationships, avoidance may prevent the person benefiting from important psychological support provided through close relationships with others.

In reviewing past experiences, therapy creates space for the client to grieve for loss, or express anger about attachment-related experiences. However, it is important that this goes beyond expressing feelings (often termed catharsis in the therapy literature). For example, a therapist may ask a client to reflect on how growing up with parents who frequently criticised his behaviour and were cold and distant might influence his current behaviour and beliefs about himself and other people. In this instance, the client may believe deep down that he is stupid and expect others to criticise him. However, typical of someone with a dismissing attachment style, he may strive to avoid criticism by overachieving and tell himself that he does not need other people. Once the client understands the influence of his past on the present, the therapist may tentatively explore possible downsides to the client's striving and avoidant behaviours. Ultimately, the therapist wants to encourage the client to develop closer, more fulfilling relationships with others, so that he can learn that not all people are cold and critical, and he can be loved and valued for who he is rather than his achievements.

As we have seen in previous chapters, insecure attachments can be associated with incoherent or distorted accounts of attachment-related experiences, poor reflective function and mentalizing skills (i.e., developmental capacity to interpret own and others' behaviour in terms of mental states), and difficulties in emotional regulation. Therapists may therefore need to probe the clients' dialogues of attachment-related experiences to help them to develop more emotionally charged (e.g., showing appropriate emotions when talking about distressing events rather than talking about them without showing any emotions) and/or coherent accounts of the past (e.g., a reasonable explanation of the effects of experiences on self). Offering interpretations that are attuned to the client's emotional state is thought to strengthen the client's self-reflection and capacity to understand their own thoughts, feeling and behaviour ("meta-cognition" or "reflective functioning"). For example, the therapist may reflect that a client with a preoccupied (or anxious) attachment style may be feeling rejected when talking about a caregiver being emotionally unavailable. Ultimately, this understanding is thought to lead to a more coherent account of the influence of past caregiving experiences on the present self. With this insight comes an awareness of one's vulnerabilities and the need to find alternative ways of being.

In terms of empirical evidence, Transference Focussed Psychotherapy and Mentalization-Based Therapy, both attachment-informed interventions, are shown to improve narrative coherence and reflective functioning in people with Borderline Personality Disorder (also known as Emotionally Unstable Personality Disorder) (Fonagy & Bateman, 2006; Levy et al., 2006). Levy and colleagues' (2006) study also looked at whether these therapies helped clients resolve past trauma and loss. Despite the participants having high levels of trauma and loss, there was only limited change found. Levy and colleagues explain this finding in terms of the fact the therapies place more emphasis on discussing the here and now relative to discussing past traumatic experiences.

THERAPISTS' OWN ATTACHMENT HISTORIES

Bowlby (1977; 1988) highlights that therapists might experience a client's need for a secure base as highly demanding as the client may unknowingly draw on the therapist to play out the role of earlier attachment figures. Consequently, the therapist must be aware of their own attachment issues, so that they are able to function as effective attachment figures for clients. For example, there is potential for therapists who are dismissive of their own and clients' attachment issues to be insensitive towards clients' needs and invalidate their experiences. There is also a possibility that clients' inadequate experiences of care can remind therapists of their own and if therapists are not aware of this, they can respond unempathically and be misattuned to clients. Another common scenario that can be played out in therapy is the potential for therapists to re-traumatise or rescue clients with a history of abuse. In this latter scenario, the therapist may sacrifice their own needs to help the client which is detrimental to the therapist themself and also prevents the client from learning to help themself.

As we indicated above, there is some emerging evidence that therapists with secure attachment styles are more likely to develop positive therapeutic relationships with clients (Degnan et al., 2016). However, therapists with anxious attachment styles may also form good relationships with clients, possibly as a result of over-compensating for their own anxieties about rejection from others through attempts to please others including clients. Nonetheless, it might be predicted that over time that the anxious attachment styles of therapist have an adverse effect on therapeutic relationships, with therapists catastrophising normal ruptures and mis-attunements in the therapy relationship.

There is also evidence from one research study assessing therapeutic interactions between mental health workers and clients, which suggests that securely attached mental health workers are less likely to be pulled into ways of behaving that maintain clients' attachment difficulties (Dozier et al., 1994). For example, they are less likely to avoid emotive topics of conversation with clients with avoidant attachment styles and less likely to fall into the trap of fostering dependence in clients with anxious attachment styles.

SEPARATION AND ENDINGS IN THERAPY

Breaks and endings in therapy can be important for assessing clients' experiences of attachment-related losses and helping the person to develop a more positive experience of these. In this respect, it is important for the therapist to normalise feelings of anxiety or other negative feelings about loss and endings and encourage clients to express these feelings. For example, therapist holidays and the ending of therapy can be particularly anxiety provoking for clients with insecure attachment styles and therefore need to be addressed and anticipated at the outset. This may involve anticipating relapses in mental health problems as breaks or the ending approaches, how to deal with these, considering attachments outside the therapeutic relationship, reviewing what skills the client has learnt in therapy, ensuring that the ending is gradual and that there is clarity about the contact the client can have with the therapist after therapy.

WORKING WITH DIFFERENT ATTACHMENT STYLES

Clients with different attachment styles may have different needs in therapy and may respond better to different styles of therapy at different stages during the therapeutic process (Mallinckrodt, 2000). As we highlighted in Chapter 2 and Chapter 6, anxious or ambivalent attachment is associated with experiences of inconsistent care giving, a preoccupation with attachment-related events and low self-efficacy. Consistency and reliability of the therapist are therefore particularly important with this group of clients, as it helps them recognise their strengths and express their needs which may have previously been denied through fear of abandonment. Therapists also need to be clear about boundaries, power and responsibility in the therapeutic relationship and avoid the pull to be overprotective towards the client or frustrated with his or her dependency. In some instances, clients with anxious styles may mask anxiety by accepting therapy too readily, so therapists need to help them find their own investment in the work. For example, the therapist may help the client to weigh up the pros and cons of engaging in therapy at this moment in time, while being explicit about some of the potential risks and downsides.

Exploratory therapies, which the client may perceive as unstructured and unpredictable, may intensify anxiety and therefore for clients with anxious attachment styles, therapies which develop skills in cognitive reflection may be more beneficial. For example, Holmes (2001) emphasises that therapists need to introduce frequent "shaping" remarks or punctuations, for example, "we'll come back to what happened to you as a child in a minute; first let's hear about what is troubling you right now."

As we outlined in Chapter 6, avoidant attachment styles are associated with an apparent lack of care in attachment relationships in adulthood, limited expression of emotion and the devaluing of relationships. To avoid reinforcing the client's self-sufficiency and lack of emotional expression, therapists must not fall into the traps of rejecting and neglecting the client, talking about superficial or non-threatening topics, or intellectualising, or even prematurely discharging the client. Clients with avoidant attachment styles may also discredit, compete with or adopt a superior stance to the therapist. These behaviours enable clients to continue to avoid intimacy and emotional exploration, and cause therapists to feel incompetent, discharge clients or even act defensively by emphasising the importance of therapy to clients. Therapists need to watch out for the pull to respond in these ways and resist them as these responses are detrimental to the therapeutic relationship and reinforce attachment working models that other people are rejecting.

In the case of clients with avoidant attachment styles, it is particularly important that therapy is at the client's own pace, even if this makes progress more gradual. For example, offering reflective comments on plans and feelings of key others in the environment, as a first step to mind-mindedness about his or her own motivations and emotions. Therapists should also be more proactive in disclosing their own thoughts and feelings to avoidant clients as a way of encouraging clients to show their own vulnerabilities later on in therapy and modelling skills in mentalizing.

Purely cognitive approaches may be less helpful for clients with avoidant attachment, owing to the risk of reinforcing their need for self-control rather than helping them feel difficult feelings. Conversely, interventions, which help clients understand and feel emotions rather than control them, may be more useful for the avoidant client. For example, Holmes (2001) emphasises that the therapist needs to search for detailed images, memories and examples that bring perfunctory stories to life, for example, "what was your mother like?", "Where in your body do you experience unhappiness?" as a way to help clients identify emotions.

In terms of disorganised/unresolved attachment, the beginning of therapy should be aimed at managing personal safety, teaching skills to keep emotional levels tolerable and ensuring that the therapist is consistently supportive. Direct treatment of traumatic memories should be approached only after the client has some coping skills in place and has given informed consent to the potentially anxiety-provoking experience of remembering and talking about past events. Wallin (2007) also highlights the way in which clients with disorganised attachment can behave in unpredictable ways and how this can worry, confuse or overwhelm the therapist. It is important to remain concerned, but not be overwhelmed or frightened by strong emotions and shifting symptoms. With the disorganised client, the therapist must tolerate oscillation, for example, missing sessions, drops outs, and still proactively try to engage the client until he or she is ready. This may involve writing to or phoning him or her following missed appointments. With disorganised clients, therapists must also work especially hard at repairing frequent alliance ruptures or breakdowns in the therapeutic relationship (Holmes, 2001; Wallin, 2007).

CASE ILLUSTRATION: DAVID

David was a twenty-seven-year-old man referred to the psychology service by his GP. Over the past year, David had been experiencing symptoms of low mood, lack of energy, no interest or pleasure in activities, difficulty sleeping, poor appetite and increased irritability. He reported that these symptoms started after finding out his girlfriend was pregnant. That child was now six months old.

David cancelled the first two appointments with the psychologist, owing to work commitments. When he did attend, he arrived late, as a result of heavy traffic. During the first meeting with the psychologist, David described feeling low in mood and unmotivated in relation to his job and social activities. He reported that he derives little pleasure from anything in his life and does not feel that he is a good father. When the therapist asked David if he felt anxious about attending therapy session, he said not.

David described his childhood as happy but was unable to provide any specific examples of positive memories. He grew up with his mum, dad and two brothers. He described his mother as unaffectionate, and he had not been able to approach her for comfort or reassurance as a child. He stated that he dealt with worries and problems on his own. David suspected that he was a 'mistake'; his brothers were significantly older than him and his father in particular had not wanted him. He described his father as strict and said that he knew very little about him as a person. His father enforced discipline by hitting David and his brothers. David described an incident where his dad punched him in the face, knocking him to the floor, although he could not remember what he had done wrong. David's father was diagnosed with cancer when David was thirteen years old. He was ill for a number of years before he finally died when David was eighteen. David describes his father as miserable, argumentative, demanding and extremely irritable during his illness. His mother's time was taken up in caring for his father, but the family did not talk about the illness or the prognosis. David reported that he was unaffected by his father's death and that he did not talk to anyone about it.

David did not feel close to his brothers when growing up and they had their own friends and interests. He describes being bullied in school and that his brothers were aware of this but did not stick up for him. He had few friends when he was younger. He went to a religious school, which involved travelling several miles each day and was not allowed to play out with other children after school.

David obtained good grades at school and went to university. However, he dropped out after six months because he was not enjoying the course. This coincided with the death of his father, although he did not make a connection himself. He returned home to his mother's house after leaving university and started an IT job in a local office. He is still with the same firm but had worked his way up to a more senior position. He reported that he does not enjoy his job and often feels annoyed with colleagues as he feels they do not like him and accuse him of being moody and aggressive.

David has a few friends from work but reported a history of difficulties in maintaining friendships with others. He feels that other people aren't bothered about being friends with him and says he can't be bothered to make all of the effort. He has had several short-term relationships with women from work. David felt that these women pursued him and that he feels uncomfortable being in close relationships. He prefers his own space.

David was seeing the mother of his child for six months before she became pregnant. He describes the pregnancy as an "accident" and that he saw the child's mother relatively infrequently. He minimised contact with the mother during the pregnancy but offered to support her financially. He reported that he never wanted children, although when the baby was born, he felt that he wanted to have contact with him. He currently sees the child twice a week. He says he would like to be more involved in the child's life but finds it hard to know how to interact with him. The child doesn't seem to know him or seem to respond to his attempts to stop him from crying or play with him. He worries that the child will grow up hating him. Despite attending the first session with the psychologist, David reported that he did not feel optimistic about change as he believes that talking about problems can't change the way you feel.

Throughout the session, he also often avoided emotive subjects by changing the topic to something more neutral or talking about potentially distressing events such as his father's death or bullying in a very neutral way. Following the first session, the therapist was left feeling pessimistic about working with David, as he did not seem keen to engage or open up. The therapist felt that he was rejecting her efforts to try to engage him.

The therapist hypothesised that David had an avoidant attachment style which he had developed as a result of his mother's lack of capacity to care for him and protect him from this father's abuse and maltreatment. Following the death of this father during adolescence, David's avoidant strategies also meant that he was not able to emotionally process and successfully grieve the loss. The therapist speculated that David's parents may also have had avoidant styles of relating to others by virtue of the fact his father's death and emotional reactions were not openly discussed and he found it difficult to get emotional support from them. It was hypothesised that David's avoidant attachment style was further played out within peer and romantic relationships and prevented him from getting close to others and appreciating the positives that could be gained from relationships. Although David had been able to avoid feelings and function relatively well into his twenties, it was hypothesised that the birth of David's first child, an attachment-related event, had triggered difficult feelings for him that were previously suppressed. David continued to use suppression to manage difficult feelings, but that strategy was becoming increasingly overwhelming for him to maintain.

The therapist was aware that David might find it difficult to engage in therapy and any direct focus on emotional topics and attempts to get to know him better might be rebuffed. However, it was positive that David had attended one session and clearly had some motivation for seeking help. As he had voiced the goal of wanting to develop a better relationship with his son, the therapist decided to start therapy focused directly on this relationship. Although David's previous relationships undoubtedly had an impact on his current problems, the therapist felt that focusing too prematurely on these emotive issues would lead him to disengage altogether. The therapist spent early sessions with David talking to him about ways to play with his son using material from positive parenting interventions. The focus here was on using play to build up positive parent-child interactions and a secure attachment relationship. The intervention was skills-based in the sense that the therapist and David would think up games he could play with his son which he could then put into practice at home. The therapist felt that this focus on behaviour, as opposed to emotion would feel safer for David and allow him to develop some sense of trust in her and the therapeutic relationship. Over time, David started to feel more confident in knowing how to interact with his son and he found these encounters more rewarding. This success gave the therapist confidence to try to broach other more difficult topics with David, such as the possible impact of early relationships at home with family and with peers. The therapist was tentative in instigating these discussions and quickly pulled back if she sensed David shutting down or being too overwhelmed. Over time, the therapist even felt able to reflect back to David that he was shutting down/pulling away from the conversation and they were able to think together about what may have triggered the response in him. The therapist and David built up a shared formulation of the impact of his earlier relationships on his cold and distant nature with others, including the costs and benefits of this way of relating. David was able to see the importance of letting others in, in order to overcome his fears of intimacy and he could see the benefits of doing so in order to demonstrate more helpful ways of relating to his son. This included allowing him to share thoughts and feelings with the therapist. Towards the end of the sessions, David was able to contemplate emotionally investing in a relationship with a new partner more than he had done with his previous girlfriends.

SUMMARY

A key goal of an attachment-informed therapy should be helping the insecure client develop more secure attachment working models. There may also be other important outcomes, such as symptom reduction or improved functioning, which may occur in addition to or following changes in attachment styles. There is some evidence that attachment styles can change as a result of therapy and some evidence that changes in attachment styles are associated with changes in symptoms. Certain therapist characteristics and strategies are likely to create a "secure base" in therapy. These include being attuned, sensitive and responsive to the client's needs and demonstrating empathy, acceptance, understanding and unconditional positive regard in relation to distressing thoughts and feelings.

The therapeutic relationship is a key factor that promotes client change in attachment-informed therapy. Therapists therefore need to be aware of the potential to be drawn into re-enacting the client's previous attachment experiences and the influence that their own attachment style can have on the relationship. If managed well, the therapeutic relationship and in particular separations and endings can be used to directly challenge the client's previous expectations of attachment relationships and ways of relating to others.

It is likely that different types of clients will have different types of needs in relation to therapy. Attachment theory can contribute to all types of psychotherapy, although the degree to which therapists draw on the theory is likely to be influenced by the degree to which clients demonstrate insecure attachment styles, clients' experiences of attachment-related loss and clients' therapy goals. Disrupted attachment is certainly not the whole story where psychological distress is concerned, but we think that attachment theory offers a well-established and theoretically coherent way to investigate empirically the main medium of therapy (the therapeutic relationship) across different therapeutic models.

RECOMMENDED READING

Berry, K. & Danquah, A. (2016). Attachment-informed therapy for adults: Toward a unifying perspective on practice. Psychology and Psychotherapy: Theory, Research and Practice, 89: 15–32.

Danquah, A. & Berry, K. (2014). Attachment theory in adult mental health: A guide to clinical practice. Routledge.

REFERENCES

Berry, K. & Danquah, A. (2016). Attachment-informed therapy for adults: Toward a unifying perspective on practice. *Psychology and Psychotherapy: Theory, Research and Practice*, 89: 15–32.

Bowlby, J. (1977). The making and breaking of affectional bonds II. Some principles of psychotherapy. *British Journal of Psychiatry*, 130: 421–431.

Bowlby, J. (1988). *Clinical applications of attachment theory: A secure base.* Routledge.

Degnan, A., Seymour-Hyde, A., Harris, A. & Berry, K. (2016). A systematic review of the role of therapist attachment, therapeutic alliance and outcomes. *Clinical Psychology and Psychotherapy*, 23: 47–65.

Dozier, M., Cue, K. L & Barnett, L. (1994). Clinicians as caregivers: Role of attachment organisation in treatment. *Journal of Consulting and Clinical Psychology*, 62: 793–800.

Fonagy, P. & Bateman, A. W. (2006). Mechanisms of change in mentalisation-based treatment of Borderline Personality Disorder. *Journal of Clinical Psychology*, 62: 411–430.

Holmes, J. (2001). *The Search for a Secure Base. Attachment Theory and Psychotherapy*. Routledge.

Levy, K. N., Meehan, K. B., Clarkin, J. F., Kernberg, O. F., Kelly, K. M., Reynoso, J. S. & Weber, M. (2006). Change in attachment patterns and reflective function in a randomized control trial of Transference-Focused Psychotherapy for Borderline Personality Disorder. *Journal of Consulting and Clinical Psychology*, 74: 1027–1040.

Mallinckrodt, B. (2000). Attachment, social competencies, social support, and interpersonal processes in psychotherapy, *Psychotherapy Research*, 10: 239–266.

Mallinckrodt, B. (2010). The psychotherapy relationship as attachment: Evidence and implications. *Journal of Social and Personal Relationships*, 27: 262–270.

Martin, D. J., Garske, J. P. & Davis, M. K. (2000). Relation of the therapeutic alliance with outcome and other variables: A meta-analytic review. *Journal of Consulting and Clinical Psychology*, 68: 438–450.

Rogers, C. R. (1965) *Client-centred therapy*. Houghton Mifflin Company.

Taylor, P., Rietzschel, J., Danquah, A. & Berry, K. (2015a). Changes in attachment representations during psychological therapy. *Psychotherapy Research*, 88: 1–20.

Taylor, P., Rietzschel, J., Danquah, A. & Berry, K. (2015b). The role of attachment style, attachment to therapist and working alliance in response to psychological therapy. *Psychology and Psychotherapy: Theory, Research and Practice*, 88: 240–253.

Wallin, D. J. (2007). *Attachment in Psychotherapy*. Guilford Press.

13

DEVELOPING SERVICES AND SYSTEMS USING ATTACHMENT THEORY

Professor Katherine Berry

INTRODUCTION

This chapter outlines why and how attachment theory should be used to inform the design and delivery of health, social care and education organisations. Attachment theory promotes key concepts such as trust, safety and support as prerequisites to exploration and endeavour in the wider world. This chapter explains how these concepts apply to the leadership, culture and work of caring and helping professions and their staff. We conclude with two examples of attachment-based systems from British schools and adult mental health services.

WHY USE ATTACHMENT THEORY TO INFORM SERVICE DELIVERY?

Attachment theory emphasises the importance of safe and secure relationships for emotional well-being. Therefore, in principle, any organisation which aims to provide support to others through relationship building may have something to learn from attachment theory. Relationships are built on a foundation of attachment, it is the principal frame for all our relationships, with trust and safety at its core, so services which are cognisant of attachment are immediately more in tune, connected and more likely to be able to engage people.

The attachment system is designed to be a help-seeking system (Bowlby, 1969), so there are fundamental links between the ways

DOI: 10.4324/9780203703878-13

in which people seek help and the ways in which service providers care for and respond to people during times of distress. Research has shown that people's attachment histories influence how they approach health and social care services and the staff who work within these systems (Bucci et al., 2015). For example, people with an avoidant attachment style may find it difficult to approach services and engage with the services that are made available to them. This pattern of behaviour may lead people to be labelled as "hard to engage", but their reluctance to seek out and accept help may be understandable given histories of being let down or mistreated by others in times of distress. Alternatively, people with anxious (or ambivalent) attachment styles may be perceived as being overly dependent on services, frequently seeking reassurance and help, owing to lack of confidence in their ability to solve their own problems and difficulties in regulating their own feelings. Service providers can see this dependence as demanding and emotionally draining, but again this pattern of engaging is likely to make sense when you consider people's attachment histories.

Attachment theory not only gives insights into how people relate to organisations and service providers, but it also helps to understand how organisations can play a role in perpetuating insecure patterns. For instance, in the above examples, those with dismissing attachment may be neglected by services particularly if staff have busy caseloads, while those with anxious attachment styles may be 'rejected' by services which are not able to meet their high levels of need. Some authors have talked about the role organisations can play in retraumatising people when they have trauma and loss both "being absorbed in and seeping out" (Bloom & Farragher, 2010; Treisman, 2017). Traumatised systems supporting traumatised people and families can perpetuate and compound the trauma. Below are two examples.

EXAMPLE 1: VISHAL

Vishal, a mental health nurse working on an acute mental health ward, had become disillusioned with seeing the same patients time and time again and felt hopeless about his capacity to make a difference. Although he was turning up to work and completing all necessary tasks, such as dispensing medications and observation checks, he felt detached from the people he worked with and had given up trying to help people develop goals for the future. This detachment mirrored Vishal's approach to coping with problems outside of work when feelings overwhelmed and was reflective of his avoidant attachment style. The detachment was also mirrored with the hospital where Vishal worked which was significantly under resourced. There was a pressure to discharge people from hospital as soon as possible to free up a bed for another person in acute crisis and little investment was made in staff development, training and supervision.

EXAMPLE 2: ADEBAYO

Adebayo, a ten-year-old boy who had experienced multiple traumas, including physical and emotional abuse by his birth mother and sexual abuse while in foster care. Adebayo was angry and hostile in his approach to the world and to services which he felt had let him down. He rejected any help that was offered and multiple foster placements in foster care had broken down as carers did not feel able to handle Adebayo's behaviour. Adebayo's social worker, Sally, felt hopeless and helpless in working with him which fed into her own anxieties about not being a good enough social worker and a sense of pressure she felt from her organisation to find foster placements. Her insecure anxious attachment style meant that is she was easily overwhelmed by these negative emotions, and she found it hard to see Adebayo's unmet attachment needs hiding behind his angry persona.

In the above examples, staff were unsupported by their organisations and did not have access to supervision which encouraged them to reflect on the feelings that their work elicited in them and the impact of these feelings. As a result, staff were experiencing what is sometimes referred to as burnout or compassion fatigue (Treisman, 2017). Treisman discusses a number of reasons why caring professionals might be more susceptible to experiencing burnout including: i) the fact that those who go into caring professionals may be more likely to have a desire to rescue and help people as a result of their own unmet attachment needs in childhood (which may not always be possible or curtailed, owing to other external pressures); ii) being exposed to and needing to contain lots of difficult and painful feelings with little opportunities for respite; c) the fact that organisations are more and more driven by performance indicators, the need to save costs and administrative work, resulting in a lack of focus on the human costs and staff feeling devalued; and d) public opinion and the media naming, shaming and blaming caring organisations such as health, social care and education services.

Despite these vulnerabilities within staff teams and organisations, attachment theory does give us insights into how services can be designed and delivered to create and maintain effective systems of care particularly for those who have experienced relational or developmental trauma. For example, attachment theory explains how certain behavioural patterns develop in the face of stress and distress. When health, social care and education practitioners face irresolvable stress in their workplace, it is inevitable that attachment patterns begin to surface in their work with service users. The value in supervision is not just in helping staff restore their own reflective functioning, but to watch out for times when stress in the system is compromising the emotional safety for service users. The ways in which attachment theory can inform the design and delivery of services will be the focus of the next section.

WHAT CAN ATTACHMENT THEORY TELL US ABOUT THE DESIGN AND DELIVERY OF SERVICES?

To develop a successful attachment-informed organisation, all aspects of the system need to be considered (Bucci et al., 2015). In an environment where trust and emotional safety are established as organisational culture by leaders, this "secure base" allows emotions to be expressed and regulated, preventing them building up and being played out as unhelpful team dynamics, or worse, toxic behaviours. Where leaders actively co-create trust and safety across a system, they provide individual services the freedom and autonomy to be creative and flexible in making decisions about delivery of the service at a local level, but offering support when needed (Bucci et al., 2015).

Relatedly, staff who work in public services also need to feel secure and stable in their own job roles in order to enable them to meet the emotional needs of those they work with. Lack of support during service changes, threats to job security and high workloads, owing to financial cutbacks can activate understandable anxieties which if left unaddressed can compromise staff's ability to support others, particularly in those staff who have insecure attachment patterns. In these vulnerable moments, organisations need to provide adequate psychological care to staff, not least so that they do not re-enact any potential lack of compassion they might have experienced themselves within their own childhoods or places of work. On a basic level, this could be actively reducing caseload numbers during times of stress, investing money in the office décor or equipment so people feel valued, and organising wellbeing and self-care activities as part of the working week.

Within an attachment-informed organisation, attachment should provide a focal lens through which to understand people's needs. Staff within attachment-informed organisations should be aware of the deep-seated influence of attachment histories, such that they are constantly alert to the attachment needs, patterns and risks of people they provide services for, and to any indication that current relationships may be unsafe and harmful. This means paying attention to the risks of relationships: staff should follow the local guidance about when and how to ask about past and present emotional, sexual or physical abuse. They should also be informed and confident about the steps that may need to be taken following a disclosure of abuse or harm.

In addition, attachment issues need to be considered during routine assessments and formulations (a term psychologists use to describe the process of understanding, or theorising about, the person or family's presenting difficulties, needs and resources). Within mental health settings, trained clinicians might use various approaches, including structured clinical interviews, questionnaires and drawing on their own observations and the individual's history to assess adult attachment styles and help people understand the impact of their attachment patterns on current psychological distress.

In attachment-informed organisations, staff who do not have professional training in mental health or psychotherapy should be trained in the basic ideas of attachment theory, including the function of the attachment system, different types of attachment styles and how these might play out in relationships with others, and how to provide sensitive and responsive care. However, this is not so that staff can diagnose or treat attachment difficulties, but so that they can better understand themselves, their relationships with the people they help, the patterns of relationships and behaviour they may encounter in others, and the fundamental importance of safety and trust in all aspects of service delivery. Shemmings (2018) cautions against the use of "attachment" in records and reports so that relative novices do not inadvertently step beyond the bounds of their competencies.

If staff are to provide sensitive and responsive care that will promote the attachment security of those they support, they need to be made aware of and helped to pay attention to the following:

a Empathy and validation of individuals' distress by careful and attentive listening. For example, a teacher taking a ten-year old child aside, who finds it hard to sit still in the classroom, to ask her how she experiences the classroom and reflecting back the frustrations the child expresses to show understanding.
b Opportunities for staff to spend sufficient one-to-one time with those they support so they can fully understand their needs. For example, a mental health ward manager making sure that each patient gets time with a staff member each day to engage in social activity either on or off the ward.
c Providing consistency and continuity of care. Ways of achieving this within health and social care systems might include: assigning each person a nominated practitioner rather than adopting "corporate caseloads"; protecting and prioritising continuity of care for service users during service reorganisation; ensuring staff retention by creating a positive working environment; offering more flexible intervention options to break down barriers to engagement which could interrupt service provision (e.g. briefer sessions, telephone contacts, written contacts, and on-demand services); ensuring support outside normal working hours when people are particularly vulnerable and are most in need of help and most at risk.
d Providing people with positive relational experiences that may challenge and modify insecure internal working models. For example, staff members who show confidence in a person,

who focus on their strengths and recognise their value and worth, but who can also create and maintain healthy boundaries, can go some way in deconstructing negative and unhelpful mental representations that service users may hold about themselves and others.

SUPPORTING STAFF THROUGH AN ATTACHMENT LENS

Implementing an attachment-informed organisation tests the internal resources of staff because many service users will bring into relationships with staff patterns of behaviour that result from negative attachment experiences.

There are a number of ways in which staff can be supported to respond to attachment difficulties including (but not limited to): a) staff training and supervision focused on increasing awareness of attachment theory and trauma-sensitive care with an emphasis on the potential impact of the work on their own wellbeing (Adshead et al., 2005; Seager, 2013; Treisman, 2017); b) staff reflective practice groups that focus on attachment styles, behaviours and needs, as well as an opportunity to reflect on difficult situations and evoked emotions (Barber, et al., 2006; Berry & Drake, 2010; Treisman, 2017); and c) teams appointing champions around self-care and stress management with clear policies to support these and a culture of continuous professional development (Treisman, 2017). Furthermore, supporting staff to identify their role in maintaining unhelpful cycles by helping them recognise their own attachment styles and how these influence their perceptions of, and relationships with those they care for is also important. As Wallin (2013) has highlighted, difficult attachment histories may in part motivate involvement in caregiving and helping professions. Personal therapy or carefully conducted attachment-informed clinical supervision are two ways in which staff can be supported to understand how their own attachment style might contribute to interpersonal relationships.

In some mental health services, one strategy for offering staff support to manage these demands and avoid falling in the trap of behaving in ways that might maintain service users' problems is the increasingly popular practice of team formulation. This is the process of facilitating a group or team of staff to develop a shared formulation about an individual they are supporting (Johnstone, 2014). The British Psychological Society's Division of Clinical Psychology "Good practice guidelines on the use of psychological formulation" developed by Lucy Johnstone and colleagues recommend, in line with trauma-informed practice, that all formulations should consider "the possible role of trauma and abuse along with the possible role of services in compounding the difficulties" (Johnstone et al., 2011, p. 29). Practitioners have developed models of team formulation that include attachment styles and relationships on the part of both staff and service users as a central feature of the discussion (Berry et al., 2016; Johnstone, 2014). Attachment-informed team formulations, along with education about the impact of trauma and adversity, help staff to provide the emotional environment that is so central to healing from trauma, including relational trauma (Clarke, 2015).

ENDINGS AND TRANSITIONS IN SERVICE DELIVERY

Acknowledging the impact of endings and transitions and planning for these events can be particularly problematic for individuals with attachment difficulties. In education, this might range from the start or end of a new school year to an unexpected supply teacher or change of classroom. In social care, this might be an unplanned move to a new care home or a change of social worker. The issue of discharge planning from mental health services is particularly important in light of the known high suicide rates following discharge from inpatient mental health care settings (Crawford, 2004).

An attachment-informed organisation must support careful planning for transitions and endings in advance, as these are times when an individual's attachment system, or bond with the organisation or member of staff, is threatened. Problems evident around discharge or transitions could be reduced, or sometimes even prevented by graded discharge or outreach work (Seager, 2013), arranging ongoing professional and lay support for the person (Barber et al., 2006), and/or by ensuring, where possible, that service users are discharged into the care of an attachment figure to minimise the possibility of harm. Endings and transitions have been shown to be especially significant for service users who may have suffered multiple past losses (Adshead et al., 2005). This is why, for example, children who have already suffered losses or attachment traumas can find a change of class teacher so unsettling; learning that their proxy secure base is in fact insecure can activate substantial anxiety.

Below, we provide two examples of how attachment theory can be applied to systems or services: the first to schools, and the second to adult mental health services.

APPLYING ATTACHMENT THEORY TO SCHOOLS

A number of schools have trained staff in attachment theory with the aim of encouraging a greater understanding of the emotional and relationship needs of children and adolescents (Bomber & Hughes, 2013; Geddes, 2006; Marshall, 2014). The goal is for staff members, and the school itself, to become a secure base that can promote and maximise children's learning and development. Developers of these programmes have argued that incorporating ideas from attachment theory within schools can improve the wellbeing of pupils and therefore their academic performance, and by helping school staff understand and respond to disruptive behaviour as evidence of emotional insecurity, the rate of exclusions can be reduced. These are important implications as children who have experienced relational and developmental trauma have an increased likelihood of absenteeism, difficulties with school adjustment, exclusion and lower academic attainment.

Although such initiatives may be especially important for children who are, or have been, looked after by the local authority, it can also be equally important for those children who are at home and have currently difficult relationships with caregivers or who have experienced past traumas. Schools can provide many protective factors including academic success, intelligence and a positive teacher-child relationship (Treisman, 2017). Importantly, children spend a significant amount of time in school, maximising the potential role that the educational system can play (Treisman, 2017).

A review paper by Bergin and Bergin (2009) concluded that the principles of attachment theory can be applied in schools in two ways. First, to the teacher-pupil relationship and, second, to the functioning of the school as a whole.

1 TEACHER AND PUPIL RELATIONSHIPS

A secure teacher-student relationship is one where the teacher is trusted by the student and the teacher is attuned to the student's emotions and needs. As described in Chapter 4, children who have experienced relational and developmental trauma are more likely to experience behavioural and emotional difficulties which can show themselves within the school settings. These difficulties might include impulsiveness, hypervigilance to threat, aggressive outbursts, poor motivation and difficulties developing relationships.

Despite these difficulties, the student should feel safe to seek help from the teacher and the teacher should be able to provide the necessary emotional support required. Teachers should have time to develop supportive relationships with their students, have high expectations of pupils and facilitate pupil autonomy (in terms of being sensitive to the child's agenda, capabilities and choice). If a child has experienced developmental trauma and/or has an insecure style of attachment, teachers may encounter difficulties in building a trusting relationship. For example, children who have experienced trauma perpetrated by supposedly trusting adults may find relationship building with school staff highly anxiety provoking. As Treisman (2017) highlights, although the school environment and staff-student relationships may be 'safe', this does not mean that those who have experienced relational traumas will feel and believe it is safe. School procedures need to be put in place to ensure that safety is paramount, for example, clear guidelines around issues such as confidentiality and boundaries, with a place of safety or person for the child to go both physically and in imagination.

Teachers need to be enabled and supported to continue to develop positive relationships with students despite the setbacks they may face with students who are fearful of relationships. In order to help them foster relationships with such students, teachers may need support to help understand the developmental antecedents to the child's behaviour (for example, to see emotional outbursts as difficulties in managing emotions as a result of trauma as opposed to angry defiance, or lack of motivation as resulting from low self-esteem and hopelessness for the future as opposed to laziness). In this respect, behaviour is seen as a means of communication which is key in being able to think about appropriate interventions, getting to know the child behind the behaviour, linking the behaviour to a learnt survival strategy as opposed to taking it personally and reducing negative labelling of students (Treisman, 2017). In helping these students cope with the difficulties of school life, teaching staff may also need to appreciate the struggles student with developmental trauma and attachment difficulties may face in relation to highly structured school system which are characterised by rules and routines and spending long periods of time away from attachment figures within the home. Similarly, children who have experienced developmental trauma often respond in line with their social and emotional age as opposed to their chronological age particularly in the context of perceived threat, meaning that teaching staff need to pitch goals and interventions accordingly (Treisman, 2017).

2 WHOLE-SCHOOL APPROACH

A whole-school approach means thinking about how everyone in the school, including non-teaching staff, relate to the children and each other. The rationale for a whole-school approach is to achieve a bottom-up and top-down cultural shift which will have wider reach than targeting specific 'problem' children (Treisman, 2017). It involves schools working towards a secure base with ripple effects for teachers, parents and the community and incorporates many of the ideas discussed above in relation to attachment-informed organisations in other care settings. For example, in terms of the whole-school approach, members of the school leadership team should encourage a positive social and emotional climate, with a culture of respect. Continuity of both people and place is important in terms of creating a sense of security and as such essential transitions (across years and schools) should be recognised as significant events and supported. Schools that are embedded within their communities are more likely to promote close relationships between staff and students and parents and closer bonding between students themselves. Schools should explicitly and implicitly convey a message that welcomes and values all students. In this respect, they should develop a commonly agreed language which avoids negative stereotyping labels and problem-focused talk. Inclusive extra-curricular activities are also seen as beneficial in terms of promoting more enriching environments and relationship building particularly for those students who are not able to access these opportunities via other means.

APPLYING ATTACHMENT THEORY TO ADULT MENTAL HEALTH SERVICES

There have been a number of positive developments in the application of attachment theory to the organisation of health care, such as the British Department of Health national advisory group on mental health, safety, and well-being (Seager et al., 2007) agreeing that secure attachments and relationships are key to mental well-being. The concept of recovery which is now a key paradigm within adult mental health services is also important in this context. Recovery is not defined as the remission of symptoms in the traditional psychiatric sense of the word but is defined by service users' perspectives. These perspectives emphasise safety, consistency, hope, building a meaningful life and provision of choice (Pitt et al., 2007), ideas that are consistent with the central tenets of attachment theory. Similarly, "relational security", a concept developed in secure mental health settings (Drennan & Alred, 2013), emphasises the importance of safe and secure staff-service user relationships.

Despite these developments, there has been comparatively little practical examples of applying attachment to mental health service delivery, and limited change in the commissioning and delivery of mental health services which across the world remain dominated by the diagnostically driven "medical model" (Bloom & Farragher, 2010). Fortunately, a closely related concept, that of being trauma-informed, has gained popularity as a frame within which to think about service design and delivery. Trauma-informed services are, like attachment-based services, based on the assumption that the core role of the staff and the system is to provide secure and consistent relationships within which traumatic experiences can be heard, understood, and processed safely. They recognise that the majority of people treated by public mental health and substance abuse services have trauma histories and that the first duty of any healthcare service is not to re-traumatise the people it sets out to help (Harris & Fallot, 2001; Treisman, 2017). This is a helpful development because trauma-informed services help everyone through the widespread adoption of sound, relationship-centred principles of care. In addition, those who have been traumatised by their own attachment experiences benefit from the deeper understanding of how persistent relational trauma can be and how corrective relational experiences can help.

SUMMARY

Effort and involvement are required by all stakeholders to ensure successful implementation of new practice, including an attachment-informed way of working. It takes time for changes to practice to be operationalised and embedded within service delivery. Considering the continual obligation for commissioners to develop effective services that provide value for money, an attachment-informed service model may need to demonstrate the potential to recoup any extra initial investment in the long term. However, developing an attachment-informed organisation will have implications for the support needs of staff. Supervision, training, consultation, reflective groups, caseload management, team building, team formulation, and additional managerial support are among the methods that can be used to enable staff to offer compassionate caregiving. Attachment theory provides a universal evidence-based theory that we believe should inform organisational health policy to promote psychologically 'safe' services.

RECOMMENDED READING

Bucci, S., Roberts, N., Danquah, A. & Berry, K. (2015). Using attachment theory to inform the design and delivery of mental health services: A systematic review of the literature. Psychology and Psychotherapy: Theory, Research and Practice, 88: 1–20.

Treisman, K. (2017). Working with relational and developmental trauma in children and adolescents. Routledge.

REFERENCES

Adshead, G., Charles, S. & Pyszora, N. (2005). Moving on: A group for patients leaving a high security hospital. *Group Analysis*, 38: 380–394.

Barber, M., Short, J., Clarke-Moore, J., Lougher, M., Huckle, P. & Amos, T. (2006). A secure attachment model of care: meeting the needs of women with mental health problems and antisocial behaviour. *Criminal Behaviour and Mental Health*, 16: 3–10.

Bergin, C. & Bergin, D. (2009). Attachment in the classroom. *Educational Psychology Review*, 21(2): 141–170.

Berry, K. & Drake, R. (2010). Attachment theory in psychiatric rehabilitation: informing clinical practice. *Advances in Psychiatric Treatment*, 16: 308–315.

Berry, K., Haddock, G., Kellett, S., Roberts, C., Drake, R. & Barrowclough, C. (2016). Feasibility of ward-based psychological intervention to improve staff and patient relationships in psychiatric rehabilitation settings. *British Journal of Clinical Psychology*, 55: 236–352.

Bloom, S. L. & Farragher, B. (2010). *Destroying sanctuary: The crisis in human service delivery systems*. Oxford University Press.

Bomber, L. M. & Hughes, D. A. (2013). *Settling to learn*. Worth Publishing.

Bowlby, J. (1969). *Attachment and loss, Vol. 1: Attachment*. Basic Books.

Bucci, S., Roberts, N., Danquah, A. & Berry, K. (2015). Using attachment theory to inform the design and delivery of mental health services: A systematic review of the literature. *Psychology and Psychotherapy: Theory, Research and Practice*, 88: 1–20.

Clarke, I. (2015). The Emotion Focused Formulation Approach: Bridging individual and team formulation. *Clinical Psychology Forum*, 275: 28–32.

Crawford, M. J. (2004). Suicide following discharge from in-patient psychiatric care. *Advances in Psychiatric Treatment*, 10: 434–438.

Drennan, G. & Alred, D. (2013). *Secure recovery: Approaches to recovery in forensic mental health settings*. Willan.

Geddes, H. (2006). *Attachment in the classroom*. Worth Publishing.

Harris, M. & Fallot, R. (Eds) (2001). *Using Trauma Theory to Design Service Systems. New Directions for Mental Health Services*. Jossey-Bass.

Johnstone, L. (2014). Using formulation in teams. In L. Johnstone & R. Dallos (Eds), *Formulation in psychology and psychotherapy: Making sense of people's problems* (2nd Ed., pp. 216–242). Routledge.

Johnstone, L., Whomsley, S., Cole, S. & Oliver, N. (2011). Good practice guidelines on the use of psychological formulation. Leicester: British Psychological Society.

Marshall, N. (2014). *The Teacher's Introduction to Attachment: Practical Essentials for Teachers, Carers and School Support Staff Paperback*. Jessica Kingsley.

Pitt, L., Kilbride, M., Nothard, S., Welford, M. & Morrison, A. P. (2007). Researching recovery from psychosis: a user-led project. *The Psychiatrist*, 31(2): 55–60.

Seager, M. (2013). Using attachment theory to inform psychologically minded care services, systems and environments. In A. Danquah & K. Berry (Eds), *Attachment theory in adult mental health: A guide to clinical practice* (pp. 213–224). Routledge.

Seager, M., Orbach, S., Samuels, A., Sinason, V., Johnstone, L., Fredman, G. & Kinderman, P. (2007). *National Advisory group on mental health, safety & well-being: Towards proactive policy: Five universal psychological principles*. Department of Health, London.

Shemmings, D. (2018). Why social workers shouldn't use 'attachment' in their records and reports. *Community Care*, 28 June. www.communitycare.co.uk/2018/06/28/social-workers-shouldnt-use-attachment-records-reports.

Treisman, K. (2017). *Working with relational and developmental trauma in children and adolescents*. Routledge.

Wallin, D. (2013). We are the tools of our trade: the therapist's attachment history as a source of impasse, inspiration and change. In A. Danquah & K. Berry (Eds), *Attachment theory in adult mental Health: A guide to clinical practice* (pp. 225–239). Routledge.

GLOSSARY

Angels in the Nursery	A phrase coined in 2005 by Alicia Lieberman and colleagues to refer to benevolent memories and ideas from parents' own childhoods which influence how they raise their own babies. Angels in the nursery balance the impact of ghosts in the nursery (see below).
Attachment	A bond or tie between a child and an attachment figure based on the need for safety, protection and comfort.
Attachment behaviour	Any behaviour by the baby that induces proximity-seeking to the attachment figure when feeling distressed, threatened, frightened or unsafe.
Attachment figure	The person (typically the parent) who cares for the baby such that the baby's chances of survival are increased.
Borderline Personality Disorder (BPD)	A personality disorder characterised by difficulty in regulating emotions, impulsive behaviours and difficulty forming stable personal relationships. *Emotionally Unstable Personality Disorder* (EUPD) is a more recent term to describe experiences formally labelled as Borderline Personality Disorder.

DOI: 10.4324/9780203703878-14

Burnout A response to chronic interpersonal stressors typically within the workplace which is characterised by overwhelming exhaustion, feelings of cynicism and detachment from the job and a sense of ineffectiveness and lack of accomplishment.

Compassion fatigue The response to helping others that results from over exposure to other people's trauma or help seeking and results in feelings of no longer caring.

Co-regulation The process of interaction between a child and caregiving adult in which the adult's attuned responses help the child to manage their feelings, restoring a sense of calm control. Over time, repeated experiences of co-regulation help the child develop a blueprint for future self-regulation.

Cortex (Also called the neocortex) is part of the mammalian brain which emerged in primates around two or three million years ago in primates and in humans around 200,000 years ago. It is the pinkish-grey crinkly area that you would recognise as the human brain. The cortex is the thinking brain or "smart brain" responsible for the development of human language, abstract thought, imagination, self-awareness, planning, organisation and reflection.

Cross-sectional research The research which measures variables of interest at the same point in time.

Disorganised attachment A behavioural pattern which emerges in children raised in unpredictable, neglectful, hostile or abusive environments. It is thought to reflect an environment in which the parent is either frightening to or frightened by the infant. Infants find themselves unable to predict their carer, hence they are unable to "organise" their behaviour in response. Infants with a disorganised attachment style show a range of unusual and contradictory behaviours including freezing in presence of mother, approaching then moving aside, disorientation, stereotyped movements such as rocking or curling up into a ball during reunion.

Dissociation The experience of feeling disconnected from yourself and the world around you. For example, feeling detached from your body or feeling as though the world around you is not real.

Formulation A term psychologists use to describe the process of understanding or theorising about, the person or family's presenting difficulties, needs and resources.

Ghosts in the nursery A metaphor first described by Selma Fraiberg to describe how unresolved negative experiences from a parent's past can influence their ability to form a warm and attuned relationship with their child.

Good enough parenting Derived from Donald Winnicott's "good enough mother". Through observations of mothers and babies he realised that babies and children actually benefit when their mothers fail them in manageable ways and are imperfect. Indeed the 'good enough parent' recognises that it's not possible to be empathic, available and attuned all of the time.

Hypothalamic-Pituitary-Adrenal Axis A complex neuro-hormonal system that manages our reactions to stressful situations. As distress or stress levels build up, a hormonal chain reaction is activated, involving the adrenals, the pituitary gland and the hypothalamus.

Infant mental health Refers to the social and emotional wellbeing of an infant as a reflection of the caregiving environment. Infant mental health develops in response to the quality of care and relationships within which the child develops. Infant mental health is therefore a field of study which focusses on parent-child and family relationships and their impact on the formative development of the brain and mind in the first few years of life.

Insecure-ambivalent attachment Infants with an insecure-ambivalent attachment style don't want to leave their caregiver to explore the room and tend to be clingy. They cry when their caregiver leaves but then when they return seem to want to be consoled but resist and seem simultaneously sad and angry.

Insecure-avoidant attachment Infants with an insecure-avoidant attachment style show little interest in their caregivers and focus on playing independently. They may show minimal upset when their caregivers leave and can seem indifferent upon reunion e.g., turning their back on them or ignoring.

Internal working model An unconscious blueprint or mental map the child develops about themselves, others and relationships based on their attachment experiences.

Limbic brain (Also called the mid-brain), the limbic brain emerged in the first mammals about 150 million years ago. It is a collection of brain areas concerned with emotions, memory, feeding, reproduction and caregiving. These include the hippocampus, strongly connected to memory, and the amygdala, which plays a central role in emotional responses and how we remember emotional experiences.

Longitudinal research The research which measures variables of interest in the same group of people at different points in time.

Maternal Sensitivity Refers to the ability of the parent to consistently pick up on his or her infant's cues and respond appropriately.

Medical model	A school of thought where mental health problems are believed to be the product of physiological factors. The medical model, which is more widely used by psychiatrists than psychologists, treats mental health problems as physical diseases whereby medication is often used in treatment.
Mentalization/Reflective Functioning	An attribute of parenting where the parent understands that infant behaviour is driven by the baby's own psychological or emotional factors. Reflective parents can reflect on both their own feelings and those of their baby and in effect balance these experiences to allow them to be responsive to the infant's needs.
Mind-mindedness	A phrase coined by Elizabeth Meins and colleagues defined as the parent's ability to read their child's mental states and verbalise this during interactions.
Recovery	A concept within adult mental health services where recovery is not defined as the remission of symptoms in the traditional psychiatric sense of the word but is defined by service users' perspectives.
Reflective practice groups	A concept developed in secure mental health settings which emphasises the importance of safe and secure staff-service user relationships.
Reptilian brain	The oldest, most primitive part of the brain. It controls vital internal functions such as heart rate, breathing, digestion, temperature and balance – all the functions that keep us alive without us having to think consciously about them.
Resilience	The ability to withstand adversity and bounce back from difficult life events.
Safe haven	Refers to a place of safety, represented by an attachment figure, that a child can return to when feeling uneasy, stressed, overwhelmed or unsafe.

Secure attachment Infants with secure attachments to their caregivers can use their caregivers, when present, as a base from which to explore their environments. When the caregiver is not present, securely attached infants show distress. During reunion episodes, securely attached infants actively seek contact with the caregiver and are genuinely comforted by that contact. A secure attachment is associated with a range of good developmental, cognitive and psychological outcomes in later life.

Secure base Refers to a place of safety, represented by an attachment figure, that a child uses as a base to explore a new environment or relationship.

Strange Situation Procedure A standardised, laboratory-based procedure to observe and assess attachment patterns in infants between the age of nine and 18 months. The procedure involves series of eight separation and reunion episodes lasting approximately 3 minutes each, whereby a mother, child and stranger are introduced, separated and reunited.

Team formulation The process of facilitating a group or team of staff to develop a shared formulation about an individual they are supporting.

Toxic stress The prolonged activation of the body's stress response systems in the absence of attachment figures or protective adults who can buffer the impact of the stress. The word toxic denotes the negative impact of toxic stress on the developing brain and body.

Transitional object A phrase coined by Donald Winnicott to refer to an object which becomes "vitally important" to a baby at times of state transition (e.g., going to sleep or managing a separation) or to help manage anxiety. Typically, a transitional object for a baby might be their preferred teddy or toy, which they want with them at times of transition or stress.

Trauma-informed services Services based on the assumption that the core role of the staff and the system is to provide secure and consistent relationships within which traumatic experiences can be heard, understood and processed safely.

Triune brain A simple model to understand the structure of the brain (MacLean, 1990). MacLean suggests we think of the brain as having three main parts: the reptilian brain, the midbrain (or limbic system) and the cortex.

INDEX

Note: Locators in *italic* indicate figures, in **bold** tables.